WOMEN'S SOURCE LIBRARY

WOMEN'S SOURCE LIBRARY

VOLUME I
The Education Papers
Edited by Dale Spender

VOLUME II
The Radical Women's Press of the 1850s
Edited by Ann Russo and Cheris Kramarae

VOLUME III
Barbara Leigh Smith Bodichon and the Langham Place Group
Edited by Candida Ann Lacey

VOLUME IV
The Revolution in Words
Edited by Lana F. Rakow and Cheris Kramarae

VOLUME V
Before the Vote was Won
Edited by Jane Lewis

VOLUME VI
The Sexuality Debates
Edited by Sheila Jeffreys

VOLUME VII
Women's Fabian Tracts
Edited by Sally Alexander

VOLUME VIII
Suffrage and the Pankhursts
Edited by Jane Marcus

VOLUME IX
The Non-Violent Militant
Edited by Carol McPhee and Ann Fitzgerald

Women's Source Library

VOLUME IV

The Revolution in Words

Righting Women, 1868–1871

Edited by
Lana F. Rakow and Cheris Kramarae

London and New York

First published 1990
by Routledge
2 Park Square, Milton Park, Abingdon, Oxon, OX14 4RN

Simultaneously published in the USA and Canada
by Routledge
270 Madison Ave, New York NY 1006

This edition first published 2001

First issued in paperback 2010

Routledge is an imprint of the Taylor & Francis Group

Typeset in Times by Keystroke, Jacaranda Lodge, Wolverhampton

British Library Cataloguing in Publication Data
A catalogue record for this book is available from the British Library

Library of Congress Cataloging in Publication Data
A catalog record for this book has been requested

ISBN 978-0-415-25669-8 (Set)
ISBN 978-0-415-25689-6 (hbk) (Volume IV)
ISBN 978-0-415-60640-0 (pbk) (Volume IV)

Publisher's note
The publisher has gone to great lengths to ensure the quality of this reprint
but points out that some imperfections in the original book may be apparent.

To Caitlin Stukel Rakow,
who was born amid The Revolution
and
To Dale Spender,
who has done so much to continue The Revolution

Contents

Contents

Contents

Contents

Contents

xi

Contents

Contents

Contents

Contents

Contents

xvi

Contents

Contents

Contents

Contents

Contents

Contents

Contents

Contents

List of illustrations

Foreword

This wonderful volume offers a treasure of selections from one of the most important documentary sources for the history of women in the nineteenth century.

The Revolution was an ambitious undertaking that would daunt women today, and one may question whether the contemporary women's movement has matched it. Sixteen folio pages per issue, in three columns of small type per page, it was packed with an astounding range and quantity of information, literature, opinion, documentary records and radical advocacy. That Susan B. Anthony, as proprietor, was left with a debt of $10,000 – equivalent to at least $100,000 today – when she turned over the paper to Laura C. Bullard in 1870 is a sad reflection on the financial struggles of any such endeavor, but it is also a testimony to the magnitude of the enterprise itself.

Issues of *The Revolution* often contained:

— poetry and fiction (such as the serialized novel, *The Born Thrall*, by Alice Cary, or the didactic serial on non-sexist education, "Dot and I," by Faith Rochester), usually occupying the first two to five pages;

— lengthy letters and signed contributions from readers and supporters on diverse subjects (many reflected in the selected excerpts in this volume);

— "Foreign correspondence," comprising long reports from abroad on women's status and the struggles for women's rights in England and Europe, and occasionally other parts of the world, such as India, including documentary reports of major meetings, parliamentary petitions and proceedings, and so on;

— "Editorial correspondence," recounting the activities and observations of the editors and authors, on their lecture tours and other travels, reflecting the concerns and responses of women in many local communities around the country;

— extensive records of the founding and proceedings of the National Woman Suffrage Association and the abortive "Union Woman Suffrage Association" (a failed effort to replace the moribund Equal Rights Association with a merger of the NWSA and the American Woman Suffrage Association), including announcements and conference calls, stenographic records of the speeches delivered and other conference proceedings, testimony before a Congressional committee, reports of meetings, elections and so on;

— reports from around the country, California to Boston, on the formation and activities of women's rights and suffrage associations;

— editorial commentaries by the editors (signed and unsigned) on all the topics reflected in this volume, and more;

— news of women's advancement or problems in all spheres (see below);

— announcements and commentaries about new radical periodicals or organizations (for example, *The Indiana Radical*, edited and published by J. H. Julian, announcing that it would "advocate as a Natural, Inalienable right, Universal Suffrage, without qualification of Race, Sex, Creed, Education or condition," and that it would "stand by the rights and interests of the Laboring Classes against the exactions of capital and the pretensions of Snobocracy");

— brief literary notices of recent books and periodical literature (in even smaller print than the main text);

— the "Financial Department," carrying articles on monetary and trade policies under a disclaimer from the editors of responsibility for the views expressed;

— and, finally, a page or two of advertisements, interesting as documents in themselves both for their explicit content and for what they represent in the relationships between potential advertisers, various constituencies of readers, and *The Revolution*.

No single volume of ordinary size and readable print could possibly encompass all this, and the editors of the present collection modestly claim only the hope that readers will find it a "rewarding introduction" to the periodical itself. Indeed, it is more than that, offering its own analysis and reconstruction of *The Revolution*, built around issues represented in the newspaper that are still salient to the current women's movement, and to our understanding of the painful controversies and exhilarating struggles of the years in

Foreword

which *The Revolution* appeared.

The debates over the Fifteenth Amendment, racism in the suffrage movement, and the personal and political conflicts among the suffrage leaders that sometimes hovered behind the scenes, sometimes emerged explosively in the pages of *The Revolution*, are carefully dealt with in the section "Onward *The Revolution*" and in several of the introductions, notes and other selections. These conflicts were rooted in the wide-ranging consciousness of political, economic, social and intellectual issues expressed by the contributors to *The Revolution*.

The editors have sought to represent the scope and content of this consciousness by organizing the main body of the selections around a thoughtfully constructed topical scheme, often using *The Revolution*'s words to define the themes: the suffrage struggle itself ("Aristocracy of Sex"), forced maternity, abortion and prostitution ("Hester Vaughanism"), economic and labor issues ("The Bread Question"), dress reform and health issues ("Going to Unfashionable Lengths"), challenging masculine domination ("Man's Sphere"), women's oppression in the home and child care issues ("What About the Babies?").

The editors have also given us a provocative selection of extracts placing some aspects of the contemporary movement in historical perspective: anti-feminist women ("All the Rights I Want"), "Man/Dated" language, and the creative forms of direct action adopted by women in the struggle ("Becoming Perfect Nuisances").

Piqued by the selections offered here, I returned to a volume of the original that I acquired years ago and have cherished as precious, yet not mined for its content until now – and, of course, found my own gems, as every new reader will. I would like to dwell a bit on some of what I found, to emphasize the richness of this source and its potential for further study, the kind of activity Rakow and Kramarae clearly hope will result from readers' use of this volume.

Though the achievements of "women worthies" are not regarded as very interesting in feminist scholarship today, it is clear that *The Revolution* considered it important to publicize and document women's entrance into new fields and project a sense of women's history. I was impressed by the innumerable details provided toward this end, even in the few months contained in my one slim volume (January through May, 1870). Many entries note, for example: appointments of women to public office (such as Martha West as Justice of the Peace in Wyoming; women as engrossing clerks for the state legislatures in Iowa, Kansas and Wisconsin; Harriet A. Tenney as State Librarian of Michigan; Lydia Sexton as chaplain at Leavenworth penitentiary); educational achievements (such as the opening of the University of Michigan to women, Emma Jones' receipt of a California State educational diploma and appointment to the Faculty of the University of the Pacific, Charlotte E. Ray's admission to the Howard University Law School); the granting of suffrage to women in Wyoming and Utah; and women's service as jurors in Wyoming and the furor of debate about it.

As a historian, my attention was caught by a poem by L. Both-Hendriksen, "A Voice from the Temple of Clio," in the February 17, 1870 issue. This poem also celebrates "great women" of the past in a way that has gone out of fashion among women's historians today (though reminding us of some, like Aspasia and Hypatia, who are only recently being restored to attention), but it gives evidence of a remarkably contemporary insight into the loss of women's history. Beginning with a lament on the bound status of women in the past, "blind and untaught," with "Powers which yet are unknown, which no mortal hath ever developed, – " it breaks off to declare: "Nay, here I err; not unknown, unrevealed are the gifts of my sisters."

One important aspect of *The Revolution* that is almost impossible to represent in a collection of short excerpts is the philosophical and theoretical content of some of the longer essays. For example, Elizabeth Cady Stanton's statement that "political equality and religious liberty have always preceded social freedom" (speech of May 10, 1870, reported May 19) is embedded in a pragmatic context ("the subjection of woman to man [in the home] as dependent") which is well represented in the selections in this volume. But the theoretical character, background and implications of her assertion deserve separate analysis. To collect and assess the ideas of contributors to *The Revolution* in the context of their relationship to traditional political philosophy is a challenging task which remains before us.

Stanton's reference to religious liberty also calls to mind a subject touched on in some of the selections here: the multifaceted relationships of religion to women's oppression or liberation. Here again we may be startled by how little we have advanced today:

> In many of the churches women are permitted to vote on all business matters, to speak and pray in their meetings, to fill the office of deacon, and even to be ordained as pastors of congregations (to draw salaries), and administer the ordinances. . . . Leading minds of the church are now giving new and more liberal interpretations of the Bible, recognizing the equality of the sexes, making the declarations of Paul and Moses subordinate to the greater facts of progressive humanity. (May 19, 1870)

This could be 1990.

The editors of this volume emphasize the significance of *The Revolution* as a resource for a new history of women's communications:

> From a woman-centered perspective on communication history, we can see *The Revolution* not simply in terms of its use as a tool by Anthony and Stanton to advance their own cause of women's suffrage, but in the web of its interconnections with other periodicals, women's organizations, women's parlour or "picnic" discussion groups, readers and writers, and other means of communicating used by women.

This "web of interconnections" was not only national, but also international, or rather transnational, crossing and even repudiating national boundaries. In addition to the regular "Foreign correspondence" section of *The Revolution*, the paper carried other contributions and announcements from abroad. Unexpectedly (though of course it should not have been unexpected), my own gems included a number of items relevant to my current research interests, falling in this category of transnational communication.

To cite first a rather esoteric example, *The Revolution* carried on May 5, 1870 an excerpt from Louis Jaccolliot's *La Bible dans l'Inde* (included perhaps for its critical perspective on the Bible), which provided me with a long-sought clue to the background for certain ideas of Céline Renooz, founder and editor of the *Revue scientifique des femmes* (Paris, 1888–9) and author of two multi-volume works, *La Nouvelle Science* (1883–98) and *L'Ere de Vérité* (1921–8), foreshadowing contemporary radical feminism in its most iconoclastic attacks on male-created culture, knowledge, religion, language, science and institutions.

A more mundane but perhaps more broadly relevant example is the appearance of announcements from the International Women's Association founded in 1868 by Marie Goegg in Geneva, Switzerland (*The Revolution*, January 27, 1870 and May 5, 1870). This was twenty years earlier than the founding of the International Council of Women, generally regarded as the first international organization for women's rights. Since Elizabeth Cady Stanton and Elizabeth S. Miller were reported to comprise the American committee affiliated with Goegg's international association, it seems noteworthy that Stanton's biographer and other sources represent the International Council of Women as the first of its kind.[1]

Marie Goegg's call to women to join the international association illustrates especially well the theme of interconnection and communication among women. Its aims were not only to work for the equality of women "in all social and political rights," but also to create among "women of all countries and all social conditions, a bond of union and a *solitarité* of moral interests which shall destroy the systematic isolation in which women have lived in respect to one another, and to constitute for them a rallying centre. . . ."

The present collection, offering its own vision and reconstruction of *The Revolution*, is an indispensable step in the processes of research and interpretation of our past, in search of what they offer for the present and the future. Like Marie Goegg's international association, and as part of its interconnecting web of communications among women, *The Revolution* worked to "destroy the systematic isolation in which women have liven in respect to one another," and constituted for them in their time – and perhaps again for us today in ours – a rallying centre, for the theory and practice of social revolution.

Note

1 Elisabeth Griffith, *In Her Own Right: The Life of Elizabeth Cady Stanton* (New York: Oxford University Press, 1984); 192–4; Edith F. Hurwitz, "The International Sisterhood," in Renate Bridenthal and Claudia Koonz, eds, *Becoming Visible: Women in European History* (Boston: Houghton Mifflin, 1977), 327–329. See, however, Sandi E. Cooper, "Women's Participation in European Peace Movements: The Struggle

to Prevent World War I," in Ruth Roach Pierson, ed., *Women and Peace: Theoretical, Historical, and Practical Perspectives* (London: Croom Helm, 1987), 54; Cooper considers Goegg's Association International des Femmes as "the first women's peace society on the continent," rather than in the context of the international women's movement.

Berenice A. Carroll

Acknowledgements

Feminist scholars recognize that scholarship is always a collaborative matter; at the least, it is built on the work of other thinkers and writers who have gone before. The editors recognize that we are indebted to the many feminists of the nineteenth and twentieth centuries who put together materials and arguments upon which this work rests.

In addition, thanks belong to several individuals who helped in the preparation of the manuscript. Susan Sorenson's excellent computer and typing skills made work with the manuscript manageable. She remained enthusiastic about the project even in the face of rearranged deadlines and barely legible type (ours and the type of the 120-year-old newspapers). John Rock, Kim Kranich, Beth Stafford, Sandy Weidner, Mary Ann Terry and Ann Russo deserve thanks for their help in finding materials.

The University of Wisconsin-Parkside, the University of Illinois at Urbana-Champaign and the Center for the Study of Women in Society at the University of Oregon provided financial and other kinds of support for this project. The Smithsonian Institution, the Library of Congress and the New Hampshire Historical Society are thanked for providing the photographs that appear in this volume. Philippa Brewster, Candida Lacey and Dale Spender gave us encouragement and the kind of useful advice they have given to so many other authors and editors working with women's historical materials. We also thank Cecelia Cancellaro and Janice Price for their support of this project during the final transformation into book form.

Lana Rakow
Cheris Kramarae

Key

Title   The double asterisks indicate that the title is not in the original periodical, but has been created for this volume. Many of the essays, letters, and speeches were untitled, or had plain headings naming the author or general subject. We worked with the phrasing and tone of the articles to provide titles which would give readers guidance to the style and subjects of the excerpts.

[Author]   The brackets indicate that the author's name is not given in the original, but can be assumed on the basis of content and context.

. . . .   Ellipses are used to indicate that we have omitted material from the original text.

The Revolution.

PRINCIPLE, NOT POLICY: JUSTICE, NOT FAVORS.—MEN, THEIR RIGHTS AND NOTHING MORE. WOMEN, THEIR RIGHTS AND NOTHING LESS.

VOL. II.—NO. 3. NEW YORK, THURSDAY, JULY 23, 1868. WHOLE NO. 29.

The Revolution.

ELIZABETH CADY STANTON,
PARKER PILLSBURY, } Editors.
SUSAN B. ANTHONY, Proprietor.

OFFICE 37 PARK ROW (ROOM 20.)

MISS ANTHONY IN THE DEMOCRATIC CONVENTION.

The republicans appear to have a real Quaker Concern over the reception of Miss Anthony and her memorial for woman's right of suffrage, by the recent Democratic Convention. Many of their journals are snarly and snappish about it as cross puppies. In her innocence, she forgot to ask republican leave to go before the democrats to beg a boon which, when she asked of Congress, she was snubbed by pompous republican senators, in some instances, and in others virtually denied the sacred right of petition at all, by the manner in which the petitions were presented ; keeping the fact that they were from women and for women, out of sight. Suppose, as the New York *Tribune* says, the memorial of Miss Anthony was received by the Convention with "derisive cheers," and "uproarious laughter ;" it was respectfully received by the president, and handsomely read by the secretary ; and if the audience cheered and laughed at the good points made against the republicans, that was no fault of Miss Anthony. Her points were well made and defended. No republican, editor or speaker, has attempted to

latiff, and that the corrupt tribunals would condemn every journal bold enough to denounce these abominations.

It is in history, that a hundred years ago, gouty and debauched old seigniors, were recommended to use warm baths of infants blood to restore their bleached and shrunken energies, and that the remedy was adopted. And yet the world wonders at, and curses to this day the Revolution which was precipitated by such enormities.

WOMAN'S WAGES.

The demand of "The Revolution" is, equal pay for woman for equal work, whether as tailors, teachers, household help, or the higher callings, as some callings are called, for some reason. If God the Creator, be "no respecter of persons," the created need not be of honorable and useful employments. The Western and Eastern journals are telling how liberal and progressive is the city of Chicago on the subject of Education. Comparatively, all may be true that is said, but here are some figures. Chicago employs about 400 teachers ; there is a general superintendent with a salary of $4,000 ; the principal of the high school has $2,500 ; he has some 12 assistants at $2,000 for the men and $1,000 for the women ; the heads of the district schools, men, have $2,000 salary ; the women principals and chief assistants have $1,000, and other women assistants $450 for the first year, $550 for the second and $700 for the third.

The *men* may call this liberal ; but if the women are competent teachers, they surely are most shabbily paid. Recently we saw in a large

THE WAY THE INDIANS ARE FED.

Sergeant Haynes, of an Iowa cavalry regiment, lately testified before the Indian Peace Commission of the way he had seen rations issued to the savages. He said :

The Winnebago and Santee Indians were fed as follows at the Crow Creek Agency in 1864 : A large vat was constructed of cotton-wood lumber, about six feet square and six feet deep, in connection with the steam saw-mill, with a pipe leading from the boiler into the vat. Into the vat was thrown beef, beef heads, entrails of the beeves, some beans, flour and pork. I think two barrels of flour were put into the vat each time, which was not oftener than once in twenty-four hours. This mass was then cooked by the steam from the boiler. It was dipped out to the Indians with a long-handled dipper made for the purpose. I cannot say the quantity given to each. It was about the consistency of very thin gruel. The Indians would pour off the thinner portion and eat that which settled at the bottom. I have often there when it was being issued, and it had a very offensive odor ; it had the odor of the contents of the entrails of the beeves. I have seen the settlings of the vat after they were through issuing it to the Indians, and it smelt like carrion—like decomposed meat. Some of the Indians refused to eat it, saying they could not, it made them sick—that it was only fit for hogs, and that they were not hogs. The quantity of food issued them per day did not exceed eight ounces per head—man, woman and child.

WOMEN'S WORK AND WAGES.

It is to be regretted that the Working Men's Union do not more readily grasp the idea that all their efforts for self-extrication and elevation are vain, until the claims of the more oppressed working women are recognized. Woman has fought her way into every religious, political, social and educational advantage she enjoys,

---

The Revolution, a radical woman's rights periodical, was published from 1868–71, first by Elizabeth Cady Stanton and Susan B. Anthony and then by Laura Curtis Bullard.

Introduction

This book is an act of retrieving for contemporary women *The Revolution* and the women who wrote and read it. *The Revolution* is not entirely a stranger to feminist historians and communication scholars, but for most academics and twentieth-century feminists, this nineteenth-century woman's rights newspaper is little more than a footnote or, at the most, paragraph in history. Scholars may know that the paper was started in 1868 by Elizabeth Cady Stanton and Susan B. Anthony, with the financial help of George Francis Train and the editorial help of abolitionist Parker Pillsbury. They may know that this radical voice for woman's rights, embroiled in a controversy over suffrage for Black men and all women and in a disagreement with other righting women about strategy, lasted only a few years. Little is widely known beyond that.[1]

The few feminist historians and communication scholars who have had occasion to sit in sometimes dimly lit and dusty libraries peering at the faded type of this nineteenth-century woman's rights periodical on microfilm know the rewards its contains.[2] In fact, one sister scholar wrote to us, "I don't know how many times I laughed out loud over one of the articles – not an easy task when one is doing dissertation work on microfilm." For those who have not yet experienced *The Revolution*, we hope the excerpts we have chosen will be a rewarding introduction.

Before readers enter the pages of *The Revolution*, they might take a few minutes first to enter the world of the women who wrote and read these words. Other scholars have documented the lives of women in the nineteenth century (we recommend the bibliographies at the end of our introductory remarks to each section) and others have described the prescriptions and arguments about their natures that women faced from ministers, physicians, politicians, editors and scientists (see Rosenberg, 1975; Newman, 1985; Ehrenreich and English, 1978; Welter, 1976; Smith-Rosenberg and

1

Rosenberg, 1975). Let us simply remind readers that *The Revolution* was written and published by women at a time period when women were pronounced to be less evolved than men, incapable of intelligence and rationality, helpless and physically inferior to men, in need of men's protection and, in fact, the property of their fathers or husbands. They were, in short, neither citizens nor fully human persons. They were presumed to be organized biologically and – as a "natural" consequence – socially around reproduction. As industrial capitalism constructed a supposedly amoral world of individual, competitive men, women were assigned the moral world of family, home and emotion.

Women generally were denied access to higher education, particularly in the professions; hence they generally lacked access to the means of creating and challenging knowledge and to admittance into men's arenas of power. They did not have the same access to transportation and communication systems which men had, even though what was available may seem "primitive" according to our standards. They rode trains and wagons and carriages or went on foot to women's meetings, if they could get their husbands' and fathers' permission to travel or had the funds to do so, but even so there were sanctions against women traveling alone and at night, and many hotels would not rent rooms to unescorted women. Few women – with notable exceptions – wrote for men's newspapers and magazines, but a number of women *were* successful writers of novels and essays published as books and tracts. They did not yet have the typewriters and telephones that could have speeded up their writing and diminished distances, two technologies soon to become particularly associated with women.

Women labored under all manner of prescriptions against their speaking, traveling and even showing signs of thinking about "men's" issues. They experienced ridicule, harassment, physical abuse or the threat of it, and arrest. These were often effective methods for controlling women who spoke out, wrote boldly, dressed in defiance of convention and walked the streets unescorted.

Economic exploitation and economic vulnerability were possibilities faced by both wage-earning women and their housebound sisters. Few occupations were open to women. They were kept out by male workers and unions as well as by employers and by public disapproval. Women's wages were terribly low – much less than men's – but in many cases even those wages and any property they might accumulate or inherit legally belonged to their husbands (women's property rights laws were being fought for and slowly

2

won by women). Women who are labeled by contemporary scholars as middle class might have had more material comfort than their wage-earning sisters, but they suffered similar economic vulnerability. They had no guarantee of their husband's earnings or his estate, or even of the custody of their own children, since children belonged to their father as his property. A financially benevolent and healthy father or husband was often all that separated these women from the fate of other women.

Yet, despite these conditions, many women survived and fought back, always an inspiring discovery for contemporary feminists. They challenged, argued, resisted, organized, spoke and wrote. While this period of women's resistance is usually characterized as the suffrage movement, and *The Revolution* is usually thought of as a suffrage periodical, we need to understand fully what suffrage meant to these women. As Ellen DuBois (1978: 17–18) argues, the suffrage movement has been underestimated. It was not simply a movement for a limited and, as now perceived, ineffectual reform. It was not about getting women the vote, *per se*. It was really about redefining women and men.

An important project for nineteenth-century righting women was to demonstrate that "woman" as then conceived was not the fragile, protected, empty-headed, half-human property and object of display men supposed, but was the oppressed creation of men's fantasies and purposes, stifled and abused. Their goal was to redefine "woman" as human, worthy, competent, an active creator of her own and her society's destiny.

Of course to understand how women had been defined and in order to define them differently required considerable attention to "the white male," whose unnatural exercise of power and exploitation of other groups had somehow gone unnoticed. He needed to be described, held up for scrutiny and held accountable. To redefine women, men would have to be redefined as well, a revolutionary proposition.[3] In much the same way, white and Black abolitionists were attempting to redefine race and the meaning of being Black (see McPherson, 1975). These redefinitions became the point of contention between some abolitionists and some advocates of (white and Black) women's rights. Would being a Black man and a Black woman be redefined in terms of dominant white definitions of manhood and womanhood, or would being a Black person be redefined as being a full human being and full citizen? (See Horton, 1986; Sealander, 1982; Jones, 1985.) The women of *The Revolution* resisted the first possibility in favor of the second. While these women were indeed racist (as we now recognize as racist many of the other abolitionists), much of what has been described as their racist actions, alliances and words actually can be traced to a commitment to this particular redefinition.

The history of *The Revolution* has generally been told in relation to the biographies and philosophies of Elizabeth Cady Stanton and Susan B. Anthony. Certainly they were important figures in the birth and life of the newspaper, but we suggest there is a need to move on from this approach to history in terms of "women worthies" to one that sees *The Revolution* in a richer context of women's history and women's communication. In fact, we suggest there is a need to rewrite the history of communication in the nineteenth century (and other centuries, as well) from a woman-centered perspective. Thanks to the efforts of feminist scholars in communication, literature and history, we are learning a great deal about women's networks, women's periodicals, women's journalistic careers, women as public speakers, women as fiction writers, but we need an integration of this information into broader accounts of how women communicated with and supported each other, challenged their prescribed destinies, fought against their oppression with their voices and pens, created prospects for alternative realities, celebrated their wisdom, made meaning of their experiences.

What would a history of communication in the nineteenth century look like from a woman-centered perspective? It would need to be an integration of linguistics, literature, interpersonal communication, organizational communication and mass communication – typically discrete areas of study, but meaningless divisions to account for the experiences of any individual or group. It would look at women's networks, friendships, and associations – their collaboration and support across distances – rather than at particular individuals, a legacy of men's approach to history. It would look at the editors, writers and readers of books, periodicals and articles as active makers of meaning, often challenging and resisting prescriptions as well as using those prescriptions to their own ends. It would look at the relationship between writers and readers as fluid and dynamic, looking for the dialogue rather than the monologue, for the shifts from reader to writer and back again.

It would not be a history of technological innovations *per se* but of arguments, access to cultural and material resources, resistance and redefinition. It would look at the role of men and their means

4

of communication used to keep women silent by their restrictions against speaking and against women's access to their media. It would look at the means women created to communicate with each other and with larger audiences – their publications; women's rights conferences and annual meetings; their study groups, clubs and organizations; their public speaking; their letters to each other and to periodicals (often sent out by the thousands to alert women to meetings and to crises); their fiction and nonfiction, books, tracts and pamphlets; their articles appearing in men's publications; their petitions (an important communication device for women with few other means of political redress) and other collective actions such as marches to the polls; their arguments in courtrooms and before legislative bodies, medical examiners, school boards and principles. It would look at the ease or difficulty with which white and Black women could safely travel to family, friends and conventions. It would look at the material, legal and social conditions that silenced women and those that made it possible for them to speak.[4]

From a woman-centered perspective on communication history, we can see *The Revolution* not simply in terms of its use as a tool by Anthony and Stanton to advance their own cause of woman's suffrage, but in the web of its interconnections with other periodicals, women's organizations, women's parlour or "pic-nic" discussion groups, readers and writers, and other means of communicating used by women.

The Revolution was, among other things, a strong voice of and for women in the public forum of the time period, a forum of debate that largely ignored women's opinions and their real rather than mythical experiences while men's publications reprinted speeches of other men, commented on news items, published commentaries, notices and letters, and in general debated their political and moral questions of the day. Publication of *The Revolution* meant that women's voices were more widely represented in those debates; in fact, it was one of the few sources of women's rights arguments to come to the attention of male politicians, ministers and newspaper editors, if their commentary reprinted in *The Revolution* gives us any indication. And not only did *The Revolution* insert women's voices and opinions into public debates on many subjects, but it also insisted that women's rights be the major topic of the day. By daring to be controversial and "outspoken," the women who wrote and produced it attracted attention and readership from a spectrum of individuals.

The Revolution was intended as a national newspaper to support not only suffrage, but also equal pay for equal work and many other "necessary changes" in the life and laws of the people; its purpose was to revolutionize, to change social relationships fundamentally. When other newspaper editors read the lively and deliberately controversial paper and criticized the editors and publisher for "meddling" not only in questions of women's rights but also in other social and political affairs, the editors of *The Revolution* responded by writing that "meddling" was the express purpose of the paper. "It is our intention to turn the State, the Church and the Home inside out, and let the people see the utter rottenness of our political, religious and social life" (March 26, 1868).

Even though the paper functioned as a voice representing women, however, we should not think of it as presenting uniform, uncontradictory positions. The pages of *The Revolution* were put together with an eye and an ear to its varied readership. While its writers were always conscious of being read by the opponents of "woman's rights" (the descriptive term used by nineteenth-century women's rights campaigners), an equally important function was to provide a forum for women to address each other. It was a place to make and hear arguments and pieces of news from editors, regular contributors and readers. The relationship between writer and reader was fluid. Many of the readers were part of a network of friends and woman's rights workers. A reader might meet with other of *The Revolution*'s readers and writers at a woman's rights meeting, read a report of the meeting in *The Revolution*, contribute a letter, and have a public speech she gave in a lecture hall reprinted in its pages. Even editor Elizabeth Cady Stanton, when she was off on a lecture tour, became a reader, once reacting angrily in a later issue to an editorial written by Parker Pillsbury criticizing Mary Lincoln.

Unfortunately, however, many of the readers *and* writers of *The Revolution* are anonymous to us. Until someone undertakes a study to find out, we can only guess at the significance of the paper to the women who read it. Letters to the editor – most from the northeast and midwest – suggest that the paper was very important to many women, who may have read it when it was passed on by a friend because they could not afford it or because they were prevented from having it arrive at their house because of the opposition of their fathers or husbands. Their letters indicate that the paper was a comfort and a companion, a piece of evidence to women that they were not sick or evil in their discontent, a source of encouragement and legitimation to boost their morale, a source of arguments to be used against their own opponents. It is unlikely that readers were solely "middle class" (a treacherous label when writing about women), for some letter writers described their conditions of poverty and employment. Certainly the women of *The Revolution* believed that the paper should be for all women, regardless of race or class.[5]

The Revolution was another connecting link for many women who had worked and visited with each other at temperance, anti-slavery and woman's rights conventions; corresponded with each other; provided forums for woman's rights speakers; canvassed for petition signatures; and published and wrote for women's news-papers. While Stanton and Anthony receive much of our attention today (because of their highly visible, long-time devotion to women's issues, and because of the wit and strength of their arguments), they always worked closely with other women. For example, Paulina Wright Davis' brief appearances from time to time in the pages of *The Revolution* do not indicate the extensive connections she had with the publisher, editors and other contributors. By 1840, she had already worked with many other women in the anti-slavery movement. In the 1840s she gave lectures on female anatomy and hygiene throughout the eastern and midwestern states, using (to the disgust of many critics) a female anatomical model for illustrations. Some of the women doctors mentioned in *The Revolution* had been encouraged to study medicine by her lectures. In the 1850s and 1860s she helped organize many of the woman's rights conventions. She invested several hundred dollars in *The Revolution*, cancelling that debt before she died in 1876.

Davis' publication *The Una*, begun in 1853, was one of the earliest publications devoted exclusively to woman's rights, and it was an early forum and source of support for some of the women who later worked on *The Revolution*. But Davis was not the only woman affiliated with *The Revolution* to publish or edit a woman's rights paper in other times and places. Contributor Mathilde Franziska Anneke published the *Deutscher Frauenzeitung* in 1852 in Milwaukee, Wisconsin. English correspondent Lydia Becker pub-lished *The Woman's Suffrage Journal* in England from 1870 to 1891. French correspondent Marie Goegg edited the *Journal des Femmes* in Paris and Geneva during the same time that *The Revolution* was being published. Contributor and supporter Matilda Joslyn Gage went on to edit *The National Citizen and Ballot Box* in 1878, a

publication of the National Woman Suffrage Association. Abigail
Scott Duniway read and wrote to *The Revolution* editors before
beginning her woman's rights newspaper, *The New Northwest,*
which she published for sixteen years in Oregon, beginning in
1871. Other contributors and supporters, such as Mary Clemmer
Ames and Lizzie Boynton were prominent journalists; others were
poets, fiction writers and novelists, such as Eleanor Kirk, Lillie
Devereux Blake, Laura Bullard, Augusta Larned, Emily Ford and
Harriet Beecher Stowe; and others were predominately lecturers,
such as Anna Dickinson. Many, such as Charlotte Wilbour, who
lectured, wrote literature and organized woman's rights meetings,
were accomplished in a number of these areas.

Our interest in these relationships among women and the
connections among their various forms of communication illustrates how we approached this project. Our primary objective was
to recover women's voices as they were heard in *The Revolution,*
making them available to other feminists and scholars. We chose
selections from the newspaper, when it was under the leadership of
Stanton and Anthony and later under Laura Bullard, that presented
unexpected arguments, strong stands, biting and humorous commentary. We could not include every issue, writer or position
published in *The Revolution*; however, our choice of ten general
topic areas reflects the most important themes and issues that
appeared in its pages. We judged them to be most important
because they were the issues most discussed and debated in the
newspaper's pages; they were the most talked-about subjects of the
day. So while columns of international news and long essays on
religion by Stanton may be of historical interest to us now, material
of this kind did not generate letters to the editor, commentary in
other newspapers and repeated news items, and, in fact, represented
only a minor part of the newspaper. Instead of focusing on what
contemporary historians have *assumed* to be the major interests of
the time period, we were guided by the principle of choosing
excerpts that illuminate the issues most talked about in *The
Revolution,* choosing material not likely to be known about or
available elsewhere. To help reconstruct the conversations about
those issues, we have grouped our selections in each section around
sub-themes, putting related excerpts next to each other, rather than
using a strict chronological ordering. Because of this process of
selecting and ordering, we realize that we have given *The Revolution*
a particular shape and interpretation for our readers. We recognize
this as unavoidable, however, since any rendering of the material

into another volume would require a similar process, and any contemporary reading of the newspaper is not occurring under the conditions within which it was originally read. We have tried, however, to help the reader become immersed in the time period in order better to hear and understand the voices of these women.

Though we deleted much, we indicate with ellipses where material has been left out preceding, following or in the middle of an excerpt. We hope scholars who want the complete context will use our excerpts as guides into the actual pages of *The Revolution*. We have made minor editorial notations in editorial brackets, such as indicating a first name or a misspelling in the original.

In some cases we have given the excerpts new titles (indicated with typographical markers★★) to be more helpful to readers by relaying quickly the content and spirit of the material. We attempted to give readers a background in what may be unfamiliar issues and people of the time period through our brief introductions to each section and with brief explanatory annotations. In a short volume, justice could not be done to the complex and detailed aspects of the time period, but we hope our introductions and annotations will be helpful in providing a context for understanding the selections. A final help may be the Appendix of biographical sketches of women (along with a few men) who were part of the network of those who published, wrote and read *The Revolution*; we feel we have come to know many of them through our encounters with them in the pages of *The Revolution* and in obscure biographies and histories. Women with sketches in the Appendix are those who were part of *The Revolution's* inner circle or who were formally listed in *The Revolution* as contributors. Other important figures are annotated in the text.

Our sections pull together major topics and ideas that we saw as recurring patterns in the pages of *The Revolution*. Section 1, "Onward *The Revolution*," contains selections about an important topic in *The Revolution* – the newspaper itself. The women of *The Revolution* were conscious of the importance of the paper to woman's rights and of the stir it had caused among supporters and opponents. Section 2 contains excerpts that describe the arguments and controversy surrounding suffrage, in general opposing the creation of what Stanton called "the aristocracy of sex," or granting suffrage to all men but not women. The paper's position on suffrage was part of a rift among righting women that ended in two distinct suffrage organizations. The title of section 3, "Hester Vaughanism," refers to women's concerns about the oppression of women through forced maternity and prostitution. Men, not women, were to blame for these crimes, they argued. "The bread question," section 4, demonstrates the attention given in *The Revolution* to working women and women's occupations and wages. Explicit attention is given to the need for redefinition of women and men in the excerpts found in section 5, "Man's sphere." Stanton challenged women to write exposés of men's abuse of power and of women. Men were warned to get out of women's way.

Section 6, "Going to unfashionable lengths," illustrates the arguments being made by women against clothing that was physically dangerous and limiting to their activities. While *Revolution* women were sympathetic to those who still wore the "reform dress" (by the time the newspaper was published, most had given it up because of the intense ridicule they suffered), they were more likely to advocate that women wear men's clothing for protection and safety. In section seven, "Man/dated language," are excerpts that surprised us with their forcefulness in critiquing man-made definitions and with their wit and sarcasm in advocating new words and new naming and speaking practices.

"What about the babies?" (section 8) was a frequent and tiresome argument to which righting women were subjected. They countered the claim that women could not vote because they had to take care of their domestic responsibilities by pointing out how insincere was such a concern for children. Not only could women take care of babies *and* vote, the babies would be better off if they did. Another argument these women encountered came from other women who claimed they had "All the rights I want" (section 9). Women of *The Revolution* wasted no time in pointing out that the rights women had – to work at drudgery, to be abused by men, to enjoy no legal and economic security – were rights that women should do without. Finally, our section 10, "Becoming perfect nuisances," is a wonderful testament to the fortitude and creativity of righting women in carrying through their opposition in ways that made sense in their own time period – "knit-ins" in saloons, petition drives, mock votes, speeches. Any deviation from women's culturally prescribed sphere was a courageous act.

In doing this project, we came to realize how much work is yet to be done if feminists are to reconceptualize and understand the integrated relationships of women's means of communicating in the nineteenth century and elsewhere, especially the role of periodicals published and written by women. We learned to be suspicious of many historical accounts which give interpretations of personalities and motives, interpretations that there is little evidence to support.[6] Perhaps one of our biggest lessons in this came when we realized we had accepted the pronouncement of historians that *The Revolution* became dull and innocuous after it was taken over by Laura Bullard, a pronunciation which has led to an earlier death certificate for *The Revolution* than is warranted. *The Revolution* under Laura Bullard was less biting and more accommodating than it was under Stanton and Anthony, but when we looked at it with fresh eyes we found strong stands taken on many of the same issues, along with its share of wit and wisdom.

Women's history is a recurring source of surprise and frustration – surprise and delight at the strength of women's opposition and vision but frustration at the familiar-sounding arguments and tactics used 'to keep women in their place. While we do not accept an essentialist position on gender – that an inherent core identity of man and woman has existed in all times and places – we none the less find these excerpts to be sometimes stunning in their application to our own time.[7] If nothing else, they should alert us to the full extent to which our place as women continues to be constructed for us under the guise of naturalism and how we are kept there through ridicule, harassment, and legal and economic sanctions. *The Revolution* is in our hands, now.

Notes

1 More detail about the newspaper is given in the introduction to section 1.

2 Fortunately, *The Revolution* has been reproduced on microfilm by Greenwood Publishing Co., making it generally available. The newspaper will also be included in a microfilm edition of the papers of Stanton and Anthony, a project of Patricia G. Holland and Ann Gordon (*The Papers of Elizabeth Cady Stanton and Susan B. Anthony*, Wilmington, Del.: Scholarly Resources, Inc., forthcoming).

3 DuBois (1975) makes a related argument. She does not argue that the women were attempting redefinition, but she does say that they saw themselves being different people when they got suffrage. But note, not only would *they* be different people but also other people would see them differently. Steiner's work (1979), a comprehensive discussion of how women's rights periodicals appealed to different women, says journals such as *The Revolution* presented new *models* for these women. We do not think they simply presented "role models," implying something to imitate or learn from; these women were arguing for

different cultural definitions. NeSmith (1987) shows a similar project by women to redefine "womanhood" and "manhood" in a turn-of-the-century clubwomen's paper.

4 NeSmith (1986) and Allen and Densmore (1977) give additional discussion of the problem of understanding women's communication history and the directions it might take.

5 The accusation that the women of *The Revolution* and of the woman's rights movements at the time were middle class, aiming to serve middle-class interests or to improve their own personal status, is a common and pernicious one. Clearly white and Black impoverished and working-class women had even less access than did the women who produced *The Revolution* to the material and cultural resources that made it possible, but we must remember the problem of labeling women with the class status of their husbands, particularly in a period in which women's legal and economic position was obtained only through the goodwill and fate of their fathers and husbands. Though the women of *The Revolution* were not without their classism and racism, which should not be excused or condoned, to belittle their efforts on that basis plays into the argument that women are not oppressed *as women* but only on the basis of their membership in a particular class or race. This argument they fought then and we need to resist now. Dale Spender (1982: 298) reminds us, "We simply cannot afford to collude in this practice of the denial and disparagement of women."

6 Dale Spender (1982) came to a similar suspicion in her research on early women thinkers. Her critique of histories of Stanton, Anthony and Matilda Joslyn Gage bear reading alongside this volume.

7 Joan Wallach Scott's discussion (1988) of feminist history is relevant here. Some feminist historians find it useful to examine how distinct notions of gender are in different time periods; we find it useful, also, to remind ourselves how much they are the same.

Bibliography

Allen, Donna, and Dana Densmore. 1977. "Call for Research." Washington, DC: Women's Institute for Freedom of the Press.

Barry, Kathleen. 1988. *Susan B. Anthony: A Biography of a Singular Feminist*. New York and London: New York University Press.

DuBois, Ellen. 1975. "The Radicalism of the Woman Suffrage Movement: Notes Toward the Reconstruction of Nineteenth-Century Feminism." *Feminist Studies*, 3: 63–71.

DuBois, Ellen. 1978. *Feminism and Suffrage: The Emergence of An Independent Women's Movement in America, 1848–1869*. Ithaca, NY: Cornell University Press.

Ehrenreich, Barbara, and Deirdre English. 1978. *For Her Own Good: 150 Years of the Experts' Advice to Women*. Garden City: Anchor Books.

Horton, James Oliver. 1986. "Freedom's Yoke: Gender Conventions Among Antebellum Free Blacks." *Feminist Studies* 12, No. 1 (Spring): 51–76.

Jones, Jacqueline. 1985. *Labor of Love, Labor of Sorrow: Black Women, Work, and the Family from Slavery to the Present.* New York: Basic Books.

Masel-Walters, Lynne. 1980. "To Hustle with the Rowdies: The Organization and Functions of the American Woman Suffrage Press." *Journal of American Culture* 3, No. 1 (Spring): 167–83.

McPherson, James M. 1975. *The Abolitionist Legacy: From Reconstruction to the NAACP.* Princeton, NJ: Princeton University Press.

NeSmith, Georgia. 1986. "Through a Gendered Eye: Notes Toward a Socialist Feminist Critique of Media History." Paper presented at the International Communication Association Conference, Chicago.

NeSmith, Georgia. 1987. "Gender and Progressivism: Voices from *The Courant,* 1899–1904." Paper presented at the International Communication Association Conference, Montreal.

Newman, Louise Michele, ed. 1985. *Men's Ideas/Women's Realities: Popular Science, 1870–1915.* New York: Pergamon.

Rosenberg, Rosalind. 1975. "In Search of Woman's Nature, 1850–1920." *Feminist Studies* 4, Nos 1/2 (Fall): 141–54.

Scott, Joan Wallach. 1988. *Gender and the Politics of History.* New York: Columbia University Press.

Sealander, Judith. 1982. "Antebellum Black Press Images of Women." *Western Journal of Black Studies* 6, No. 3: 159–65.

Smith-Rosenberg, Carroll, and Charles Rosenberg. 1975. "The Female Animal: Medical and Biological Views of Woman and Her Role in 19th-Century America." *Journal of American History* 59: 331–56.

Spender, Dale. 1982. *Women of Ideas (And What Men have Done to Them).* London: Ark.

Steiner, Linda Claire. 1979. "The Women's Suffrage Press, 1850–1900: A Cultural Analysis." Doctoral dissertation. University of Illinois, Urbana-Champaign.

Welter, Barbara. 1976. *Dimity Convictions: The American Woman in the Nineteenth Century.* Athens, Ohio: Ohio University Press.

1
Onward *The Revolution*

Introduction

The appearance of the first issue of *The Revolution* on January 8, 1868, must have been as exciting to its readers as the appearance of *Ms* magazine in July 1972 was to contemporary feminists. At last, letter writers responded, a publication that dared to say what they had been thinking all along.

After the Civil War, women needed a national publication to give them a voice. A number of radical, woman's rights newspapers had been published by women since the 1850s, but most had ceased publication by the time of the Civil War. (*The Sibyl*, 1856–64, a dress reform and woman's rights periodical was an exception.) Susan B. Anthony, Elizabeth Cady Stanton and Lucy Stone had talked about the need for a journal for some time, even unsuccessfully soliciting funds to begin one. The money to begin *The Revolution* was offered by George Francis Train, who made the offer while campaigning for women's suffrage in Kansas with Anthony. Other abolitionists and suffragists were already alarmed that Stanton and Anthony had accepted Train's campaign help – he was called a "Copperhead," a southern sympathizer – so his assistance in starting a journal, called by a less than timid name, gave the journal immediate attention from a mixed readership.

Train came to be involved with Stanton and Anthony at a time when two referenda were going to the ballot in Kansas – one which would give Black men the vote and one which would give women the vote (presumably only white women unless the other amendment was also adopted). State Republicans launched an anti-woman suffrage campaign, while abolitionists refused to endorse women's suffrage, using the justification that they did not want to jeopardize the amendment for Black men's suffrage. Train, a Democrat, financier and activist for Irish independence from England, was well-known as a flamboyant speaker and dresser. In his speaking tour with Anthony, she would argue for passage of

14

both amendments, while he would argue that if only one group could get the vote first, it should be white women.

The condemnation Stanton and Anthony received because of their association with Train might have been due in part to his racism, but it must be remembered that other abolitionists and women's suffragists were also racists (Henry Blackwell, for example). Using recently discovered correspondence hidden for more than a century, Kathleen Barry (1988) concludes that Blackwell and a colleague conspired for their own political purposes, first to arrange that Train offered his campaign help in Kansas, and later to use Anthony's association with Train to try to discredit her as a woman's rights leader. These actions, unknown to Stanton and Anthony, may have been important factors in the painful and damaging split in the woman's movement in 1869, Barry suggests. What the Republican men did not anticipate was that Train would offer financial support for a radical newspaper. Anthony and Stanton knew there were powerful forces working for abolition but few representatives for woman's suffrage. Certainly most of the men they had worked with in the abolition movement were either indifferent or antagonistic to woman's rights arguments. Anthony and Stanton thought there was no hope for their campaign unless they accepted what small offers of support were given them.

Actually, Train gave little support. Though Train's affiliation with the journal was a source of conflict with other abolitionists and suffragists, his actual involvement in the journal was limited. The week the first issue of the journal was published, he sailed for England, only to be arrested and confined for almost a year. The journal's financial pages, handled by Train's friend David M. Melliss (financial editor of the New York *World*), continued to reflect Train's radical financial theories such as Greenbackism (establishing greenbacks as the national currency along with a fixed national rate of interest), and Train continued to send letters which the editors published. However, the substantial financial support that he pledged never materialized. He ultimately contributed approximately $3,000 and Melliss $7,000 toward its support.

Without a stable source of financial support, the journal was always in a precarious position. In its pages, Anthony exhorted readers to get more subscribers (subscriptions peaked at 3,000, though her goal as she publicized it in *The Revolution* was 100,000), offering those who sold a substantial number of subscriptions such inducements as a copy of John Stuart Mill's *The Subjection of Women* and a sewing machine. She chastised newspaper editors who wanted free subscriptions (she claimed that the journal exchanged with 6,000 other newspapers). Yet she and Stanton would not compromise on the kind of advertisements they would accept. Unlike other publications of its day, they refused patent medicine advertising. In addition, other advertisers generally were uninterested in advertising to women, in a controversial journal, especially when they could advertise in general circulation, conservative and moderate newspapers. The yearly price of the paper was kept at $2 as long as possible to keep it affordable to more women, was raised to $3 on June 17, 1869, but was returned to $2 after Stanton and Anthony left the paper.

In the short time that the journal was issued by Stanton and Anthony, its offices were housed in three locations, each appointed by the women with such attractions as portraits of Lucretia Mott and Mary Wollstonecraft. Initially the offices were located in the New York *World* building in what were the headquarters of the American Equal Rights Association. The extent of the physical difficulties the women endured in putting out the journal is illustrated by the fact that their offices were on the fourth floor of a building several blocks from the fifth floor office of their printer's elevatorless building. In May 1869, the journal's offices were moved to the Woman's Bureau (49 East 23rd Street, near Fifth Avenue), a building purchased by Elizabeth B. Phelps for the use of women's organizations. *The Revolution* occupied the first floor of what must have been a much more pleasant, convenient and inspiring setting. Unfortunately other organizations were apparently reluctant to be housed in the same location as the radical *Revolution*, so the arrangement only lasted one year. In April of 1870 the offices were moved to 27 Chatham Street.

The Revolution was not only a centralizing and organizing force for its readers but its offices were also a rallying place for like-minded women to gather, talk and support each other. Contributors to its pages as well as other supporters included Anna Dickinson, Paulina Wright Davis, Lucretia Mott, Elizabeth Smith Miller, Matilda Joslyn Gage, Eleanor Kirk [Ames], Rebecca Moore, Lillie Devereux Blake, Alice Cary, Phoebe Cary, Laura Curtis Bullard, Elizabeth Tilton and Mary Anthony (Susan's sister). (Other contributors during Anthony and Stanton's tenure with the paper are listed in the excerpt, "Prospectus of *The Revolution* for

16

1870." For biographical information on those who had direct involvement with the paper and those listed as contributors, see the biographical Appendix.) Parker Pillsbury was a loyal editor (along with Stanton; Anthony was the "proprietor" or publisher) until he left for a time in 1869 for a more lucrative position, returning in 1870 on an appeal from Anthony when she went on a Lyceum tour to earn money for *The Revolution* and get new subscribers. Paulina Wright Davis, who had edited *The Una*, a woman's rights periodical of the 1850s, served as corresponding editor beginning January 1, 1870.

Given the lack of signatures on many articles and our lack of knowledge of the day to day operations of the newspaper, it is difficult to know who was responsible for writing much of the content. In at least one case of an editorial with Stanton's initials on it, she claims in her autobiography, *Eighty Years and More*, not to have written it (presumably she was referring to the excerpt in this chapter called "Garrison Crucifies Democrats, Train, and the Women of '*The Revolution*'"). Regardless of authorship, the paper was bold, crisply written and well printed, and was evidently intended to be a lasting contribution to the woman's rights movement. (The newsprint used was of good quality and bound volumes of six months' worth of issues were advertised as available from *The Revolution* office.) The editors and contributors laid out long arguments in editorials, commented on reprinted news items and speeches and provided a forum for letter writers. The newspaper attracted considerable attention – in the form of both praise and condemnation – from other newspaper editors, and it filled a void for its women readers, who must have cheered often at the boxed ears of ministers, politicians and editors. In all, *The Revolution* was a public display of a strong women's movement.

Unfortunately, the paper was not to continue. Though Stanton drew no salary, Pillsbury a very small salary, and Anthony only her expenses, debts continued to mount. Given *The Revolution's* precarious financial situation and its burden to Anthony, a project to create a stock company of several wealthy women for the financial foundation of the newspaper was begun. Isabella Beecher Hooker and Harriet Beecher Stowe discussed with Anthony and Stanton becoming editors, bringing their substantial personal influence to the paper. They were dissuaded from insisting that the name of the paper be changed in order for them to affiliate with it, but in the end *The Revolution's* unabashed position taken in favor of a divorced woman whose former husband had killed her lover (known as the Richardson-McFarland case) dissolved the relationship.

Despite its frequent assertion by contemporaries, it is doubtful that Anthony and Stanton gave up the paper because of competition from *The Woman's Journal*, begun by Lucy Stone and others in 1870. Subscriptions to *The Revolution* were increasing at the time the paper was passed on to other hands. But with Parker Pillsbury eager to be released to a better paying position, Stanton busy with lecturing, and Anthony increasingly burdened with the paper's debts, Anthony reluctantly transferred possession of the paper after its May 26, 1870 issue to editor Laura Curtis Bullard and publisher Edwin A. Studwell (chairman of the Union Woman Suffrage Society at the time) for one dollar, a dollar that ironically was stolen from Anthony's wallet a few days later. Anthony assumed the paper's $10,000 debt, which she paid off in six years through lecture tours and donations.

Under Bullard's editorship, the journal's motto changed from "Men, their rights and nothing more: Women, their rights and nothing less" to "What therefore God hath joined together, let not man put asunder." Perhaps it was this new motto that has led to the contemporary assessment that *The Revolution* ceased to be of interest after it was no longer associated with Stanton and Anthony. But the motto – and Bullard – were perhaps bolder and more clever than is apparent at first glance. In an editorial in the September 15, 1870 issue, Bullard explained that the motto not only referred to marriage but also to the need to restore women's equal participation in society: "[Woman] has been systematically divorced from [man] from the beginning of time: she is now to proclaim and enforce her marriage rights. She is to be joined with him in all the great ventures of human life. She is to have an equal place with him in the trades, in the colleges, in the lyceum, in the press, in literature, in science, in art, in government, in everything."

The newspaper now contained more pieces of fiction, more poetry, and woman's rights literary criticism (for example, reviews of woman's rights books by G. F. Ball and reviews of women characters in fiction by Emily E. Ford). It contained a great deal of material from foreign correspondents and travelogues from Bullard and others traveling outside the country. Well-known women were featured in biographical essays, including Margaret Fuller, English printer and *Revolution* correspondent Emily Faithfull and other journalists. Phoebe Cary and Augusta Larned provided Bullard with substantial editorial assistance, particularly when Bullard was traveling out of the country. The names of other women – Celia Burleigh, Lillie Devereux Blake, Lizzie Boynton, Rebecca Moore, Laura Holloway – appear frequently in the paper's pages, suggesting a sustained support from women who had been contributors under Anthony and Stanton. Stanton on occasion provided strong articles.

The writing in *The Revolution* under Bullard's editorship was more literary than argumentative, but none the less most of the same issues continued to be presented. Bullard, in fact, took strong opposition to criticism in *The Woman's Journal* that her paper should stay out of all issues but suffrage. She was, however, willing to be more placating than her predecessors had been. The change in tone and style (no longer featuring "words as hard as cannon-balls," as Anthony desired from her contributors) may help account for the pain that Anthony and Stanton felt about the newspaper during this time period. Though Bullard asked Anthony to come back to the paper and manage its affairs, Anthony's 1870 diary indicates that despite her interest she was unwilling to do so alone. Bullard gave up *The Revolution*, she said in a farewell editorial, because her travels took her away too much. She was also a fiction writer, who may have found that the pressure of publication interfered with her primary interest.

With the October 28, 1871 issue, the paper was transferred to J. N. Hallock, publisher, and Revd W. T. Clarke, editor. Its motto became "Devoted to the Interest of Woman and Home Culture," reflecting the editor's insistence that the home is the center of every "true woman's" world. Clarke advocated woman suffrage, but he made it clear that he objected to women in the movement who blamed men for their abuse of women. "He has not wronged her because she was woman, but because she was weak," he claimed (October 28, 1871); "Most men are exceedingly kind to women, and treat them with too much tenderness rather than too little. More women among us are injured by indulgence than injustice." Perhaps mercifully, *The Revolution* was soon dissolved. In the last issue, published February 17, 1872, the publisher announced that because of the resignation of the editor and the limited financial success of the newspaper, *The Revolution's* subscription list was being merged with that of the publisher's other newspaper, the *Liberal Christian*. *The Revolution*, which had ceased to be revolutionary under Clarke's editorship, no longer existed even in name.

Bibliography

Anthony, Katharine. 1954. *Susan B. Anthony: Her Personal History and Her Era*. Garden City, NY: Doubleday.

Barry, Kathleen. 1988. *Susan B. Anthony: A Biography of a Singular Feminist*. New York and London: New York University Press.

Dorr, Rheta Childe. 1928. *Susan B. Anthony: The Woman Who Changed the Mind of a Nation*. New York: Frederick A. Stokes.

Filler, Louis. 1946. "Parker Pillsbury: An Anti-Slavery Apostle." *New England Quarterly*, September: 315–37.

Griffith, Elisabeth. 1984. *In Her Own Right: The Life of Elizabeth Cady Stanton*. New York: Oxford University Press.

Harper, Ida Husted. 1969. *Life and Work of Susan B. Anthony, Vol. 1*. New York: Arno and *The New York Times*.

Lutz, Alma. 1959. *Susan B. Anthony, Rebel, Crusader, Humanitarian*. Beacon Hill: Beacon Press.

Masel-Walters, Lynne. 1976. "Their Rights and Nothing More: A History of *The Revolution*, 1868–1870." *Journalism Quarterly* 53, No. 2 (Summer): 242–51.

Steiner, Linda Claire. 1979. "The Women's Suffrage Press, 1850–1900: A Cultural Analysis". Doctoral dissertation, University of Illinois, Urbana-Champaign.

The Revolution: The Organ of the National Party of New America

PRINCIPLE, NOT POLICY – INDIVIDUAL RIGHTS AND RESPONSIBILITIES

THE REVOLUTION WILL ADVOCATE:

1. IN POLITICS – Educated Suffrage, irrespective of Sex or Color; Equal Pay to Women for Equal Work; Eight Hours Labor; Abolition of Standing Armies and Party Despotisms, Down with Politicians – Up with the People!

2. IN RELIGION – Deeper Thought; Broader Idea; Science not Superstition; Personal Purity; Love to Man as well as God.

3. IN SOCIAL LIFE – Morality and Reform; Practical Education, not Theoretical; Facts not Fiction; Virtue not Vice; Cold Water not Alcoholic Drinks or Medicines. It will indulge in no Gross Personalities and insert no Quack or Immoral Advertisements, so common even in Religious Newspapers.

4. THE REVOLUTION proposes a new Commercial and Financial Policy. America no longer led by Europe. Gold like our Cotton and

Corn for sale. Greenbacks for money. An American System of Finance. American Products and Labor Free. Foreign Manufactures [sic] Prohibited. Open doors to Artisans and Immigrants. Atlantic and Pacific Oceans for American Steamships and Shipping; or American goods in American bottoms. New York the Financial Centre of the World. Wall Street emancipated from Bank of England, or American Cash for American Bills. The Credit Foncier and Credit Mobilier System, or Capital Mobilized to Resuscitate the South and our Mining Interests, and to People the Country from Ocean to Ocean, from Omaha to San Francisco. More organized Labor, more Cotton, more Gold and Silver Bullion to sell foreigners at the highest prices. Ten millions of Naturalized Citizens DEMAND A PENNY OCEAN POSTAGE, to Strengthen the Brotherhood of Labor; and if Congress Vote One Hundred and Twenty-five Millions for a Standing Army and Freedman's Bureau, cannot they spare One Million to Educate Europe and to keep bright the chain of acquaintance and friendship between those millions and their fatherland?

. . . TERMS – Two dollars a year, in advance. Ten names ($20) entitle the sender to one copy free.

ELIZABETH CADY STANTON, PARKER PILLSBURY, Eds.
SUSAN B. ANTHONY, Proprietor and Manager.
37 Park Row (Room 17), New York City.

January 8, 1868

★★The President Subscribes★★

Monday night George Francis Train and Susan B. Anthony were invited to address the people at Rahway, New Jersey, by the Athenaeum Society, on the Enfranchisement of Women. . . . Miss Anthony having just returned from Washington, where she had been introducing her new journal, *The Revolution*, Mr. Train interrupted her by asking about the capital. . . .

TRAIN – Whom did you see at the Capital?

ANTHONY – Everybody.

TRAIN – What did Everybody say to you?

(Laughter.)

ANTHONY – They said as Revolutions never go backward, they would all subscribe for the new organ of the age. . . . (Applause.)

TRAIN – Did you go to the White House?

ANTHONY – Oh, yes. . . . Johnson stood at his desk. Said "No," had a thousand such applications every day; more papers than he

21

could read. I told him he was mistaken. That he never had such an application in his life. You recognize, I said, Mr. Johnson, that Mrs. Stanton and myself, for two years, have boldly told the Republican party that they must give ballots to women as well as negroes, and by means of *The Revolution* we are bound to drive the party to logical conclusions, or break it into a thousand pieces as was the old Whig party, unless we get our rights. (Applause.) That brought him to his pocket book, and he signed his name Andrew Johnson, with a bold hand, as much as to say, anything to get rid of this woman and break the radical party. (Loud applause and laughter.)

January 8, 1868

Salutatory

A new paper is the promise of a new thought; of something better or different, at least, from what has gone before.

With the highest idea of the dignity and power of the press, this journal is to represent no party, sect, or organization, but individual opinion; editors and correspondents alike, all writing, from their own stand point, and over their own names. The enfranchisement of woman is one of the leading ideas that calls this journal into existence. Seeing, in its realization, the many necessary changes in our modes of life, we think "*The Revolution*" a fitting name for a paper that will advocate so radical a reform as this involves in our political, religious and social world.

With both man and woman in the editorial department, we shall not have masculine and feminine ideas alone, but united thought on all questions of national and individual interest.

But we do not promise the millennium in journalism, from this experiment, or in politics from the enfranchisement of woman, only a new, and, we hope, a better phase of the existence, which, to those who are tired of the old grooves in which the world has run so long, is something to be welcomed in the future. With the moral chaos that surrounds us on every side, the corruption in the State, the dissensions in the church, the jealousies in the home, what thinking mind does not feel that we need something new and revolutionary in every department of life. Determined to do our part in pushing on the car of progress we begin with the new year, a new life work, hoping the world will be the better for the birth of "*The Revolution*."

January 8, 1868

Onward The Revolution

The Revolution

The name speaks its purpose. It is to revolutionize. It is Radicalism practical, not theoretical. It is to effect changes through abolitions, reconstructions and restorations. It is to realize ancient visions, answer long uttered prayers and fulfil old prophecies. Former things are passing away. Old Faïths, Philosophies and Philanthropies are to be extended, and new principles discovered and applied to human enfranchisement. New America is discovered. . . .

January 8, 1868

Garrison Crucifies Democrats, Train, and the Women of "*The Revolution*"

January 4th

Dear Miss Anthony:

In all friendliness, and with the highest regard for the Women's Rights movement, I cannot refrain from expressing my regret and astonishment that you and Mrs. Stanton should have taken such leave of good sense, and departed so far from true self-respect, as to be travelling companions and associate lecturers with that crack brained, harlequin and semi-lunatic, George Francis Train! . . .

It seems you are looking to the Democratic party, and not to the Republican, to give success politically to your movement! I should as soon think of looking to the Great Adversary to espouse the cause of righteousness.

Your old and outspoken friend,
Wm. Lloyd Garrison

We publish the above letter as a fair type of a few we have received from leading abolitionists during the last two months. . . .

Mr. Garrison has watched and criticised all political parties, during the last thirty years, solely with reference to their action on the question of African slavery. He has taken no note of what they said or did on commerce or finance, homestead laws or protection, prison discipline, temperance or woman's rights. – Whatever their action on all these questions, he has ever praised Republicans and Democrats alike for every true word and legislative act in favor of the black race.

If Mr. Garrison may judge parties by their action on slavery alone, is it not equally fair for us to judge them by their action on woman alone? Applying this test to the Republican party of to–day, where does it stand?

It is the first party in American history that ever proposed to introduce the word "male" into the Federal Constitution; that ever insulted the women of the republic as petitioners, by apologizing for their presentation, and so garbling the petitions that no one could tell who petitioned, or what they asked. It has blocked the discussion of this question in every possible way; shut us out from its journals, and denied us a hearing in the House of Representatives, the only time we have ever asked for its use. In the Constitutional Convention of New York it gave us a sham hearing, having decided in caucus [chaired by Horace Greeley], beforehand, that it would report against our rights. In Kansas, it ignored our question in the State Convention; yet leading Republican politicians, with black men, stumped the State against striking the word "male" from its Constitution.

The Democratic party on the contrary, has done all it could to keep our question alive in the State and national councils, by pressing Republicans, in their debates on negro suffrage, to logical conclusions. They have respectfully presented our petitions, and called attention to them in every possible way. They have franked our documents, from one end of the Union to the other, made us liberal donations, helped us to secure 9,000 votes in Kansas, and to establish a journal through which we can speak, with their motives for such action we have no more to do than with the motives of Republicans, in pressing negro suffrage while they ignore woman's suffrage. . . .

Elizabeth Cady Stanton
January 29, 1868

A Charming Surprise

We promised our readers a new idea in journalism, and now they have it. On Monday morning our metropolitans were all agog with the appearance of six little Irish girls, dressed in their national colors, quietly marching through our fashionable streets, selling "*The Revolution.*" To Madame Demorest* we are indebted for the admirable style of the outfit. This beautiful pageant now to be seen daily in our streets is but the herald of the good time coming, when "*The Revolution*" will have a magnificent building, owned by women, with women in every department – writing editorials, setting type, working the press, cutting, folding – and with little girls selling in every city in the Union, young and old

Onward The Revolution

alike in comfortable costume, a happy, healthy class of self-supporting, educated, enfranchised citizens.

January 29, 1868

[★ Demorest was also president of the Woman's Tea Company in New York, and her paper, *Demorest's Monthly*, originated the sewing pattern business.]

What the People Say of Us

Springfield, Iowa

RESPECTED FRIENDS: I have received "*The Revolution.*" As it is a bloodless one and just such a one as I have been wanting for years, I send two dollars to further it on, with the expectation of having the pleasure of reading something the ensuing year (if life and health permit) that will not insult my dignity as a woman. I rejoice in the prospect. Go on and revolve the whole wheel! . . .

Yours,

Ann L. Raley

Chicago

DEAR MRS. STANTON:

Women do so need an organized and well-established centre around which to rally. A paper which for character and influence should come to be a power in the land, and which should deal justly and impartially with woman – her claims and interests on the one hand, and her ignorances and wrong doings on the other – would, it seems to me, help on social progress more than any other one thing which I can think of. . . .

Very sincerely yours,

Caroline F. Corbin★

Weymouth

DEAR MISS ANTHONY:

I am delighted to learn that we are to have a paper. It is what we most need. When we have a paper and a party we shall have weapons to fight with. . . .

Yours sincerely,

Olympia Brown★

Stubois, Mich.

God speed you in the cause of justice, Equal Rights, and human

25

liberty. *"Revolution!"* How I *like* that name, and how gladly
welcome the paper. I am a co-worker with you in the noble cause
of Suffrage for Woman. Inclosed my subscription for one year.

Miss Elvira Wheelock
February 5, 1868

[* Author Caroline Corbin was one of the founders of the
Association for the Advancement of Women and later became
president of the Illinois Association Opposed to Woman Suffrage.
Olympia Brown was a minister and suffrage leader who cam-
paigned with Stanton and Anthony in Kansas.]

Lesser of Two Evils

. . . It would have been a sadder mistake if we had chosen to have
had neither Train or *"The Revolution"* to spread our opinions, and
thus been without a mouthpiece.

March 5, 1868

Meddling With Everything

From the *Waterloo* (Canada) *Chronicle*:

> *"The Revolution"* – Miss Susan B. Anthony of New York, has
> favored the *Chronicle* by sending us her new weekly paper, *"The
> Revolution,"* a journal devoted to "Woman's Rights." . . . In
> addition to the advocacy of "Woman's Rights," *"The Revolution"*
> meddles with a number of other questions, some of which are
> not likely to give it much popularity outside of the states. We
> regret this. . . .

We thank our Canada friends for all kindly suggestions, but every
paper, like every family, knows its own business better than
anybody else possibly can. We might suggest to the *Chronicle* to
shut out of its columns all quack advertisements as we do; but
perhaps the *Chronicle* has a reason for their publication. We might
advise the *Chronicle* to fill its columns with one subject, and not
wander into reform, theology and politics, but the *Chronicle*,
having a variety of readers to please, would, no doubt, say to us,
we do not publish our paper to suit the taste of one man, but many.
"The Revolution" started for the express purpose of "meddling"
with everything. It is our intention to turn the State, the Church

and the Home inside out, and let the people see the utter rottenness of our political, religious and social life. Do not suppose, Mr. *Chronicle* that we are "a Una," "a Lily," or "a Sybil,"★ and that we started a paper to sentimentalize about love, moonshine, and women. No such thing! We intend to talk about trade, commerce, finance, Ireland, Abyssinia, Bismark, Napoleon, science, government, schools, children, cooking, bread and housekeeping. Believing that the universe was not made for man alone, we shall take the liberty of looking at the land and sea and sky and all things that dwell thereon and therein, and describing what we see in "*The Revolution.*"

March 26, 1868

[★ These are names of earlier US woman's rights journals, which were more radical than their titles suggest, and for which Stanton was a contributor.]

Wall Street

Many of our subscribers ask us why we publish all that nonsense about Wall street, as they do not see the point in it. We do not suppose that the honest, unsophisticated children of men, on the granite hills of New England, or on the far-off prairies of the west, do see the point of all this financial trickery and knavery. But, dear friends, we are simply turning Wall street inside out, as we intend to do everything else. Its denizens see the point. They buy up "*The Revolution*" by the hundreds, the moment it is out. They sit and read it, laugh over it, swear over it, and wonder at the women of "*The Revolution.*" . . . If the people of this nation only knew all the swindling that is done in these stock-gambling alleys, they would rise in their wrath. . . . Wall street is nothing more or less than a grand gambling saloon on a large scale. . . .

Elizabeth Cady Stanton
April 16, 1868

★★Poison Pen★★

From the *Memorial and Rock*, Plymouth, Mass.:
. . . [*The Revolution*] proves conclusively that for caustic sharpness and pointed pungency, a woman's pen fully maintains the reputation of her tongue.

April 23, 1868

The Revolution in Words

★★We Have Come to the Revolution★★

From the *People's Journal*, Greenwich, N.Y.:

"*The Revolution.*" – Before us is a copy of a new applicant for the favor of the reading public. It is "something new under the sun." Woman's Rights are advocated, and their ways portrayed in language of force and reason, while the great political principles which agitate the public mind are handled with no little power.

Yes, sir, it is "something new under the sun" for women to talk about finance, capital, labor, politics, religion and social life. The time has passed for "Lilys, Sybils, Unas, May Flowers, Dewdrops," etc., and we have come to "*The Revolution.*"

April 30, 1868

"Why Don't You X?"

In reply to the many calls we receive from editors in all parts of the country to exchange with them, it is with great regret we find ourselves compelled to refuse. Our rapidly increasing circulation takes all that we publish in advance.

Remember gentlemen, 6,000 editors are asking us to exchange. Those who hold the fat offices under government, who have all the advantages and opportunities of life open to them; who have the national, state and county printing and advertising, ask us, a disfranchised class, shut out of all the profitable and honorable posts of life, to give the ruling class $12,000 a year. We have been so cordially welcomed to the field of journalism, that we are truly sorry to refuse so small a favor, but as our price is very low, only $2.00 a year, we hope there is enough chivalry in the press, to contribute this sum to sustain the only journal in the nation that advocates Universal Suffrage in the reconstruction.

May 21, 1868

★★Man "Sticks Out" Everywhere★★

From the *Weekly Kansas Radical*:

"*The Revolution.*" – A paper with this title has been started in New York city. It is well conducted editorially, and mechanically

28

is a model of taste. The "woman" "sticks out" in both departments. . . .

. . . Seeing that the man "sticks out" everywhere in the Bible, constitution, laws, in every journal in the two hemispheres, it seems to us time that there should be such a Revolution in mundane affairs that the "woman should strike out" somewhere, and let the "white male" know that he does not constitute all the elements necessary to the state, the church, or the home. . . .

June 11, 1868

What the Press Says of Us

From the *Commercial Advertiser*, New York

"*The Revolution*" – This paper, the organ of the Women Suffrage movement, and edited by Mrs. Stanton and Parker Pillsbury, has now reached the age of five months, and is as lively a child as was ever reared. It is independent, chatty, personal and intensely self-conscious. Its notices from the press, both good and bad, it parades and comments upon in the spirit in which they are uttered. It has a thoroughly Amazonian liking for a fight.

And like all lively, willful children, everybody is telling us to subside. We have more sympathy than ever with "little Johnny," whose fidgetty mother is continually saying "don't do this," "don't do that," for everybody seems to be in a state of chronic alarm lest "*The Revolution*" should do or say something it should not. One says, "let politics alone; just talk Woman's Suffrage;" as if this demand, and all the arguments to maintain it, did not lend us at once into that forbidden realm. Another says, "for Heaven's sake, let political economy alone. What does a woman know of finance, capital and labor, free trade and protection? Talk about women's work and wages." Just as if woman, taxed to pay the public debt, taxed for every foreign product she eats and wears, and paying double for everything made at home, the victim of monopolists, capitalists and bondholders equally with man, should not inform herself on all these points. If woman knows nothing about these questions, then that is the very reason we should discuss them in "*The Revolution*." . . . We publish the comments of the press as a matter of history, for the women of the next generation to see the crude notions that the men of our day have on woman. . . .

June 18, 1868

The Revolution in Words

★★Going By Train★★

Susan Anthony says woman is going ahead. All right; ladies should not be compelled to go afoot. – *N. Y. Express.*

We are not – we have taken the Train!

July 2, 1868

Price of *"The Revolution"*

When you advanced the price of your paper to ten cents, I dropped it, perceiving that the women are no better than men, and no more fit to rule. It is avarice and extortion to charge twice what a paper is worth.

J. P. M.

. . . . We fixed our subscription at two dollars per year, much below a *"fair price,"* that we might place our paper within the reach of the *working people* – especially all *women* who earn their own living. . . .

July 19, 1868

The Politics of *"The Revolution"*

A friend writes us that as Miss Anthony, in the midst of a speech in the New York State Teachers Association at Owego, recommended *"The Revolution"* to the women teachers, a schoolmaster, anxious to confuse the audience and confound Miss A., asked, in a triumphant tone, "what are the politics of '*The Revolution*';" to which, with her usual promptness, Miss A. replied, "Exact and Equal Justice to every human being under the government of the United States."

August 20, 1868

The Old Year is Gone

. . . With the opening of the New Year, *"The Revolution"* celebrates its first birthday. As it is now a hale and hearty child and is welcomed and praised by the press of both continents, we may as well confess that when it came into the world with such a startling cry of defiance and prophesy, and received its bloody baptismal name, *"The Revolution,"* with such an erratic world-known and

30

abhored ¼god father as George Train, and was given to our care and keeping, it was not without grave fears and distrust of our wisdom and capacity that we undertook the management of what we clearly saw was destined to be a wayward, willful sprite. . . .

"*The Revolution*," all tell us, meets a want that no other paper does, and to fill this niche is our highest ambition.

There are plenty of journals to advocate science, politics, theology, agriculture and amusements; plenty devoted to elegant extracts, to prose, verse, polite literature, art, dillitanti morals, fashions and customs; papers that studiously avoid all "vexed questions;" "too deep for popular thought before which the great and wise stand trembling and appalled;" plenty of papers to tell the people what they are pleased to hear. "*The Revolution*," as its name indicates comes to tell the people what they ought to know; not to *reflect*, but to *make*, public sentiment. It is our purpose to show the causes and remedies of ignorance, poverty, misery and crime; to stir the Stygian pools of human woe and degradation to their lowest depths; and to exalt the glory of the "three fine arts" as Ruskin calls them, "how to feed and clothe, and house the poor."

With a deeper study of the science of government, of political economy and finance, we see it is not the ballot alone that woman needs for her safety and protection, but a revolution in our political, religious and social systems; in fact the entire reorganization of society. Such being our policy, the names of distinguished men and women who write only for money and popularity will not be found in our columns, which in the future as in the past will be kept sacred for the earnest words of voluntary contributors who have no other outlet for their advanced thoughts. . . .

Elizabeth Cady Stanton
December 31, 1868

The Revolution on Finance

During the recent visit of Miss Anthony to Washington, the opinions published in *The Revolution* on finance were much canvassed by some of the leading senators. . . .*

Senator – Miss Anthony, your *Revolution* gives great prominence to finance. . . .

Susan B. Anthony – Senator, . . . I am for justice to all, in finance, as well as in suffrage, without regard to color or sex. One lawful money for all alike – government, bond-holder and people. Why not, Senator?

Senator (laughing) – Well, Miss Anthony, you put the question, woman-like, in a very conclusive form to suit your view of the case, by mixing things that ought not to be mixed. Government, in our extremity during the rebellion, contracted to pay the interest of our bonds in coin, and, in order to do so, we were forced to make the Custom Duties payable in gold coin, or, as you express it, to have two kinds of money.

S.B.A. – This is the old plea, Senator, of expediency in the place of principle. Want of faith in principle, and the terrible earnestness of the people to put down the rebellion was the first fatal mistake that government made in its financial legislation. It began discrediting its own money or promises to pay, by making two kinds of money current in its own receipts and disbursements. . . . In the first place, as we have paper money, and must continue to have it, even when we return to specie payments, let us have but one kind, and that the best and cheapest. . . . So, Senator, my first plank in *The Revolution* is – Greenbacks and fractional currency direct from government as the only lawful paper money in the country.

Senator – You take rather a contracted view of this question, and lose sight of what the country owes to the National banks for their services during the rebellion. . . .

S.B.A. – . . . The National bank notes and the $20,000,000 gold interest paid annually to the National banks for their use is a direct robbery of the people. The next plank in *The Revolution*'s financial platform, is to keep gold and silver, like our cotton and tobacco, always articles of merchandise to be sold at the highest possible price to foreigners.

Senator – . . . I am no friend to the old state banking system, which, as you say, always failed to redeem their notes in every crisis; but when we do resume specie payments this time, the National banks will be compelled to keep, by law, so large a reserve of specie, that there will be no fear of their failing to redeem their notes on demand.

S.B.A. – Perhaps so – certainly so, if I have my way, and my way is this; The best way, Senator, to guarantee that the National banks shall always redeem their notes on demand is to have no National bank notes at all. . . . The people would then be safe. Otherwise I have no more faith in them than in the old State banks. No, Senator, the true remedy is, no paper money but greenbacks and fractional currency issued direct by government.

February 4, 1869

Onward The Revolution

[* One biographer of Anthony suggests this conversation did not take place, that it was written by Train (Katherine Anthony, *Susan B. Anthony: Her Personal History and Her Era*, New York, Garden City, 1954, p. 221). Though their biographers have claimed Stanton and Anthony were not interested in the financial issues covered in the paper, we do not know this for a fact.]

Revolution's Twin Sister

. . . On the trains [to Milwaukee, Mrs. Mary Livermore] told me her plans in regard to her new paper, the *Agitator*. Having decided to call such a journal into being, what its name should be was the question. Accordingly a council was held of the wise men and wilful women of Chicago over the baptismal font of the new comer. The men, still clinging to the pleasant illusions that everything emanating from women should be mild, gentle, serene, suggested "The Lilly," "The Rose Bud," "The New Era,"' "The Dawn of Day;" but Mrs. Livermore, always heroic and brave, now defiant and determined, having fully awoke to the power and dignity of the ballot, and stung to the very soul with the proposed amendment of "manhood suffrage," declared that none of those names, however touching and beautiful, expressed what she intended the paper should be – nothing more or less than the twin sister of *The Revolution*, whose mission is to turn everything inside out, upside down, wrong side before. With such intentions, she felt the *Agitator* was the only name that fully matched *The Revolution*.

Elizabeth Cady Stanton
March 18, 1869

The Woman's Bureau

By the 1st of May *The Revolution* will be in splendid quarters up-town where women can visit us without climbing up three long flights of stairs, encountering at every turn the smoke and juice of the vile Virginia weed.

Our new office will be found at No. 49 East 23d street, second door from the Academy of Design and directly opposite the Young Men's Christian Association. And will not *The Revolution*, staring those young male Christians in the face, be a standing prophecy that the great wheel of time may possibly revoke their recent decision that no *Daughter of Eve* shall be admitted within their charmed circle?

33

The "Woman's Bureau" is to be a kind of Woman's Exchange, where the Sorosis [a woman's club founded in 1868], the Suffrage and Working Woman's Association can hold sweet counsel together, have weekly receptions in the elegantly furnished parlors.

This large four-story brown stone building had just been purchased by Mrs. Elizabeth B. Phelps for the special purpose of establishing *Headquarters* for the Woman Movement. Mrs. Phelps is a woman of cultivation, generosity and rare financial ability, who, Mr. [Horace] Greeley says, never makes a mistake. She intends hereafter to devote her wealth, time and talents to the education, elevation and enfranchisement of her sex. She has long been contemplating some plan to aid woman; and this experiment is but the beginning of what she proposes to do in the no distant future.

April 22, 1869

The Tribune in Hysterics

. . . We hold, with some reserve as to persons and things, that the movement for Woman's Rights springs from good motives, and may be fairly expected to produce some good results. We may be pardoned if we do not fail to perceive its comedy as well as its earnestness. And while Mrs. Stanton's imperial eloquence charms us, it is enough to give able-bodied men hysterics to see the angels making men of themselves. [The New York *Tribune*]

Oliver Wendell Holmes once wrote some humorous lines which so affected an "able-bodied man" that he laughed nine days and nights and died; since that time, the Poet tells us that he never "dared to write as funny as he can."

If it be true that "my imperial eloquence" has thrown the able-bodied editor of the *Tribune* into hysterics, such is my high regard for that noble man, and so important do I feel that his life is to this nation, that with true Holmes magnanimity, I vow never again to be as eloquent as I can. Whatever I do hereafter with pen and tongue, let all men understand that it is not a tithe of what I could do if I were not afraid of convulsing and collapsing the *Tribune*.

Elizabeth Cady Stanton
June 3, 1869

"The World" Forsakes Us

. . . [The *World*] says, "there [in England] the movement is more like a crusade, while here it is carried on like a picnic; there the women sit still and listen, and able men plead their cause, while here the women are their own advocates; there they are earnest, logical and reasonable, while here the light artillery of wit and ridicule plays round our rulers' heads until they are fairly dizzy." . . .

The *World* innocently asks us the question, why, like the Englishwomen, we do not sit still in our conventions, and get "first class men" to do the speaking? We might, with equal propriety, ask the *World's* editorial staff why they do not lay down their pens and get first class men to edit their journal? . . .

Elizabeth Cady Stanton
August 12, 1869

Those Ridiculous Headings

A lady said [at the Women's National Suffrage Association meeting] that the New York *Tribune* of September 3 headed its report of the meeting of the Working Woman's Association as "The Wars of the Women." Beside that report thus designated stood the report of the Twenty-third Street Union Republican General Committee without a heading, though that might have appropriately been called the "wars of the men," as you will see, she continued, if you allow me to read one resolution passed at that meeting. The speaker read the resolution referred to, and then said: In fact, one cannot take up a paper these beautiful early September days that is not filled with the wars of the men; too many entirely for our peaceloving and sensitive hearts or heads to understand. The only way in which I can account for the omission of headings to these reports of the wars of the men is that these captions are written by some masculine wit, who is decidedly partial to jokes on women. . . .

Mrs. Stanton said the best thing they could do was to start a daily paper of their own, and then treat men as they were treated by them, and then she thought they could give them all they desired. . . .

September 16, 1869

★★Harvard Needs Revolution★★

Cambridge, Sept. 18, 1869.
Dear Revolution: The students of the Divinity School in Harvard

35

University are very desirous of seeing your paper, and they have asked me to aid them in obtaining it for their reading room. They are unable to subscribe for it. Can it be sent to them gratuitously?

Edward J. Young
Hancock Professor

To be sure we will send it to you FREE. . . .

Though the daughters of the land in darkness and ignorance sit weeping at the college doors, still barred against them, yet women will be true to you. . . .*

October 7, 1869

[* This request elicited a number of ridicules in subsequent issues. An embarrassed Harvard eventually declined the subscription.]

A Most Unjust Charge

Rev. Mrs. [Phebe] Hanaford* writes to Miss Anthony from Massachusetts as per the following extracts: . . .

"Alexander Troupe, Secretary of the Troy Union Cooperative Linen Collar and Cuff Company said he hoped to see none but real, active women engaged in work, and he also hoped that the working women themselves would give no countenance to such women as Miss Anthony, of *The Revolution*, who paid the female type setters in her office less wages then were being paid in any other printing office in the city of New York.

"Now, Susan, is it *true* that you pay your women type-setters less than they can get elsewhere? I shall not believe that it is true, till you say so, for I do not believe you would be thus unjust to your own sex, which it has been your lifelong labor to elevate and bless."

Thanks to Mrs. Hanaford for calling attention to what, but for her, might not have been seen. Miss Anthony, in the first place, employs no women nor men as printers, and never did. She has her paper printed by contract, as do many other proprietors of newspapers. But Mr. Johnston, who does her work, makes no distinction in prices between men and women, and never has; believing firmly in *The Revolution* doctrine of Equal Pay for Equal Work.

November 4, 1869

[* Phebe Hanaford was a Universalist Church minister, lecturer and writer. She edited the *Ladies' Repository* for three years.]

Onward The Revolution

To Correspondents

Don't preach. Don't even exhort. Don't philosophize. Above all, don't sentimentalize. For the two former we have no need. Of the third, not more than ten men and women are capable in any generation. For the fourth, this globe of granite and stern fact has no room, time nor patience. *Give us facts and experience*, in words, if you please, as hard as cannon-balls.

January 6, 1870

The Woman's Journal

. . . *The Revolution* gladly welcomes this new and valiant auxiliary to the field of conflict.* But it is more glad to assure it that its prospect is quite other than it would have been two years ago, when woman's voice had been silenced and her claim suspended during the five year's clash of battle with rebellion. Now, she is herself in the field, and with a might unknown before. She has made herself heard from the Atlantic to the Pacific ocean. . . . [L]et our new ally rejoice with us, woman's triumph is already assured! indeed, as compared with our own beginning, seems almost won.

January 13, 1870

[* *The Woman's Journal*, begun by Lucy Stone and others more conservative in their approach to women's rights than were Stanton and Anthony, continued publication until 1917.]

Don't Know Its Mother!

Though like Mrs. Stowe's "Topsy," the newborn of Boston doesn't know its mother. *The Revolution* knows all its children. First, *The* (Ohio) *Woman's Advocate*, a brave, sturdy youth already running alone. Second, *The* (N. Y.) *Woman's Advocate*, a demure, staid body of a twelve month. Third, *The* (Chicago) *Agitator*, of less than a year. Fourth, and latest, *The* (Boston) *Woman's Journal*, proper in every line, without even a speck on one of its fair pages. What a splendid family! God speed each and all the dear ones now set up for themselves. Good friends, send each of them your subscription. It will help make easy the hard, rough road before them. And while you bless the younglings of the flock, don't forget that their good old weather beaten Dame still lives. . . .

Susan B. Anthony
January 13, 1870

To the Friends and Patrons of The Revolution

May not *The Revolution* at this time renewedly present its claims to a far wider patronage than hitherto it has received? Its friends, as is well known, are a multitude that no man can number, but they are not all its patrons and subscribers. It has never made one special, well-directed and vigorous effort to increase its circulation. It has relied too much, perhaps, on the goodness of its cause and the generosity of its friends. It has been too well satisfied with its moral results to be even properly and suitably careful about its more material and moneyed affairs. . . .

. . . No truly Reform journal ever made its owner rich. None ever can. It can only become popular by the triumph of its principles, and then it is no longer needed. Let every well-wisher to the cause, every earnest worker in it, keep this in mind when making out the list of newspapers to be continued or subscribed for in the current year.

Parker Pillsbury
April 28, 1870

Prospectus of the Revolution for 1870

The Revolution is a weekly journal demanding Suffrage for Women.

The demands for women everywhere to day, are for a wider range of employments, higher wages, thorough physical and mental education, and her civil rights of person, property, wages and children. While we yield to none in the earnestness of our advocacy of any of these, we make the broader demand of woman's enfranchisement as the only way by which all special privileges can be permanently secured. No class of citizens, either men or women, can ever feel a proper self-respect, or command the respect of others, until their political equality – their citizenship be fully recognized.

In discussing, as we shall incidentally, the many sides of all questions of national life – of science, philosophy, society, religion, and politics, of finance, trade, capital, labor and land monopoly, of sanitary, educational and prison reform, we propose to educate woman for an intelligent expression of opinion at the polls, where, in the march of civilization, she is so soon to share in the grave responsibilities of government.

While we would not refuse even an occasional word in our columns, yet as masculine ideas have ruled the race for six thousand years, we specially desire that *The Revolution* shall be the mouth-piece of women, that they may give the world the feminine thought in politics, religion and social life; that ultimately in the union of both we may find the truth in all things.

On the idea taught by the creeds, codes and customs of our times, that woman was made for man – his toy, drudge, victim, subject, or even mere companion – we declare war to the death, and proclaim the higher truth that, like man, she was created by God for INDIVIDUAL MORAL RESPONSIBILITY and progress here and forever, and that the physical conditions of her earthly life are not to be taken as the principle evidence of the Divine intention respecting her as an immortal being.

Our special contributors this year are: Paulina Wright Davis, Isabella Beecher Hooker, Harriet Beecher Stowe, Alice and Phebe Cary, Olive Logan, Mary Clemmer Ames, Elizabeth B. Tilton, Celia Burleigh, Eleanor Kirk, M. E. Joslyn Gage, Charlotte B. Wilbour, Laura C. Bullard, Elizabeth Smith Miller, Madame [Mathilde] Anneka, Madame [Jenny] D'Hericourt, Kate N. Doggett, Isabella Grant Meredith, Phebe Couzens, Lilie Peckham, Lizzie M. Boynton, Helen Ekin Starrett, Mary W. Sawtell, Elizabeth T. Schenck; FOREIGN: Rebecca Moore, Lydia E. Becker, Madame Marie Goeg [Goegg]. ★

In announcing this brilliant array of contributors for the coming year, we wish to say to our readers that as *The Revolution* is an independent journal, bound to no party or sect, those who write for our columns are responsible only for what appears under their own names. Hence if old Abolitionists and Slaveholders, Republicans and Democrats, Presbyterians and Universalists, Saints, Sinners and the Beecher family find themselves side by side in writing up the question of Woman Suffrage, they must pardon each other's differences on all other points, trusting that by giving their own views strongly and grandly, they will overshadow the errors by their side.

Elizabeth Cady Stanton, Editor
Susan B. Anthony, Proprietor
November 18, 1869

[★ See the Appendix for biographical information on contributors.]

Who Shall Fill Our Places

With the next number we shall introduce to our readers, a new editor, young, brave, brilliant and beautiful who will bring to her duties rare culture, clear moral perceptions, enthusiasm, untiring industry and a liberality that comes from extensive travel, reading and thought. Instead of the name of Susan B. Anthony will appear that of a young gentleman of wealth, influence and rare executive ability as the future Manager of this Journal. Under the new auspices we confidently predict a long and prosperous voyage for the plucky little *The Revolution.* . . .

Our good friend Susan, writing from Chicago, says of the transfer of *The Revolution,* "I feel a great calm sadness like that of a mother binding out a pet child she could not support."

No! no! not so. It is rather like giving up the society of a much loved daughter to new and brilliant prospects, superior education, foreign travel, or a desirable matrimonial alliance.

For ourself, having long sought release from all reform organizations, committees and societies whatever, from manuscripts, Pindaric odes, prosy prose, and proof-sheets, in resigning all our posts of honor outside our garden gate, we have the same satisfaction of prospective repose, sitting under our own vine and fig tree today that we had, the first time we sent our three elder boys to boarding school. Do not think, dear readers, that we propose to die or pass our time in idleness; far from it, we shall speak and write in the future as in the past, not, however, at appointed times and seasons, but just when the spirit moves us.

Our little pet, that some half dozen of us have struggled so hard to support, we now resign into the hands of able sponsors, who will gladly keep its lamp of life trimmed and burning.

Elizabeth Cady Stanton

In view of the active demand for conventions, lectures and discussions on Woman Suffrage, I have concluded that so far as my own personal efforts are concerned, I can be more useful on the platform than in a newspaper. So, on the 1st of June next, I shall cease to be the *sole* proprietor of *The Revolution,* and shall be free to attend public meetings, where ever so plain and matter of fact an old worker as I am, can secure a hearing. It gives me a throb of delight to say that this journal, which has always been the idol of my heart, holding the place in my affections which a fond mother gives to a pet child, is to be here after more sumptuously cared for, more advantageously brought up and more elegantly settled in life, than I had ever dared to hope. . . .

The Revolution itself has become the joint stock property of a company of ladies and gentlemen who are worth their millions of dollars, and among whom the only poverty-stricken member of the concern is my ever beggarly self. As I never knew before what it was to have rich partners in business, my heart is lighter than a feather at seeing nine-tenths of my burthen shifted to other and stronger shoulders.

The public has already been informed . . . that Mrs. Laura Curtis Bullard★, of Brooklyn, is about to become the chief-editor of this journal; a woman who, for beauty of person, refinement of manners, knowledge of literature, acquaintance with leading minds and enthusiasm for the cause, has no superior among all the noble women who now represent the best womanhood of America.

The former Editor, my long and dearly beloved co-worker, Elizabeth Cady Stanton, who has never before been a proprietor in this journal, becomes a member in equal interest with myself of the new stock company. Her pen (which, as I think, is the best that ever was dipped into ink) being now at liberty, will flash and sparkle brighter than ever before.

Mr. Edwin A. Studwell, Chairman of the Executive Committee of the Union Woman Suffrage Society, will be the Business Manager of *The Revolution*; and I need tell nobody in these parts that he is a man of great energy, activity, and enterprise. Neither the new editor nor the new publisher will accept a penny for their services to the new concern.

This arrangement will be a further evidence to my friends of the truth of the old proverb that "*The Revolution* never goes backward." . . .

Susan B. Anthony
May 26, 1870

[★ See the Appendix for biographical information on Laura Curtis Bullard.]

The Motto of This Journal

It is not our habit to discuss theology, or to indulge in Scriptural exegesis, or to adduce the lore of the pundits in illustration of points of doubtful interpretation; but as a correspondent has asked me why we have chosen for this journal the Scriptural motto which stands at the head of it, we will endeavor to show the propriety of our selection. The words are, "What therefore God hath joined together, let not man put asunder." They were spoken by a Great Teacher, who, whether we regard him as God or as man, is still the Master of us all. . . .

, . . . We use it at the head of our columns because it is a time-honored form of words expressing not only one limited idea but many other noble meanings.

In the first place, not to be misunderstood, let us say that the view of marriage which it describes, and which it protects as with a sacred shield, is the true and only idea which can ever satisfy a pure heart, whether in woman or man. . . . On the subject of marriage, therefore, we say (as we have all been Christianly taught to say) "What God hath joined together, let not man put asunder."

Furthermore, this motto not only serves a noble purpose in furtherance of the great reform in behalf of which we use it, but it served a similar purpose in the great reform which ended in breaking the chains of four million slaves. One of the great cruelties of slavery was, that it separated parents and children – tearing the babe from its mother's bosom – violating that divine right of human nature which makes the mother the lawful ministrant and guardian to her child. And to-day, not in slavery but in freedom, not in squalor but in refinement, not in degradation but in the highest social positions, are thousands of mothers who are as thoroughly debarred from the control of their children as were the slave-women of the South; and it is in behalf of all such that we quote the great law of nature, "What God hath joined together, let not man put asunder."

So, too, no words seem to us more fitly to describe the natural equality which exists, or should exist, between the sexes, whatever the situations in which they are placed – whether in society, in the family, in the church, or in the State. We believe that God designed, in the creation of man and woman, that these two chief personages in the world's history – very similar, yet very dissimilar, in their nature – should be always and everywhere together. Man without woman, or woman without man, presents a spectacle which, wherever one sees it, is a lamentable distortion of the divine idea; for the divine idea was expressed by Him who said, "What God hath joined together, let not man put asunder."

Take the serious question of the education of the sexes. From time immemorial, the great colleges of the world have been built and administered on the plan of giving to men an education, and of keeping women in ignorance. Oxford and Cambridge, Yale and Harvard – these institutions are the world's testimonies to the importance of intellectual discipline to men. They pay an illustrious tribute to the inherent dignity of the masculine intellect. They are another way of saying that the chief person on earth is man, and that woman is his plaything, or ornament, or slave, but not his equal. This old idea of education is fading away. . . . And this is part of our general meaning when we say at the head of our columns, "What God hath joined together, let not man put asunder."

Walking in the streets of New York or Brooklyn, and seeing in each business section of these cities a thousand signboards indicating that merchandize is bought and sold by men who make princely fortunes by such buying and selling, our hearts sometimes yearn, almost to aching, for the time when there will be the same chances for women to acquire wealth. . . . We want to see equal rights, privileges and emoluments in all trades for women and men. If a man finds that the dry goods business is the way to a competence, a woman has the same right as he to follow the same path to success. And our notion is that all this is implied in the maxim, "What God hath joined together, let not man put asunder."

Not to multiply instances, we say in brief, that the great want of our times is the co-equal participation of man and woman in all the great social, industrial, civil, educational, political and religious interests of the human race. . . . And we respectfully inform our correspondent that all this, and a good deal more beside, which we will not now stop to mention, is what we meant, and still mean, by keeping at the head of our sheet a saying which, more fitly than any other, whether human or divine, characterizes the great movement in which this journal is engaged – "What God hath joined together, let not man put asunder."

[Laura Curtis Bullard]
September 15, 1870

The Revolution: Prospectus

The Revolution is a journal devoted to the welfare of Woman.

If its name be thought too ungentle to represent the sex for whom it speaks, let us explain in what sense its purpose is revolutionary. . . .

Not to lengthen the catalogue of illustrations, we say in brief, that every law of the State, every limitation of wages, every inadequate system of education, every tyranny of custom, every equal conventionalism of society, and every other incubus which bears unjustly and injuriously on woman, to cripple her growth and hinder her progress; – any and every obstacle which prevents her realization of the high ideal to which God predestined woman by creating her soul for an immortal equality with man's; – all this we aim to revolutionize.

Called into existence to utter the cry of the ill-paid, of the unfriended and of the disfranchised, this journal is woman's voice speaking from woman's heart.

Shall it not be heard? Is it not entitled to the sympathy and support of the women in America? Ought it not be received as a welcome guest into their homes and hearts?

Let every earnest woman who reads this Prospectus subscribe for this paper.

The Revolution is published not for any pecuniary gain to its responsible contractors, for they receive no compensation for their services. Its proprietors are a joint-stock company, who have supplied it with a capital of fifty thousand dollars, and who mean to publish it at its actual cost, without a penny of profit.

The subscription price is only Two Dollars a year – one dollar less than heretofore. Clubs of ten or more copies, $1.75. Single numbers, five cents each. Terms, cash in advance.

You are respectfully invited to subscribe at once.

The office of *The Revolution* is at No. 31 Union Place, corner of Sixteenth street and Broadway, New York; and Branch Office at No. 11 Fulton street, near Fulton Ferry, Brooklyn. . . .

Mrs. Laura Curtis Bullard
October 20, 1870

What Flag Shall We Fly?

It grieves us to find certain organs of the woman's movement narrowing down our great reform to the mere dimensions of a demand for the elective franchise. The *Woman's Journal*, for instance, lifts its hands in gentle shudder at the impropriety of what it regards *The Revolution*'s latitudinarian discussions, and warns us to "stick to the point." What are these discussions, and what is this point? The discussions for which we are criticized run over the whole range of woman's needs and demands, rights and wrongs, opportunities and enterprises – including her work, her wages, her property, her education, her physical training, her social status, her political equality, her marriage, and her divorce. The "point" to which we are asked to stick is the single one of woman's suffrage.

We reject the advice – not because we do not respect its source, but because we do not believe in its wisdom.

In the first place, the *Woman's Journal*, in attempting to reduce the woman's movement to the square-inch of a ballot, writes itself down in 1870 as more conservative than the originators of the movement were in 1848. It turns back the sun on the dial. It makes not even the crab's progress, which is sidewise, but goes directly to the rear. This will be clearly seen by any one who takes pains to refer to the proceedings of the original woman's rights conventions at Seneca Falls, held in July, 1848 – more than twenty-two years ago. The utterances of that convention were far in advance of the customary editorial comments of the *Woman's Journal* of the present day. . . .

. . . In undertaking the conduct of this newspaper, we took into our hands a harp of more than a single string. Instead, therefore, of sticking to the solitary point which the *Woman's Journal* indicates, we hereby dedicate these columns anew to each and all the multitudinous interests connected with the industrial, social, intellectual, civil, political, moral and religious progress of the disfranchised half of the American people.

[Laura Curtis Bullard]
October 27, 1870

Valedictory

With the present number of this journal my editorial connection with it ceases. My frequent and necessary absences from America render it impossible for me to do justice to *The Revolution* or myself, and makes it imperative upon me to yield the conduct of the paper into other hands.

I am happy to say that my successors,* though they cannot bring a more zealous adherence to the cause of woman's rights than myself, will, at least, be able to devote to its advocacy a larger amount of time and more constant labor.

The Revolution, under my editorship, has claimed for woman not only civil but social equality with man. Not woman suffrage alone has been inscribed on its banner, but woman's rights – and first and foremost among those rights is that of self development, which

God has imposed upon her in common with man as the highest duty; to this end I have claimed for her, as the first step which must lead to it, freedom of mind and person; freedom to work out her career unbiased by any one calling her master; freedom to think her own thoughts and to shape her own destiny; freedom to educate herself untrammelled by the schools; freedom to choose a congenial employment and to earn a living at it; freedom to marry, and, having married, to be her husband's equal and not his subject in the marriage bond; freedom to remain unmarried without loss of her social prestige; freedom in all that pertains to her physical growth, to her intellectual stimulus, to her social ties, and to her moral aims. . . .

Laura Curtis Bullard
October 12, 1871

[* In this issue she announces that the publisher will be Mr J.N. Hallock of New York, the editor Rev. W. T. Clark, who has "long experience, marked ability and culture."]

2
Aristocracy of sex

Introduction

The women of *The Revolution* saw their support of women's right to suffrage as championing a great and essential principle. Not everyone then and now agrees. Some others have seen the campaign as selfish, elitist, impractical and racist. *The Revolution* was born and lived out its life during a time of intense debates about suffrage, debates about the advisability and political practicality of enfranchising Black men and all women. Republicans fought Democrats, abolitionists fought racists, woman's righters fought sexists, and abolitionists and woman's righters disagreed among themselves. While Republicans, abolitionists and many woman's righters were advocating the enfranchisement of Black men, *The Revolution* provided a platform for arguments for woman's suffrage at a time when the issue received little serious, consistent airing anywhere else. Of course, *The Revolution* was about much more than votes for women (as the other sections in this volume attest), but a substantial portion of space and emphasis of the journal was devoted to forceful arguments in editorials, in editorial comments on news items, and in letters to the editor on the importance of woman's suffrage.

The consistent editorial position of *The Revolution* was to insist that suffrage for women must accompany suffrage for Black men, a position that led them to oppose passage of the Fifteenth Amendment (passed by Congress in February 1869) unless it included the word "sex" or unless it was passed along with a Sixteenth Amendment granting the vote to women (such amendments were introduced in December 1868 and March 1869). The Fifteenth Amendment prohibited the right to vote being denied on the basis of race, color or previous condition of servitude. Since the word "male" had been introduced into the Constitution for the first time by the Fourteenth Amendment, the Fifteenth Amendment would grant suffrage to Black men but not women. Beyond this general editorial position, however, positions on suffrage varied somewhat. Parker Pillsbury apparently favored educated suffrage, while Stanton in this time period usually opposed any qualifications. (A history of the conflicting interests and priorities of Stanton and others is carefully documented in Andolsen, 1986.)

We now recognize as racist some of the language, reasoning and stereotyping used in editorials by Stanton and Pillsbury to convince opponents. They were attempting to use their opponents' own arguments against them. In addition, their racism can be understood in the context of their cultural milieu; along with many others of their day, they believed in a progressive, evolutionary development of the human "race." Stanton, for example, sometimes referred to the "lower orders of mankind," an indication of her belief that education and "civilization" were needed to bring groups of people (particularly American Blacks and white working-class immigrants) out of barbarism and to the pinnacle of development. However, *The Revolution* consistently supported suffrage for Black women and editorial commentary frequently deplored racism (called "colorphobia"). Reports of the successes of Black women and men as well as their unjustified ill-treatment were carried in its pages.

Stanton was the most forceful in arguing against the creation of an "aristocracy of sex." Unlike other abolitionists and woman's righters who argued that gaining suffrage for Black men was a step forward in bringing all groups into complete citizenship, Stanton argued that granting all men the vote would solidify and more deeply embed the sexual caste system, cutting across all races and classes. To admit Black men to enfranchisement was to admit them into "manhood," making even more difficult the task of redefining citizenship (that is, full humanness and full public participation) to include women. That is, "citizen" would continue to mean "man," not "person." Black men's quest for admittance to the privileges of manhood would bolster patriarchy, not weaken it. Stanton's argument that *masculinity* – men's power and privilege – was the root problem of the ills of her day is one made by contemporary radical feminists. Once it became clear to her that universal suffrage for white women and Black men was not supported by many politicians and male reformers, she called upon women to devote themselves to their own cause.

Thus the importance of the ballot for women for Stanton and Anthony was not simply that the ballot would be a political tool for women to use but that it would represent a new definition of womanhood as fully human and of manhood as only part, not all, of the human race.

It has been easy to pin blame on *The Revolution* and its editors and publisher for the divisiveness between abolitionists and radical women and between radical and liberal women following the Civil War. They did not accept the argument that it was "politically expedient" to secure Black men's enfranchisement first. Given that women were not granted enfranchisement until 1920, it was obviously not politically expedient. If we are to understand the antagonisms of the time period, we need to recognize the deep sexism of most Republicans and abolitionists who were supposedly women's allies and the effect this sexism had on preventing a coalition of interests. Many historians have assumed that the 1868–9 internal split in the woman's movement was due to political and strategic differences about whether to work for suffrage for Black men before or at the same time as suffrage for women. However, Kathleen Barry finds evidence that the split was initiated by the abolitionist men as early as 1860 – and over the issue of divorce (1988: 388).

As a result of these differences, organizations formed, disbanded and merged. The American Equal Rights Association, founded in 1866 as a blending of abolitionist and woman's rights interests, was superseded by the National Woman Suffrage Association and the American Woman Suffrage Association, formed in 1869. The first, led by Anthony and Stanton, took the woman's movement away from its abolitionist connections toward autonomy. The latter remained closely aligned with abolitionists and the Republican party, putting Black men's enfranchisement first, and after the passage of the Fifteenth Amendment focusing narrowly on securing the vote for women. Efforts to unite the two organizations, described in *The Revolution*, were unsuccessful for the next two decades.

While the struggle for women's suffrage may seem far removed from the concerns of contemporary feminists, many of the same ideological and strategic questions confront us and sometimes divide us. Understanding the strengths and oppressions resulting from the intersections of gender, race and class is still a major challenge.

Bibliography

Andolsen, Barbara Hilbert. 1986. *"Daughters of Jefferson, Daughters of*

Bootblacks": Racism and American Feminism. Macon, Georgia: Mercer
University Press.
Aptheker, Bettina. 1982. *Woman's Legacy: Essays on Race, Sex, and Class in
American History.* Amherst: University of Massachusetts Press.
Barry, Kathleen. 1988. *Susan B. Anthony: A Biography of a Singular
Feminist.* New York and London: New York University Press.
DuBois, Ellen Carol. 1978. *Feminism and Suffrage: The Emergence of an
Independent Women's Movement in America 1848–1869.* Ithaca, NY:
Cornell University Press.
Flexner, Eleanor. 1959. *Century of Struggle: The Woman's Rights Movement
in the United States.* Cambridge, Mass.: Harvard University Press.
Giddings, Paula. 1984. *When and Where I Enter: The Impact of Black Women
on Race and Sex in America.* New York: Morrow.
Kugler, Israel. 1987. *From Ladies to Women: The Organized Struggle for
Woman's Rights in the Reconstruction Era.* New York: Greenwood Press.
Stanton, Elizabeth Cady, Susan B. Anthony and Matilda Joslyn Gage, eds.
1882. *History of Woman Suffrage, Vol. II.* New York: Fowler & Wells,
reprinted New York: Arno and *The New York Times,* 1969.

★★Aristocracy of Sex★★

Wendell Phillips has issued a pronunciamento in his two papers,
one monthly and one weekly, against those advocates of the
Woman's Rights movement who are opposed to the position in
which the Fifteenth Amendment places the women of the country.★

In asserting, as Mr. Phillips does, that the Fifteenth Amendment
affects no class, race, color, nationality but the negro, he makes a
grave mistake. In Rhode Island, for example, are twenty thousand
Irishmen not permitted to vote, because of their foreign birth. If
that state adopted the Fifteenth Amendment all these foreigners
must be enfranchised? The same results would follow in California
with the thousands of Chinese now crowding our Pacific coast. So,
too, all the ignorant men of Massachusetts, not able to read and
write, and all the races from Europe and our Southern isles, if
landed here to-morrow, would be citizens as soon as naturalized. . . .

We have no possible objection to all men on the footstool, doing
their own voting, but we do object most decidedly to any more of
man's legislation for women. We have tried that to our full
satisfaction, until we are painfully alive to its danger and to the deep
humiliation of an aristocracy of sex, making every woman the
political inferior of every man on this continent. We oppose the

Fifteenth Amendment, not because it does too much, but too little. . . .

In protesting against an aristocracy of sex, we do precisely what the shining lights in the anti-slavery movement did in Rhode Island in 1842. It was proposed at that time by constitutional enactment to extend suffrage to all white men. Stephen Foster, Abby Kelley, Parker Pillsbury and Frederick Douglass stumped the state against the proposition. To-day, owing to those efforts, twenty thousand Irishmen are disfranchised in that state, while black men vote. These persons all *graduated in the school of anti-slavery*, and yet they thought it more important to prevent an aristocracy of color than to extend suffrage to a few more white men. . . .

Just so we feel to-day in regard to the Fifteenth Amendment. . . .

Elizabeth Cady Stanton
July 15, 1869

[* Abolitionist Wendell Phillips edited the *Anti-Slavery Standard*. The Fifteenth Amendment said the right of citizens to vote could not be decided because of race, color, or previous condition of servitude, but it did not include sex.]

Alike in One Respect

. . . The Democrats said this was a white man's government; the Republicans said this was a man's government. . . .*

Lucy Stone
January 8, 1868

[* The Democrats did not support Black suffrage; the Republicans did not support women's suffrage.]

Equal Rights to All!

Mrs. E. Cady Stanton reports in "*The Revolution*" that there is a general in Washington, and a tall and stately man at that, who is willing "to extend suffrage to woman on property qualifications." This, adds Mrs. S., is the opinion of many of our best men. We suppose that she is mistaken at least in a part of her statement. The men who can properly be called the best have all long since abandoned the idea of property as a fitting qualification for the elective franchise. . . . [excerpt from another newspaper]

. . . When a man says he is willing that women should vote with an educational or property qualification, his position is not so invidious towards our sex as is that of the man who says, "woman should not be allowed to vote at all." It is just the difference between a surmountable and insurmountable qualification.

. . . Many of our best men, who are favorable to the extending of suffrage to women, express the fear that the ignorant and vicious women would rush to the polls while the educated and refined would stay away. To meet that objection we say, then begin the experiment by extending suffrage to those holding real estate.

It is a little surprising, however, that while all classes of men are permitted to make laws and levy taxes for women of refinement, wealth and education, there should be so much fear of the lower classes of women.

For our part, we prefer Bridget and Dinah at the ballot-box to Patrick and Sambo, though, with the *Sun*, we believe in equal rights to all, irrespective of sex or color. . . .

Elizabeth Cady Stanton
February 26, 1868

The Ballot

Extract from a sermon by O. B. Frothingham.*

. . . In the hands of the ignorant, the stupid, the lawless, the passionate, and the evil-minded, [the ballot] is a weapon that may be turned against the heart of society; it is a tool that may be used to pry up the foundations of the commonwealth. So far from believing that it possesses any virtue to educate, or civilize mankind in and by itself, I believe that its universal bestowment would let loose a flood of imbecility that nothing would enable us to withstand. . . .

. . . Ignorant negroes and women, may not use it wisely, for learned men do not; they may injure the cause they would serve by bad legislation, but they could not do worse than white men in the past have done for them. . . . When Mr. Frothingham says that "universal suffrage would let loose a flood of imbecility," does he mean to insinuate that women and negroes, the only disfranchised classes we now have, monopolize all the "imbecility" in the world?

Seeing that the ballot is already in the hands of "the ignorant," "the stupid," "the lawless," "the passionate," "the evil-minded," who have used it thus far to grind women and negroes to powder, might it not be a beneficial revelation to these classes to find that they no longer had a strata of society beneath their feet? . . .

Elizabeth Cady Stanton
March 26, 1868

[* Frothingham was a Unitarian minister and founder of the Free Religious Association in 1867. His sermons and pamphlets were widely distributed and discussed.]

Fudge!"

We are tired of this universal harping about "Universal Suffrage" when only half the universal family are meant. It is an unpardonable affront to all womankind, and none the less so because coming from such a source as Thaddeus Stevens [abolitionist and Representative from Pennsylvania], as below:

> . . . Whoever undertakes to make a distinction between the colored man and ourselves because of the color of his skin, or the formation of his body, has forgotten his God, and his God will forget him. In other words, you must go back now to universal and impartial suffrage as the only foundation on which the government can stand.
>   . . . [H]enceforth let us understand that universal suffrage, operating in favor of every *man* who is to be governed by the votes cast, is one of those doctrines planted deeper than the granite on which our fathers laid the foundation of their immortal work. . . .

The only answer *woman* should make to all this is, Fudge!

Ed. Rev.
April 2, 1868

Universal Suffrage

The legal disabilities to the exercise of suffrage (for persons of sound mind and body) in the several states, are five: age, color, sex, property and education. As age depends on a fixed law beyond the control of fallible man, viz: the revolution of the earth around the sun, it must be impartial, for *nolens volens*, all men must revolve with their native planet; and as no republican or democrat majority can make the earth stand still, even for a Presidential campaign, they must in time perform that journey often enough to become legal voters. As the right to the ballot is not based on intelligence, it matters not that some boys of eighteen do know more than some men of thirty. Inasmuch as boys are not bound by any contract, except marriage; cannot sell a horse, or piece of land, or be sued for debt until they are twenty-one, this qualification of age seems to be in harmony with the laws of the land, and based on common sense. As to color and sex, neither time, money or education, can make black white or woman man; therefore, such insurmountable qualifications, not to be tolerated in a republican government are unworthy [of] our serious consideration. "Qualifications," says Senator [Charles] Sumner [abolitionist], "cannot be in their nature insurmountable. A permanent or insurmountable qualification is equivalent to a deprivation of the suffrage." In other words, it is the tyranny of taxation without representation, and this tyranny, I insist, is not intrusted to any state in the Union. As to property and education, there are some plausible arguments in favor of such qualifications, but they are all alike unsatisfactory, illogical, and unjust. A limited suffrage creates a privileged class, and is based on the false idea, that government is the natural arbiter of its citizens, while in fact, it is the creature of their will. In the old days of the Colonies, when the property qualification was five pounds, that being just the price of a donkey, Benjamin Franklin facetiously asked, If a man must own a jackass in order to vote, who does the voting, the man or the jackass. If property and education were a sure guage [*sic*] of character, if intelligence and virtue were twin sisters, these qualifications might do; but such is not the case.

In our late war, black men were loyal, generous and heroic, without the alphabet or multiplication table, while men of wealth, educated by the nation, graduates of West Point, were false to their country and traitors to their flag. There was a time in England's history when members of the House of Lord's could neither read or write. Before the art of printing, were all men fools? Were the Apostles and martyrs worth $250? . . . . Such qualifications would cut off one-eighth the population at the South, and one-twentieth in the Northern states. As capital has ever ground labor to the dust, is it generous to disfranchise the poor and ignorant, because they are so, these victims of our stupidity, who, through the ages, have suffered that we might shine. . . . Oh no! if a man cannot read, give him the ballot, it is school-master. If he does not own a dollar, give him the ballot, it is the key to wealth, education and power. . . .

Elizabeth Cady Stanton
July 30, 1868

Equal Rights

. . . The world never hears us say, "this is the woman's hour," for in the world of work, as in politics, we demand the equal recognition of the whole people. . . .

Elizabeth Cady Stanton
October 1, 1868

Half a Loaf

. . . The male advocates of the Fifteenth Amendment tell us we ought to accept the half loaf when we cannot get the whole. I do not see that woman gets any part of the loaf, not even a *crumb* that falls from the rich man's table. It may appear very magnanimous for men, who have never known the degradation of being thrust down in the scale of humanity by reason of their sex, to urge these yielding measures upon women, they cannot and do not know our feelings on the subject, and I regard it as neither just nor generous to eternally compel women to yield on all questions (no matter how humiliating they may be to her), simply because they are *women*. . . .

Phoebe Couzins*
July 8, 1869

[* See the Appendix for biographical information.]

Fickle Abolitionists

. . . Most of our Northern humanitarians enjoy the theory of equality on a Southern plantation better than its practice in their own every-day life.

Abolitionists, even, cannot brook self-assertion, either in women or negroes. When Frederick Douglass, the ignorant, runaway slave, was a dependent on northern charity and protection, he, wisely in all things, reflected the opinions of those who fed him, and life, with him, moved smoothly on; but, when in the larger development of all his powers and forces, in full-grown manhood, he dared to differ with his benefactors, though he was the grandest fact that freedom could boast, Mr. [William Lloyd] Garrison denounced him and his journal, through which he uttered his gospel of the black man's rights. . . .

Just so to-day, those women who refuse to hold their claims in abeyance to say pet theories or party interests, to Temperance or the Fifteenth Amendment in this country, or the Irish Church question in England, may look for condemnation and ridicule, for they will be ostracized and persecuted by the very men who insist that, of all others, they are the truest and most earnest patrons and friends of their cause.

It is always one thing at a time in man's political economy, and woman's time never comes, and it never will, so long as she has no just estimate of her own dignity and importance in the scale of being, and invariably, in all things, yields precedence to man.

November 11, 1869

Men Everywhere

. . . Men, men, everywhere men, as it was in Tennyson's charge of the Light Brigade, where cannon were to the right of them, cannon to the left of them, cannon in front of them, so now the women of America see men everywhere about them; the civilization of the country, and the legislation of the country, shape themselves on their interests. Women are practically ignored, or especially thrust to one side, unless, indeed, where their rights or their existence come in conflict with men's desires. At such times the press proposes to *regulate* the conditions between them.

Look at the Chinese women and the laws regarding them in California. Look at the Mormon women, and the laws *dis*regarding them in Utah. Look at the poor southern black women and the laws (congressional) virtually ignoring their existence, and then ask yourselves if the time for a change has not come. Aye, look at yourselves, favored northern white women, see in how far *you* lack of being each one, the property, body and soul, of some man, and say if the time has not come to make vigorous determined effort for your recognition by government, as part of the people holding equal civil and political rights with man. . . .

January 13, 1870

White Masters

. . . The difference in the slavery of the negro and woman is that of the mouse in the cat's paw, and the bird in a cage, equally hopeless for happiness. One perishes by violence, the other through repression. If the mouse escapes it is stronger for the struggle; if the bird escapes it perishes in its native element.

There are many points of analogy in the condition of all disfranchised classes. The fact that women and negroes have no voice in the government is one strong point of analogy; that women and negroes are taught obedience to their white masters in the Bible is another; the fact that women and negroes have ever been the slaves of white man, the one to his lust, the other to his avarice, makes too many points of analogy for woman to contemplate without a deep feeling of indignation. But if there are no points of analogy in the condition of women and negroes, why did the "white man" in his wisdom make the same laws for both classes? Why are women and negroes shut out of the colleges and professions together if there are no points of analogy in their condition? Why do the telegraphic wires bring the news to-day that in Kansas and Iowa henceforth "women and negroes" are to be permitted to practice law. We have stood together in the laws and constitutions in our degradation, why not together in our exaltation? . . .

Elizabeth Cady Stanton
March 12, 1868

★Racism Answered★★

From the *Frontier Index*:

"*The Revolution*" . . . Mrs. Stanton and Miss Anthony do give the radicals particular fits. They have been to Washington and looked into the smelleriferous skulduggery being played by the niggeropolists, and are bold in saying the country is in the grinning jaws of sharks and sea-serpents. Parker Pillsbury, one of the editors, once an ultra abolitionist is stumping New Hampshire for the democracy.

Hip! hip! hip! hurrah for the telling efforts of "*The Revolution*." God bless the ladies; may their noble, patriotic, honest influence bring our poor distracted country back to peace and *white* prosperity. . . .

. . . All the stumping [our senior editor] has done has been in "*The Revolution*." As our motto is principle, not policy, we do not care much for either party, based as they both are on caste and class. We say prosperity and peace for all God's children, black and white, male and female. . . .

March 26, 1868

✶✶Ballot for Black Women✶✶

. . . The best interests of the race demand that the equilibrium of sex be restored. This will do more to hasten the onward march of civilization, than the enfranchisement of any race or class of men, than the conversion of any nation to Protestantism, than the triumph of the temperance reform, or any proposed plan of reconstruction. Just as the constituent elements of nitrogen and oxygen, make the necessary atmosphere in which man can breathe and live, and the exhausting of either is certain death, so are the male and female elements in their true proportions as necessary for our moral life, and this negation of womanhood is the degradation of our common humanity. . . . To us the black women of the south are as precious in the scale of being as the men. Woman suffers in slavery a degradation man can never know. The strongest appeals made by abolitionists in the past against slavery have been on woman's wrongs, and now, when the day of emancipation comes, shall man enter into all the rights, privileges and immunities of citizenship while the woman by his side is left without that sceptre of power, the ballot, for her protection? Wendell Phillips says that emancipation is mockery to the black man without the ballot? Have not the women of this nation suffered enough from man's unjust legislation, to know that such emancipation as he offers the black woman is a mockery also?

Those slaves have worked and suffered side by side, shared each other's sorrows, fears, and anxieties through centuries of heathenism and bondage; and now shall abolitionists consent that another race of men shall find their liberties over this fresh holocaust of womanhood? No, no. We have no reason to suppose that the black man understands the principles of equity, or will practice the christian virtues better than his Saxon masters. And our demands on the Woman's Rights platform for the last twenty years are proof sufficient that man cannot legislate wisely and justly for the woman by his side. . . .

Elizabeth Cady Stanton
April 9, 1868

Georgia Reconstruction

The legislature of Georgia asserted its new sovereignity last Thursday by expelling its twenty-five colored members.✶ In the morning one of them, a Mr. Turner, made a speech which occupied the entire session. In conclusion he said: "This thing means revolution. Look out, carpet-baggers! When we go, they will turn you out, impeach Gov. Bullock and upset the constitution." At the afternoon session, several members participated in the debate. A vote being taken, the negroes were declared ineligible by a division of 80 against 23. Turner, as he walked out, brushed the dust from his feet. Other negroes bowed to the speaker and waved their hats to the members. Of course, their right to vote will go with the rest. The states, according to the Chicago platform, must regulate their own right of suffrage. And until the right is held to be *natural, inalienable, and indispensible in a republic,* it never can be secure. And thus based, of course it includes women and men alike. . . .

September 10, 1868

[* They were unseated on the grounds that Blacks were ineligible to hold office, but their seats were restored in 1870 when Congress intervened in Georgia's affairs.]

Colored Convention in Utica

A convention of colored people was held at Utica last week to demand right of Suffrage . . . and the following letter was received and read:

Woman's Suffrage Association of America

To the President and members of the Colored Men's State Convention.
Gentlemen: Permit me in behalf of the colored women of the State of New York to urge upon you to extend your demand for the ballot to your wives and daughters – your mothers and sisters. By the laws of our State the grievances of colored women are a thousand fold greater than those of colored men. While colored men not possessed of the requisite $250 to make them voters are exempted from taxation, all colored *women* worth even $50 are compelled to pay taxes. That is, the colored man to-day is worth $200, and is exempt, he dies to-morrow, and his widow is immediately assessed as tax-payer. Then in all trades and professions, your sisters and daughters have not only the obstacles that are everywhere thrown in your way, but also the prejudices and impediments everywhere thrown in woman's way, in addition. Now, Heaven, and all colored men know that the barriers that hedge *your* pathway on every side are most discouraging; I ask you, then, to remember the women by your side, and secure to them all

59

that you claim for yourselves. Now is the time to establish the government of our state, as well as the nation, on the *one Democratic Republican principle* – the *consent of the whole people* – black women and white, as well as black men must now be brought within the body politic.

Respectfully yours, Susan B. Anthony

. . . Several attempts were made, we are told, by the friends of Woman Suffrage to bring the question before the convention . . . but they were unsuccessful, a careful canvass of the members showed they were bitterly opposed to it.★

October 22, 1868

[★ It is not clear whether the opposition was to suffrage for Black and white women or to Anthony.]

Southern Literature

The *Seminary Magazine* is a monthly just commenced in Richmond, Virginia, "devoted (its Prospectus says) to the interests of education and the mental culture of THE WOMEN OF THE SOUTH."

. . . [I]n an editorial article headed, "Education for the Masses," there is a good deal of this kind of talk:

> While statesmen are exerting all their wisdom to avoid the dangers which threaten the political fabric, there looms up in the future a *dark and appalling cloud, which must, if not wisely forstalled, ultimately invade the social circle and taint the purity of the Caucasian blood.* This idea is too delicate to elaborate, and it is only referred to in the hope that our people will pursue it to its legitimate conclusion. *It is not a pleasant thought*, and it may be that our fears are delusive, and that the history of the past few years will be reversed. Prudent forethought demands that the present generation should leave nothing neglected which will preserve the *integrity of the domestic fireside.* . . .

The word *white* inserted in the prospectus of the institution would have obviated the necessity of this whole article. The simple truth is, the southern people are shaping their whole policy, government, literature, and religion, so as most effectively to degrade and finally to crush out the whole African race.

. . . The south never hated the negro for his color, or that he was a slave. It took the north to do that. But when she had been conquered by him in battle, and is now again in his power at the ballot-box, it is not in human nature that she should love him, or seek his prosperity and happiness. Nor is it expected that she will hate him less, because in all this, he is and has been really the passive instrument of the north; accepting freedom at her hand when and where she needed him, and only then and there, and the right of suffrage exactly on the same conditions. . . . Then again in reconstruction they are wanted, with ballots instead of bullets, and so they are given the ballot. . . . In one word, north and south, the Dred Scott decision, seven times sublimed, is practically applicable to-day as it ever has been, to the colored man.* He has no rights which the white man is bound to respect. None in the government, none in literature, none in religion, none anywhere. . . .

Parker Pillsbury
October 29, 1868

[* In the Dred Scott decision in 1857, the Supreme Court ruled that free Blacks were not citizens.]

Let Blacks Rise – Lift Them

New York
December 23, 1868

Editors of the Revolution:

I desire to say a word relative to a communication of J. Madison Allen of Ancora, N. J., which appeared in your paper of the 17th inst., not so much to condemn anything said, as to set the matter before the public in a different light. The sentence is, "Let blacks rise – lift them! Let women rise – aid them!" Now, as I am personally and unmistakably identified with the class of citizens designated "*blacks*," and consequently feel a deep interest in any and every means employed to accomplish the great work of our elevation, I must be permitted to demur to being *lifted* as though we were utterly powerless. I believe such work injurious both to us and the country. All that can be done beneficially for us and the whole country is, to *aid* us in every honest and manly struggle (*womanly*, too, if you please) we make to ascend the scale of mental, moral, and religious improvement. If one half of the money given for our improvement was given to us to enable us to *improve ourselves*, a great deal more might be effected in a great deal less time. . . .

D. Wadkins
January 7, 1869

A Colored Woman's Voice

The colored women, of all other American women, should be devoted to the cause of Suffrage. One appeared in the recent Chicago Convention [Woman Suffrage Convention] to the following effect:

> I present myself to you as a composition of humanity, for there flows through my veins a combination of the blood of four distinct nations, of which the greater part is Dutch, part Indian, part African, and the lesser part Irish.* (Applause and laughter.) I am an American, because here I was born. I am true, because I love the dear old flag. I am on the right side of the question, because I believe woman was made a helpmate for man; that he is but half a man without woman (applause), and you need her help as well in political affairs as you do in private or domestic affairs. And, gentlemen, I warn you no longer to stand out in refusing the right for which we contend; in trying to withhold from these noble ladies here and their darker sisters the franchise they now demand. . . .

March 4, 1869

[* After the abolition of slavery, a binary caste system was maintained by designating anyone with Black ancestry as Black.]

Harper Defends Fifteenth

. . . [At the American Equal Rights Association Meeting, Frances Ellen Harper] (colored) . . . proceeded with her remarks, saying that when it was a question of race she let the lesser question of sex go. But the white women all go for sex, letting race occupy a minor position. She liked the idea of working-women, but she would like to know if it was broad enough to take colored women?

Miss Anthony and several others – Yes, yes.

Mrs. Harper said that when she was at Boston, there were sixty women who rose up and left work because one colored woman went to gain a livelihood in their midst. (Applause.) If the nation could only handle one question, she would not have the black women put a single straw in the way if only the race of men could obtain what they wanted. (Great applause.) . . .*

May 27, 1869

[* Black women were significantly few in number at most suffrage meetings, with the important exceptions of women such as Harper, a poet and anti-slavery lecturer, who supported the Fifteenth Amendment, and Sojourner Truth, who opposed it.]

★Oppressed Women of All Shades★★

Providence

My Dear Mrs. Stanton: Nothing but the great crisis pending in our movement would have drawn me from my retirement again into public strife and turmoil, but I feel it a duty to enter my protest with yours against the Fifteenth Amendment. Last Winter, in Boston, I could only give my vote against it, for no Sixteenth had been proposed. It seemed almost a childish, selfish thing to do, when all the eloquence of a Boston platform was arrayed on the other side, and other women rose and said they were ready to step aside and let the colored man have his rights first. Not one said we will step aside and let the negro woman (whom I affirm, as I ever have, is better fitted for self-government than the negro man) have her rights before we press our claim, I could not but think it an easy thing for them to do, never having had the right they demanded. But if they truly believe that it will do for humanity what is claimed for it, I do not see why it should be called magnanimous for a woman to say, I yield to man just what he has always asserted as his, the right to rule. You have taken a bold stand, and I thank God for it. Though still in the minority, there is hope; for a radical truth one shall chase a thousand, and two put ten thousand to flight; and ere very long, before another convention, I trust many more will see with us that the Fifteenth Amendment, without the Sixteenth, is a compromise worse by far for the nation than any other ever passed. They could be repealed, *this can not*. Once settled, the waves of corruption will swamp our little bark freighted with all humanity, the women of all shades of color, and subject to every variety of tyranny and oppression, from the cramped feet of the Chinese to the cramped brains and waists of our own higher order of civilization. . . .

Yours ever truly,

P. W. [Paulina Wright] Davis★
June 17, 1869

[★ See the Appendix for biographical information.]

Colorphobia

It used to be said and believed that when slavery should be

abolished, prejudice against color would disappear as the shadow departs when the tree is removed. But it was a sad mistake. . . .

[T]he condition of nineteen-twentieths of the colored population of the South is materially, mentally, and morally as deplorable as it was in slavery, abating only the sale and separation of families. And that leaves an awful margin of misery still endured. And that unfortunate people have no more malignant, and certainly no more dangerous enemies in the South than thousands and thousands of their professed friends, republicans mostly, from the northern and western states. Even in Washington, scenes are of constant occurrence that are a disgrace and a scandal to the civilization of the age. Here is what a correspondent of the New York *Times* wrote from there last Thursday:

> On Monday the daughter of Rev. Sella Martin was admitted to one of the schools on an admission ticket signed by Professor Vashon, a colored school trustee. As the girl and her mother, who accompanied her, are almost white, the teacher, Miss Noys, admitted the pupil without hesitation. An hour afterwards she discovered that the new-comer had African blood. Miss Noyes, immediately sent for a trustee, who ordered the girl home with instructions not to return until the full Board of Trustees has considered and determined the matter. . . .

. . . It is an insulting burlesque on the very name of government, autocratic, democratic or anything between, to talk of the condition of the vast majority of colored people in the South as in any degree tolerable, or even sufferable. . . .

Parker Pillsbury
December 2, 1869

Colorphobia Cured

It has always been held incurable. Hydrophobia was hopeful compared to it. The Colonization Society, thirty years ago, tried Christianity upon it, in allopathic doses, and declared it wholly inefficacious. And so it invented Liberia, and made haste to put the Atlantic ocean, with all its winds and waves, betwixt the negro and its nobility. Only the *free* negro, however, was thus offensive, obnoxious. A rose by any other name would smell as sweet, but not so the black man, or woman. As *slaves* they were sweet as Baltimore belles, or any other roses; but free, who could bear them? As slaves they could travel anywhere, any way, by land or sea. They and their masters or mistresses could occupy any saloon and drawing-room, car, steamboat stateroom, or inside of stage coach, with the lap-dogs, parrots, pet monkeys, or whatever stock, goods or chattels were necessary to the owner's convenience, comfort, or pleasure; but as free they used to ride in what was called the "Jim Crow car," into which no white person was permitted to enter.

But now another cure is discovered for the terrible malady. It has already cured republicans, nearly to the last man, and democracy is rapidly recovering. The black man is annointed with the *ballot* . . . it purifies him so suddenly . . . that already the democratic editors and politicians are so far recovering as to render it sure that *colorphobia*, like Judean leprosy and possession of devils, witchcraft and London plague, will soon totally disappear. . . .

Parker Pillsbury
April 21, 1870

★★Without Regard to Sex or Color★★

As a colored man, and a victim to the terrible tyranny inflicted by the injustice and prejudice of the Nation, I ask no right that I will not give to every other human being, without regard to sex or color. I cannot ask white women to give their efforts and influence in behalf of my race, and then meanly and selfishly withhold countenance of a movement tending to their enfranchisement.

Robert Purvis★
Philadephia
January 6, 1870

[★ Purvis was one of the founders of the American Anti-Slavery Society in 1833 and a leader in the Underground Railroad movement. He was one of the few Black men who remained committed to the woman's rights movement while others argued for Black men's suffrage first.]

★★Alongside Negro "Wenches"★★

Not only has Wyoming by legislative enactment given Suffrage to its women, but her neighbor, Colorado, is debating the same question in her legislative halls. . . .

. . . Mr. M. S. Taylor [is] against the proposed measure. . . . [He] asserted it was the *best looking members of the House* who favored the measure, and as he never saw anything pleasant in the glass, that fact would cause him to oppose the bill.

. . . For the life of me I cannot tell why, but a parody on certain familiar lines *will* come into my mind.

> Goosey, goosey gander, where shall I wander?
> Up stairs and down stairs in the council chamber,
> Where sits M. S. Taylor snuffing up his nose,
> Looking in the glass, preparing to oppose.

His first objection, as above stated, seems meant as playful satire, for soon comes what he evidently deems the strong meat of the occasion, for he assures us he has another objection to make, which is a "serious objection." "The bill would give *negro wenches* the right to vote." "Did they ever think of that?" he pathetically continues. Negro wenches! And still farther presenting his serious objection, he says, "Do they know they are placing negro wenches on an equality with their wives, sisters, mothers and daughters?"

O Tempora, O mores! Can we stand this?

Being on an equality with negro women now, in our equal deprivation with them of suffrage, we have hopes we could survive an equality with them in the ballot.

Matilda E. Joslyn Gage★
February 17, 1870

[★ See the Appendix for biographical information.]

★★Men Can Lump It★★

. . . Mr. [Theodore] Tilton introduced the Sybian Sybil [prophet], Sojourner Truth [at the National Woman Suffrage Association meeting]. She thought it was a shame that the women should be begging for a thing that belongs to them, the right to vote. "Woman is the very thing that ought to have *all* rights. If she doesn't have 'em, how are her sons and daughters to know about their rights, I'd like to know? I don't want children to be saying as they do to their mothers, "You're nothing but a woman! What do you know!" They learn it from their fathers. What kind of men will they make, I'd like to know? Man has no right to make a booby of himself. Let him take care of the children himself. Some of 'em ain't good for nothing else!"

Sojourner wanted to be reported in a grammatical and smooth

way, "not as if I was saying tickety-ump-ump-nicky-nacky." "Only a few years more," she concluded, "and we'll enter into Congress, and then, men, you'll get your right place. You've never had it yet. We'll have women lawyers, and your old brandy-nosed pettifoggers will have to get out of the way. If they don't like it, they'll have to lump it." . . .

May 12, 1870

Fifteenth Amendment Celebrations

The colored men have signalized it widely, but seem to have forgotten wholly their women, and all women. They have made many earnest, powerful addresses and speeches, but in not one, that I have seen, is there the least recognition of woman. Women used to work pretty hard, practice a good deal of self-denial, suffer not a little persecution, living almost the very lives of the slaves, in "remembering them that were in bonds as bound with them," but they get little credit or gratitude for it yet, from the newly-created citizenship. . . .

In their many celebrations and processions the names of many men have been emblazoned on their banners of most dubious reputation as friends of the colored race, but what woman has been so distinguished? Are the names of Sarah and Angelina Grimke, Lydia Maria Child, Maria Weston Chapman, Abby Kelley to be forgotten? not to speak of Harriet Beecher Stowe, Lucy Stone and others of later, but scarely lesser note, and some of them *colored women, too*!

Far be it from this writer to call the newly-made colored citizenship to account; or even to criticize their doings, or not doings. But, as one who, for twenty-seven years of midmanhood, had no other aim, hope, wish, or care, *but their emancipation and enfranchisement*, with their wives and children, he may be permitted to ask whether, while emblazoning aloft on so many constellations of banners the names of newly-found political divinities, the names of a few of those women . . . should be wholly ignored and forgotten?

Parker Pillsbury
May 12, 1870

National Woman Suffrage Association Report

On this our first anniversary it may be well to recall the particulars

67

of the organization of our Association and inasmuch as some very incorrect statements have been put forth by persons who were not present on that very interesting occasion, we ask the friends present to [pay] strict attention to the report of the actual facts. On Saturday evening, May 15, 1869, the friends of Woman Suffrage met for a reception, by an invitation, given in public by Mrs. Livermore, at the "Woman's Bureau," 49 East 23d Street. On that evening after they assembled in sufficient numbers to fill the parlors, halls and stairways, Miss Anthony announced that at the urgent request of the numerous delegates to the late Equal Rights Association, the reception would assume the character of a formal meeting. . . .

. . . [I]t was voted to organize a "*National Woman's Suffrage Association.*" A constitution was prepared and accepted, and about one hundred persons, both men and women, registered their names as members of this new Association. These members were from all parts of the country and appeared eager to join the first "*National Woman's Suffrage Association*" ever organized in this country. The only object of the Association was announced to be to secure the passage of a "Sixteenth Amendment." Mrs. Stanton was elected President with enthusiastic demonstrations. . . .

During the summer of 1869, a circular letter was issued by some well-known advocates of the ballot for women, asking signatures to a *Call* for a *National Convention* to be held for the sole purpose of organizing a "*Truly*" "National Woman's Suffrage Association." Mrs. Stanton, our President – received one of the circular letters, and returned an answer, in substance, that "We already had such an organization." When this call was issued, the National Association was not invited as an *association* to attend the Convention, and as far as your committee have been able to ascertain the facts in the case, after a great deal of careful inquiry, not one resident of this city who held office in the *National Association*, received an invitation. The State Association, being auxiliary to the National, did not therefore appoint any delegates to that convention. Thus the most important state in the Union was not represented in the new organization. . . .

As we foresaw, the two organizations *did* work confusion in the minds of the friends of that cause all over the country. A partisan spirit led individual members of each organization to criminate and vindicate the leading spirits of the two associations, and a great deal of valuable time was stolen from the hours which should have been devoted to the proper work of both, answering inquiries, explaining sections, defending the accused, denying charges, etc. . . .

On the 15th of March, the chairman of the Executive Committee received the following printed invitation signed by 13 names, headed by that of Theodore Tilton, editor of the New York *Independent*:

> Entertaining a warm respect for the officers of both societies, we hereby send you our friendly greetings and invite you to commission three of your number from each organization, making six, to confer with three others appointed by the signers of this letter, the nine to assemble at Fifth Ave. Hotel, in New York, on Wednesday, April 6th, at noon, to devise measures for the future union and co-operation of all the friends of Woman's Suffrage throughout the Republic.

In compliance with the invitation extended – as we believe, in good faith – your committee appointed three of its members to meet in conference as requested. Mr. Parker Pillsbury, Mrs. Josephine Griffing, and Mrs. C. B. Wilbour were the persons selected to represent the Association upon the question of a *union* of the two Suffrage Associations. From an active correspondence with its leading members, the committee were prepared to instruct its representatives to declare unreservedly in favor of *"union upon equal terms."*

The result of that conference, you already know. . . .*

At a meeting of the Executive Committee, held at the "Woman's Bureau," May 4th, at which were present Mrs. Stanton, Mrs. [Elizabeth] Phelps, Mrs. [Lillie Devereux] Blake, Mrs. [Mathilde F.] Wendt*, Susan B. Anthony and Mrs. Wilbour, it was voted that the Executive Committee, in its annual report, recommend to its association to accept the proposition of Theodore Tilton, Mrs. Lucretia Mott and Mrs. Laura Curtis Bullard, and unite in a more complete organization which shall embrace all the friends of Woman's Suffrage, North, South, East and West. . . .

Charlotte B. Wilbour*
Chairman of the Executive Committee
May 26, 1870

[* The "Peace Conference" between the National Woman Suffrage Association and the American Woman Suffrage Association (reported in *The Revolution*, April 14, 1870) ended with the refusal

The Revolution in Words

of the American Association representatives to compromise. They were Lucy Stone, Col. T. W. Higginson and George Wm. Curtis. The split in the movement was to continue for the next several decades. Ellen DuBois in *Feminism and Suffrage* (pp. 200–1) sees this as basically a positive, not a negative, outcome for the movement.

Mathilde Wendt was editing *Die Neue Zeit*, a woman's journal, in New York at this time. See the Appendix for biographical information on Charlotte Wilbour.]

★★White Male Presidents★★

Who shall be the President of the National Woman's Suffrage Association? is the question on all lips and in all letters. Ordinarily I should say some woman most assuredly. It shows a want of faith in ourselves to place any man in that position. What should we think of the intelligent, cultivated black men in this country, if in their conventions they should always choose a white man to preside over them. . . .

But unfortunately the women who have been leaders in this movement for a quarter of a century being human, are now so divided with personal jealousies and animosities that they cannot unite on any one of their own number, and women just coming into the movement shrink from the antagonisms such divisions involve, and refuse all offical positions. Hence, in the present emergency, as a *war measure*, it seems both necessary and expedient to marshal our forces under the inevitable "white male;" whether we shall ever in good time coming escape that dynasty, is yet to be seen.★

The committee that met at Fifth Avenue Hotel, April 6, nominated Theodore Tilton, one of the most deservedly popular young men in the nation, for the President of the new organization [Union Woman's Suffrage Society], and the friends in favor of union throughout the country will no doubt confirm that choice in the coming convention.

As the cause of Woman's Suffrage becomes popular and large numbers come to its support, division is inevitable. . . . The state is divided into parties, the church into sects, and to require that the 15,000,000 women in this country should move in solid phalanx in one bee-line is to suppose the millennium of harmony right at hand.

Accepting disunion then as part of the eternal plan for quickening action, and "white male" presidents as the most available for the

70

present emergencies, let us have done with all back-biting, envy, hatred and malice, and look at the pleasant features of the situation. . . .

May 5, 1870

[* A major distinction between the National Woman Suffrage Association and the American Woman Suffrage Association was the latter's interest in having men's involvement in leadership positions. The NWSA was not interested in it. The efforts to make a new organization proved abortive. It is unclear that there was ever a white male president of NWSA. (See Ellen DuBois' *Feminism and Suffrage.*)]

Side Issues

Some masculine writer in the New York *Daily Standard* and T. W. Higginson, in the *Woman's Journal*, seem to have the same yard-stick for measuring the height, depth, the length, and breadth, of the woman's rights movement, and are both agreed that, like Paganini [famous violinist], the women should play on one string; that from New Year's Morn to Christmas Eve they should sing suffrage songs, and nothing more; no solos on "side issues," especially on marriage, divorce, or other social oppressions.

If a bright young girl, wishing to study law, knocks at the door of Columbia Law School, and the authorities refuse to let her in, she must not pause to criticize the injustice of such professors, or our present false system of education, but rush at once into some woman's paper or convention, and demand suffrage.

If another young girl is arraigned and sentenced to be hung for the crime of infanticide, while her seducer walks abroad without stripes or shame, women should not call an indignation meeting in Cooper Institute, to denounce the laws and public sentiment that forced the girl to commit that crime, but humbly circulate petitions on suffrage; though the masses of women – even the Mrs. Admiral Dahlgrens and the Catherine Beechers – are to-day wholly oblivious to the power of the ballot, and fail to see the connection between political ostracism and social wrongs.

If a married woman desires to escape from a drunkard, a debauchee, or a tyrant, who holds her person, property and children at his disposal, instead of riddling a marriage institution that denies equality to the contracting parties, she must swallow her griefs and unfurl the banner of suffrage.

Of all "white male" leaders on this woman question, the New England Abolitionists are the most dangerous, because the women look up to them as gods, trusting that they will do for them what they did for the slaves on the southern plantations, forgetting that in this reform, men are themselves the slaveholders who make the creeds, the codes, the conventionalisms, for the women of their households; for the elements of mankind, that framed these laws in the beginning, are not yet wholly extinct in the sons. . . .

In the anti-slavery warfare, these same men were not so troubled about side issues. "The negro pew," "the Jim Crow cars," "colored schools," the Bible, the church, everything that was supposed to stand in the way of complete negro equality was riddled, turned, and overturned.

For years, they fought the intermarriage laws of Massachusetts, roused the people to white heat over the problem of miscegenation, took the commonwealth by the throat, and compelled it to annul those laws that forbade blacks and whites to clasp hands at the altar. But now, forsooth, because some women, who understood the ways of their sex better than any man possibly can, have seen fit to protest against the inequalities of sex in the present legal marriage relation – making man master, woman slave – Boston* is frightened from her propriety with fear of "side issues." But marriage and divorce are not "side issues" to-day; they are the kernel of the question. . . .

Elizabeth Cady Stanton
October 6, 1870

[* "Boston" refers to the American Woman Suffrage Association (AWSA), with leaders in Boston. AWSA (unlike the National Woman Suffrage Association with Stanton as president) wanted a focus on suffrage alone.]

3
Hester Vaughanism

Introduction

The injustices suffered by Hester Vaughan in 1868 epitomized to the women of *The Revolution* a host of wrongs against women, wrongs that involved double standards of sexuality, forced motherhood, economic vulnerability and legal oppression. Abortion, infanticide and prostitution were not women's crimes but the result of men's crimes against women, they argued, despite the fact that women were tried and convicted by public sentiment, as well as by the legal system.

Hester Vaughan, an English immigrant who found work as a domestic servant in Pennsylvania, became pregnant by her employer and was fired. Without money and family, she gave birth alone in an unheated room and was found, ill, three days later with a dead child. She was arrested and convicted of infanticide (child murder) and sentenced to death. When the women of *The Revolution* heard of the case, they took up Vaughan's cause. Editorials condemned a system of sexual and economic oppression that would put her in such circumstances and then convict her of them. The Working Women's Association sent a delegation to visit her in prison, and Stanton, along with her cousin Elizabeth Smith Miller, personally visited the governor of Pennsylvania to ask for a pardon. Vaughan ultimately was pardoned and returned to her family in England, helped by the financial contributions of the Working Women's Association.

Both abortion and infanticide were perceived at this time as serious social problems by those both for and against women's rights. The women of *The Revolution*, however, did not lay the blame for these acts on women's depravity, as others did, but on women's economic and sexual exploitation by men. Motherhood itself, extolled in the popular press and guidebooks, they saw as debased by women's subordinate relation to men, a relationship that meant women were the objects of men's unwanted sexual

73

advances because of the legal obligation of marriage or the economic blackmail of employment. Contrary to popular myth, they pointed out, bearing a child is not a noble activity in and of itself.

Given the high birthrate and the high risk of death or debilitation from childbearing during the time period, it is not surprising that some women were so interested in gaining control over maternity. Though the birthrate did drop from more than seven children on average per woman at the beginning of the century to more than three by the end of the century, the rate did not decline for Black women or white immigrant women. In addition, the birthrate does not include the number of pregnancies not carried to term, so pregnancy and nursing occupied substantial portions of a woman's life. The physical risk from childbirth was as high as one death for every thirty live births even at the beginning of the twentieth century, and women were subjected to intrusive and often debilitating medical practices.

Abortion has been credited by some modern observers with being largely responsible for the drop in the birthrate through the nineteenth century. At the beginning of the nineteenth century abortion was largely unregulated, under the belief that the fetus was not alive until after the woman felt its movement. By the time of *The Revolution*, however, the medical profession was increasingly insistent that the fetus' life begins at the time of conception and that abortion should be regulated. Still, increased numbers of white, married, middle class women were having abortions as a means of regulating family size. Other means of birth control – condoms, pessaries and withdrawal – continued to be used.

Neither abortions nor birth control were advocated in *The Revolution*, however, but woman's right to her own body was. Claiming a woman's right to her own body was part of the writers' efforts to redefine "woman," not as property or object, but as an autonomous and self-directing human being. They were at the same time redefining sexuality in marriage from a woman's duty to a free choice. Birth control would have accomplished the same goal of regulating pregnancies, but at the expense of intensifying men's ownership of women's sexual availability. The way in which the feminist movement and the introduction of the birth control pill were co-opted in the 1960s and 1970s into a push for women's increased sexual availability to men suggests that the nineteenth-century argument for women's control over their own sexuality was not as naive as might be thought.

The sexual double standard that created "fallen women" out of economically oppressed or sexually active women was also criticized in the pages of *The Revolution*. Despite public denunciations of prostitution, it was seen by many – physicians, the police, military leaders – as a necessity, a means for providing outlets for men's sexuality without sacrificing the purity of white, middle-class women. It is not surprising that *The Revolution* would recognize in the prostitute a symbol of men's economic and sexual exploitation of women. Prostitution was, in fact, a growing way of life for white women, though Black, Asian, Mexican and Native American women were even more likely to be sexually victimized by men. Calls to regulate prostitution by such means as forcing prostitutes to register (similar to the Contagious Diseases Acts instituted in England during the 1860s) brought a forceful and successful fight against regulation by Anthony and other women.

A more widespread response to prostitution was the attempts to reform prostitutes through "benevolent" associations such as Magdalen Asylums. As editorials in *The Revolution* pointed out, such attempts to rehabilitate prostitutes ignored men's responsibility in the activity and in creating the circumstances that fostered prostitution.

Prostitution and other violations of women's code of appropriate sexual behavior were often used as excuses for the arrest or legal harassment of women, as *The Revolution* makes clear. Of course, these were effective means of control, regulating women's physical movement and their relationships in both public and private. Radical women realized that men's power to define what constitutes a crime and to enforce codes of behavior had to be changed.

Bibliography

Baxandall, Rosalyn, Linda Gordon and Susan Reverby, comps. and eds. 1976. *America's Working Women*. New York: Vintage Books.

Butler, Anne M. 1985. *Daughters of Joy, Sisters of Misery: Prostitutes in the American West*. Urbana: University of Illinois Press.

Clinton, Catherine. 1984. *The Other Civil War: American Women in the Nineteenth Century*. New York: Hill & Wang.

Freedman, Estelle B. 1981. *Their Sisters' Keepers: Women's Prison Reform in America, 1830–1930*. Ann Arbor: University of Michigan Press.

Gordon, Linda. 1982. "Why Nineteenth-Century Feminists Did Not

Support 'Birth Control' and Twentieth-Century Feminists Do: Feminism, Reproduction, and the Family." In *Rethinking the Family: Some Feminist Questions*, Barrie Thorne, ed., with Marilyn Yalsom. New York: Longman: 40–53.

Leavitt, Judith Walzer. 1986. "Under the Shadow of Maternity: American Women's Responses to Death and Debility Fears in 19th Century Childbirth." *Feminist Studies* 12, No. 1 (Spring): 129–154.

Mohr, James C. 1978. *Abortion in America: The Origins and Evolution of National Policy, 1800–1900*. New York: Oxford University Press.

Pivar, David J. 1973. *Purity Crusade: Sexual Morality and Social Control, 1868–1900*. Westport, Conn.: Greenwood Press.

Ruggles, Steven. 1983. "Fallen Women: The Inmates of the Magdalen Society Asylum of Philadelphia, 1836–1908." *Journal of Social History* 16: 65–82.

Walkowitz, Judith R. 1980. *Prostitution and Victorian Society: Women, Class and the State*. Cambridge: Cambridge University Press.

Hester Vaughan*

Judge Ludlow, of Philadelphia, [has pronounced] a death sentence on a poor, ignorant, friendless and forlorn girl who had killed her newborn child because she knew not what else to do with it. . . .

If that poor child of sorrow is hung, it will be deliberate, downright murder. Her death will be a far more horrible *infanticide* than was the killing of her child. She is the child of our society and civilization, begotten and born of it, seduced by it, by the judge who pronounced her sentence, by the bar and jury, by the legislature that enacted law (in which, because a woman, she had no vote or voice), by the church and the pulpit that sanctify the law and the deeds, of all these will her blood, yea, and her virtue, too, be required! All these were the joint seducer, and now see if by hanging her, they will also become her murderer.

August 6, 1868

Not long ago, one day a pretty English girl, poor and friendless, was wandering in the streets of Philadelphia, seeking employment. Seeing a respectable-looking man, she asked him if he could tell her where she could find a good place to work. Yes, he promptly replied, he would take her to his country home. So she went with him and remained in his family several months.

But alas! her protector proved her betrayer, and she was turned into the street at the very time she needed shelter, love and care.

76

With the wages she had saved, for she was an industrious, frugal girl, she took a small room in a tenement house, and there, in the depth of the winter, without a fire, a bed, or one article of furniture, with no eyes, save that of Omnipotence, to witness, and no human heart to pity her sufferings, she laid one morning with a new born child, exhausted on the floor. In vain she had called for help, no one heard or heeded her cries, feverish with pain and thirst, she dragged herself to the door to beg some passerby for water, and when, at last, help came, she was found in a fainting condition, and the child dead by her side. She was taken to the station house, and soon after imprisoned for infanticide. Tried and condemned, with most inadequate proof, she now lies in a Philadelphia prison waiting the hour of her execution. . . . So long as by law and public sentiment maternity is made a disgrace and a degradation, the young and inexperienced of the poorer classes are driven to open violence, while money affords the rich the means of fraud, protection and concealment.

What a holocaust of women and children we offer annually to the barbarous customs of our present type of civilization, to the unjust laws that make crimes for women that are not crimes for men! . . .

Elizabeth Cady Stanton
November 19, 1868

. . . This case carries with it a lesson for the serious thought of every woman, as it shows the importance that women of wealth, education and leisure study the laws under which they live, that they may defend the unfortunate of their sex in our courts of justice, and, as able advocates, avail themselves of every advantage the law gives for their acquittal. . . . Had Hester Vaughan been informed of her rights and privileges, she might have challenged her jurors. . . . Women have the right to challenge all male jurors because the difference in our political position is as wide as that of noble and peasant in the Old World. . . .

If we look over the history of Jury trial, we find in all ages, and nations, the greatest stress laid on every man being judged by his equals. . . . If nobles cannot judge peasants, or peasants nobles, how can man judge woman? . . .

Elizabeth Cady Stanton
December 10, 1868

[* *The Revolution* generally used this spelling, but others have used "Vaughn."]

Infanticide

The remarkable mortality among natural or illegitimate children is a topic agitating the Press very largely just now in America, England and France. . . . It is impossible for us to shut our eyes to these facts. They tell a common story – that of extravagance, celibacy, vice, and consequent degeneration. Where lies the remedy? – *N.Y. Times*

In the independence of woman. . . .

. . . So long as woman is dependent on man, her relation to him will be a false one, either in marriage or out of it; she will despise herself and hate him whose desires she gratifies for the necessaries of life; the children of such unions must needs be unloved and deserted. When women have their own property and business, they will choose and not be chosen; they will marry the men they love, or not at all; and where there is love between the parents, children will ever find care and protection. . . .

January 29, 1868

★★Slaves to Man's Lust★★

. . . Scarce a day passes but some of our daily journals take note of the fearful ravages on the race, made through the crimes of Infanticide and Prostitution.

. . . We believe the cause of all these abuses lies in the degradation of woman.

Strike the chains from your women; for as long as they are slaves to man's lust, man will be the slave of his own passions.

Wonder not that American women do everything in their power to avoid maternity; for, from false habits of life, dress, food and generations of disease and abominations, it is to them a period of sickness, lassitude, disgust, agony and death.

What man would walk up to the gallows if he could avoid it? . . .

Elizabeth Cady Stanton
February 5, 1868

Child Murder

. . . Androscoggin county in Maine is largely a rural district, but a recent Medical Convention there unfolded a fearful condition of society in relation to this subject. Dr. Oaks made the remark that, according to the best estimate he could make, there were *four hundred murders annually produced by abortion* in that county alone. . . .

There must be a remedy even for such a crying evil as this. But where shall it be found, at least where begin, if not in the complete enfranchisement and elevation of women? Forced maternity, not out of legal marriage but within it, the complete power of the stronger over the weaker sex, must lie at the bottom of a vast proportion of such revolting outrages against the laws of nature and our common humanity.

March 12, 1868

★★Gestation Facts Needed★★

Editors of the Revolution:

. . . I am *sure* that women would rarely *dare* to destroy the product of conception if they did not *fully believe* that the little being was devoid of life during all the earlier period of gestation.

. . . Dr. [Anne] Densmore demonstrated to us fully and clearly that the fulfillment of life processes were going on from the very beginning of embryonic development. . . .★ And that even before the mother could assure herself that she was to wear the crown of maternity by realizing the movements of the child, that the educated ear of the physician could often distinguish the beating of its heart. These are the facts that women need to know. . . .

Give us *knowledge* before accusing us of crime, and do not foget to guage [sic] the calibre of our sins by the light furnished to guide us. . . .

A Teacher
March 19, 1868

[★ Densmore and other physicians were pushing for a recognition that the fetus is alive at conception, not after "quickening," or movement.]

★★Time to Conspire★★

E. Poland, Me.

Editors of the Revolution:

In a late number of "*The Revolution*" I noticed an article under this head [Child Murder], wherein the statement was made that four hundred children were annually murdered in Androscoggin county, and in a later number an article from a teacher, wherein it was proposed to remedy this evil by educating woman to the knowledge that there was life in the embryo. Now, I live in

Androscoggin county, and am personally acquainted with the physician who made the statement and several of the women who go to make up the four hundred; and though I do not wish to disturb the faith of any one in the virtue or goodness of women, I must confess that I do not think this knowledge would deter one out of ten, if it did one out of a hundred, with us from the commission of this deed. They do it with the knowledge that it endangers their own lives, but the cry is "Liberty or Death;" and could you look in upon the wretched homes where heartbroken women work day and night for the most shameful pittance, to provide food for the little ones whom the brutal lusts of a drunken husband have forced upon them, you would not wonder that they did not choose to add to their number. . . .

The *Tribune* laments over this "conspiracy against marriage," but it is time to conspire against an institution which makes one human being the slave of another. . . .

Conspirator
April 9, 1868

Is Woman Her Own?

. . . "Child Murder" . . . [touches] a subject which lies deeper down into woman's wrongs than any other. This is the denial of the right to herself. In no historic age of the world has woman yet had that. . . . [N]owhere has the marital union of the sexes been one in which woman has had control over her own body.

Enforced motherhood is a crime against the body of the mother and the soul of the child. . . .

I hesitate not to assert that most of this crime of "child murder," "abortion," "infanticide," lies at the door of the male sex. . . .

Matilda E. J. Gage*
April 9, 1868

[* See the Appendix for biographical information.]

Restellism Not the Problem

. . . When the conditions of society are so false that mothers kill their own children, the trouble lies deeper down than "Restellism." . . .*

June 18, 1868

[* The term "Restellism" for abortion came from the name of

Madame Restell, a successful abortion practitioner from 1838 until her imprisonment and suicide in 1878.]

Respecting Maternity

. . . *Whereas*, Recent developments in this city and in other places, have called the attention of Sorosis [a women's club] to the homeless and unprotected condition of those upon whom, by misfortune or crime, is laid the burden of unlegalized maternity; and . . .

Whereas, The partners in their crime, or, as is too often the case, the authors of their misery, are unrebuked by society, and are not prevented by public opinion from pursuing the same free and dishonorable career as if virtuous, while their companions, or victims, are bereft of social position and debarred from all opportunity to retrieve their error and to rise to honor and preferment in respectable communities; and as by this most unjust relative position woman is driven to despondency, loss of self-respect, and that deep despair which ultimates in recklessness and ruin; therefore, . . .

Resolved, That the first work of the committee shall be to ascertain what public provision has been made by way of hospitals and asylums, in this city and elsewhere, for the protection and care of the unfortunate woman approaching maternity in consequence, it may be, of the first downward step; and if such wise and humane guardianship shall not be found, to consider the question of the erection of such asylums and hospitals with the hope that the divine "quality of mercy" may be extended to the erring woman no less freely than to the erring man, and that the desolate and despairing, through whom society has dishonored the holy office of maternity by degrading its entire significance, and negating its most imperative and sacred claims, may be rescued from misery and vice, and her offspring saved to fill an honorable place in our great, intelligent, and virtuous commonwealth. . . .

January 14, 1869

How Man Legislates for Woman

Mr. Brush, of Duchess, introduced an important bill this morning [to the New York legislature], to suppress prostitution in the Metropolitan Police District, and for the better preservation of the public health therein.

This bill, as presented in our daily journals last winter, section by section, is a disgrace to the decency and humanity of the nineteenth century. . . .*

It requires every young girl who leads this miserable life, to register her name in a book, kept by the police, and thus announce prostitution as her profession. . . . Having registered her name, she is to be under the constant supervision of a Board of Health, *composed of men*! to be watched and kept for the safety and convenience of the depraved and licentious of their own sex. . . . What man who has transgressed the immutable laws of nature and suffers the inevitable penalties, would consent thus to register *his* name, though old in crime? . . .

For twenty years we have asked the men of this state to give us the "ballot", that great moral lever by which woman can be raised from the depths of her degradation and made to assert herself in the world of thought and action. To-day we demand it as the best "bill for the suppression of prostitution" that our rulers can present to the people of this state for their thoughtful consideration.

Elizabeth Cady Stanton
March 19, 1868

[* The bill did not pass.]

Man's Humanity

Annie Myers, a girl twenty years of age, was found wandering in the streets on Tuesday night without food or shelter. She said she had lately been an inmate of Bellevue Hospital, but when deemed well enough to leave was sent abroad, and had no money or friends. – *Morning Papers*

"Woman's sphere is home." How comes it that none of these "natural protectors" of womanhood, these "oaks" made for woman to lean upon, were ready to save Annie from cold, hunger, temptation and death? Men sent Annie from the hospital without money or friends! Men published the above facts without comment. Men picked Annie up in the streets. Men have her in charge to-day, and men make the laws for her *protection*.

April 2, 1868

Women's Pages, Men's Crimes

. . . I can grasp your hand warmly upon the "Woman's Rights" question, especially upon reading the "Decision of the Superior Court," in the "Von Glan Divorce Suit," * and in seeing, day after day and week after week, all the cases of rape, bigamy, elopements, and all other crimes or weaknesses connected with our sex, placed under the heading of "Woman," in all the issues of the Chicago *Times,* just as though *men* were in nowise connected with them, and as though they are not generally, almost universally, the prime movers in such matters. . . .

P. W. Raley
April 9, 1868

[* This perhaps refers to the bill for divorce brought by Matilda Von Glahn against her husband, August Von Glahn. At issue was whether the courts should grant a divorce if her own behavior "provoked" him to beat her (*Illinois Reports 180,* 1867).]

Black-Mailing

As the organ of woman in her lowest as well as high estate, we cannot be silent over the painful fact which has come to our notice, that there is a regular system of *black-mail* levied by policemen upon the hard-earned money of poor little street walkers. More than a year ago, a corporation ordinance was passed which rendered it a misdemeanor for such girls to solicit men in the streets. The fact, therefore, of a girl standing to talk with a man at night renders her liable to arrest, under the supposition that she is *soliciting* him for improper purposes. Taking advantage of this, many policemen compel presents from girls, with an understanding that they will not arrest them. . . .

Our readers have, doubtless, all noticed policemen talking with young women at street corners, both day and night. It rarely happens that the girls are not of the unfortunate class, and that the rascals are not pestering them for money.

October 15, 1868

Letter to Mr. Perham of Maine

Birmingham, Michigan

Sir: You propose in your bill relating to the pension law to withhold pensions from "women who live in prostitution or concubinage." The spirit of tyranny which induces the strong to oppress the weak, caused the rebellion. In that war fell the natural guardians of the homes of the unfortunate class you mention in your bill. Indirectly, they became the subjects of that same tyranny by being deprived of adequate support for themselves and children. Thus tyranny brought destitution, and destitution opened the door of crime, and you propose to oppress these unfortunates still more. Let us have equal laws for all men and women. Now, bring a bill withholding pensions from males, who are guilty of like crimes, and another reaching all men who receive government emoluments who are guilty of breaking the seventh commandment. We have put up with man's inhumanity to woman for about six thousand years, and now we intend to show a slight resistance. Divide with us the offices and professions, and their rewards. Give us endowments for universities and Colleges. Open to us those already in existence. Give us the power to help make laws, and we will see that a licentious man is put upon the same social level that his female victim is. We will distribute the occupations of life in such a way that every woman can earn a living, and not be forced into a life of shame from necessity. No doubt, Mr. Perham, you view this world through uncontaminated eyes, and so have little sympathy with any of its wretched inhabitants. If you wish to tax crime, *begin* on the man's side.

Kate E. Alexander
February 25, 1869

Police as Protectors

Mrs. Hamilton, a genteel young woman, who is employed as a boot-lacer . . . was accosted by roundsman Charles Wanderling, No. 999, who, mistaking her for a street walker, gave her three heavy blows across the back with his club. Half fainting, she staggered across the street, to Reed's dining rooms. After resting a while, she gained sufficient strength to return to her home at West Eleventh Street, where she has since been confined to her bed. [*New York Sun*]

. . . This is but one, no doubt, of hundreds of cases that are daily and hourly occurring of police inhumanity to women. He seeks to shelter himself under the plea that he supposed she was a street-walker (probably one whom he had some private spite against). Admitting the fact she was, what right had he to club a woman in that manner?

Sound this brute's name, and number, over the length and

breadth of the land, as another instance that should justify Woman's Suffrage. Charles Wandling, New York Metropolitan police officer, No. 999, has handed his name down to posterity as a forcible protector of woman's morals, viz.: a locust club two inches thick, foot and a-half long on a respectable married woman's back, going peacefully to earn an honest living by the sweat of her brow, and now seeks to screen himself under the plea, he was mistaken in the sanctity of her order. So immaculate and sure was he in the sanctity of his own purity, and of his clearance in the eyes of the law. . . .

Mrs. M. A. S.
August 26, 1869

Abandoned Men

ARREST OF ABANDONED WOMEN – For a long time [the streets] have been infested with numbers of women of the most abandoned character. . . . On Sunday night, [Capt. Jourdan] sent a number of officers in plain clothes, and within a few hours they apprehended no less than fifty-five of these abandoned women. . . . Yesterday, Justice Hogan committed the entire party in default of $300 bail each, which is tantamount to a sentence of six months on Blackwell's Island. [*Tribune*]

. . . .

Surely we have cause here for congratulation! What a sweet sense of peace ought to enter our souls when we read that "Justice Hogan committed the entire party (in our city) in default of $300 bail each, which is tantamount to a sentence of six months on Blackwell's Island."★ "Now, at least, we are safe," thought I, when suddenly, it flashed upon me that, as in the course of impartial justice, for which our city is celebrated, the case of *men of the town* is next on the carpet. I say, when *that* thought crossed my mind, I was overwhelmed, dismayed, aghast, "Who shall try the men?" I cried aloud in my anguish; "what judge, or where shall be found a jury? Where is the beginning? and where, oh where! is the end of so great a work? And, it accomplished, what a desert shall we behold! Not a man in all the length and breadth of this great town! How *could* we abide it? Where is the Blackwell Archipelago that would be needed to accommodate our dear companions of the male sex? All the South Sea Islands would not suffice. And, oh! what a melancholy sight as shipload after shipload sails from our port. Tears blind my eyes, sobs choke my utterance. Don't let us do it, dear *Revolution*, don't let us even attempt to arrest our *men of the town*, for although they could bail each other without difficulty as they hold the purse-strings, yet we should have immediately to re-arrest them on a new charge, and, in short, neither time nor space could be found sufficient to do them justice.

V.
January 14, 1869

[* Blackwell's Island was a women's prison in New York City.]

Homes for Fallen Men

Every one must see that the work of reclaiming fallen women is almost useless, while there are so many more of the opposite sex in the same condition. We should have, therefore, as soon as practicable, homes for fallen men. . . .

A majority of the men holding public offices would probably seek these homes. They would be a secure retreat for many Congressmen and lobbyists. . . .

Each home should be managed by a board of women, who should issue their orders through competent superintendents. Women would be better than men as directors, because men might be too lenient, and only the strictest conformity to established rules could work the needed reform. . . .

As soon as our poor besieged men shall be aided by these homes in keeping their virtue, the vocation of these [corrupt women] will be gone. . . .

Sarah Knowles Bolton*
September 30, 1869

[* Sarah Knowles Bolton was an author who contributed to newspapers and wrote short stories, poetry and books. She traveled extensively abroad and had a special interest in women's education.]

Male Magdalen Asylums*

Why not Male as well as Female? Certainly for every Mary Magdalen there must have been a David Magdalen, a Solomon Magdalen, an Abraham, an Isaac, or a Jacob Magdalen. There may have been more. Poor Mary Magdalen was possessed of seven devils, all *males*, of course, for the Bible always makes devils masculine. . . . But why Magdalen Asylums for the Marys and none for the tempter, the serpent, the devil that caused their fall? Magdalen Asylums are not benevolent, charitable, philanthropic, christian. They are places of punishment. Whoever enters them goes as a culprit, a criminal. The entrance, indeed, is another "Bridge of Sighs;" all hope of perfect restoration, recognition as an equal, a trusted, loved, honored member of society may as well be left behind. . . . But the seducer needs no such penitential, purgatorial discipline. He is at the top of society here; has no doubt he will be hereafter. He is the court that tries, the judge that sentences, the governor that hangs the Hester Vaughans, unless some rescuing angel interposes and snatches the prey from their very fangs. They need no Magdalen Asylums. They build them and then crowd them with victims of their own destroying. For every fallen woman there are forty fallen men. Men, many of them, fallen forty times lower, too, than any woman, because it is they who drag women down. . . . Man frames laws, society shapes its customs, fashions, occupations, compensations, so as to lure or drive woman to these terrible straits, especially poor woman, then she falls, is henceforth branded, shunned, goes forth a fugitive, a vagabond, or is consigned to, rather is confined in, a Magdalen Asylum to expiate in grief and tears the sin she was tempted, driven by force she did not create, could not control, to commit or die! . .

Parker Pillsbury
May 12, 1870

[* Magdalen Asylums were charity houses for repentant prostitutes.]

The Social Evil

It is with an indignation difficult to be expressed that we refer to the introduction into the American city of St. Louis of the French system of registering fallen women. . . .*

. . . The list has reached between six and seven hundred names, and will probably go up to a thousand.

With unreserved condemnation, we aver that this book reflects as much shame on the men who are writing it as on the women who are written in it.

The most horrible of trades is prostitution. It is a devil's business in which women and men are equal partners, and from which they should reap an equal measure of guilt and condemnation. If a woman falls, she falls because she is dragged down by a man. Woman's merchandise of her body – by which she makes a market of herself in the streets – is impossible without man's complicity in the hellish bargain. God never ordained two codes of morality – one for woman and the other for man. The same judgment is visited by the Divine Judge impartially upon each of the two participants in the sins of the sexes. He who is no respecter of persons holds both males and females to an equal and awful accountability for their mutual and infernal crime.

But what says the city of St. Louis to this just equality of guilt and penalty? It says: "We are a man's government. The power is all in the hands of our own sex. Let us therefore make a public record which shall affix the shame of prostitution wholly on women, and remove it wholly from men." This is the meaning of the ledger opened by the Board of Health of St. Louis.

Now, in the name of all that is just and equal, we maintain that there is only one way in which a government of men (if they are gentlemen) can find a decent pretext for keeping a public record of prostitutes; and that is, by adding to it a similar record of paramours. If the police must register the women, let them also register the men. Prostitution is committed on the basis of a business contract; and if one party thereto must give legal notice to the authorities, let the other do the same. Let impartial justice be dealt to both accomplices in a common crime. . . .

. . . If every house of prostitution is to be known to the police, and if every woman residing in it is to be registered in the official list, then let a policeman stand at the door, and take the name, residence and occupation (under oath) of every man who enters; and let every man who, on entering, shall swear falsely, be tried for perjury, and suffer the customary penalty for that crime. The only just system of governmental control of the social evil – the only one which can be made consistent with itself, which can have any pretext for existence, or which can be anything else than tyrannous fraud – is one which will record in the St. Louis ledger the names of the men, as well as of the women, who thus commit the unpardonable sin against society.

We make this amendment to the St. Louis plan, and have faith to believe that the plan, as amended, would prove a very short method for putting out a fire of hell which the public authorities seem to be kindling afresh in that city.

August 11, 1870

Hester Vaughanism

[* According to Catherine Clinton, the St. Louis experiment of registering prostitutes lasted four years; registration proposals in other American cities were never adopted (*The Other Civil War: American Women in the Nineteenth Century*, New York: Hill & Wang, 1984, p. 158).]

Woman's Punishment and Man's Pardon

. . . In the matter of chastity, society has one code of morality for a woman and quite another for a man.

Public opinion . . . is shocked and outraged by the portrayal of a heroine of romance who, having made a misstep, conceals it from the man whom she marries; but it has no word or thought of condemnation for the many heroes of novels who have erred in this same way. Still further, in real life, public opinion does not make it a point of honor for a man to unveil all the secrets of his bachelor life to the woman he seeks in marriage. What would be thought of the charge against a man, "In his youth he fell, yet had no hesitation in marrying an honest woman who was ignorant of his history!" It would be regarded as simply absurd. Do we not all know, in the social circles in which we move, dozens of young men who have been "rehabilitated" after not one but many "falls," by marriage with "loving, respectable and unsuspecting wives"?

Has it not passed into a proverb that "reformed rakes make the best husbands?"

When society is ready to receive the prodigal son, and kill the fatted calf in his honor, why should it have no welcoming smiles for the repentant daughter? A sinner dare plead before God no distinction of sex as a palliation for his crime? Why is such a plea allowed by mankind?

To excuse that sin in a man which, when committed by a woman is punished by her social degradation, is one of the grossest forms of injustice of which society has been guilty. . . .

October 20, 1870

More Insults

To the Editor of the Revolution:

Thanks to the powers that be that women now have an avenue [*The Revolution*] through which to discharge their pent up feelings of indignation at the gross insults that are daily perpetrated upon

89

them, by our immaculate and spotless sons of Adam, our "lords of creation," who claim to be "protectors" and "superiors." . . .

[An] estimable and highly respected lady residing in the Southwest, applied for a school and obtained it without being subjected to the . . . humiliating and harrowing method of proving her own good character . . . but it seems the trying time was yet to come with her in a manner quite unexpected. She requested the board of directors to increase her wages; they did so, but she must first pass through the fire of insult to prove herself the true metal, ere it was granted. The immaculate Judge (one of the chief directors or superintendents) called on the lady, requested a private interview, cast out some vague inuendoes which the lady failed at once to comprehend, supposing him to be a man of uprightness and respectability, and finally ended by making her indecent overtures, promising an increase of her salary by her compliance with his diabolical request. Astounded and angered, she resented with indignity such base offers, and was about to retire with disgust when he changed his tactics and expressed much pleasure at the ladies' dignified conduct, informing her that this was but an artifice of his to prove her genuine morality and virtuous principles.

Are you masculine autocrats then so pure and refined that you must needs set yourselves up as judges and criterions for poor degenerate woman-kind?

How many, think you, are there among you would be "Lords of creation" that would stand the test, or run the gauntlet of such ordeals of moral inspection unharmed or unsullied? Can *you* Mr. Superintendent of said school who dared to question an innocent woman, assert your own purity and moral rectitude unblushingly?

We should be pleased to know "by what law of morals a woman is compelled to be purer than a man." We would most earnestly request our masculine friends and "protectors" to cease their prating about feminine virtues and feminine purity, until they give us some better evidences in future of their *own* purity and uprightness. *Then* and not *till* then will it be proper *or just* for them to sit in judgment upon us.

A Woman's Rights Woman
February 9, 1871

4
The bread question

Introduction

The pages of *The Revolution* demonstrate the high priority radical women of the nineteenth century placed on changing the lack of economic security and independence that threatened all classes of women. Higher wages and better work conditions for working-class women were demanded as well as the right of all women to be trained and prepared for productive, dignified labor. The popular ideal of the leisured lady devoted to fashion and domesticity was lampooned as well as refuted, and the realities of women's struggles to feed their children were displayed and their efforts to break new ground were championed. Writers stressed that women shared a common oppression of legal and economic dependency on men as husbands and employers that made even those women who were materially comfortable vulnerable to an instant change of economic status.

The kinds of jobs open to women at this time in the nineteenth century were few and badly paid. While the popular ideal for womanhood may have called for women's full-time devotion to domesticity, the expectation was not carried out by many women, whose sheer survival hinged on the few dollars they could earn. And in actuality, Black women and most white immigrant women were expected by the dominant culture to work outside their homes or be seen as lazy. Most women (particularly Black women and Irish women) worked as domestics, at needlework and in factories. Native-born white women from families with more status were more likely to be found in more "genteel" ("Oh, how I hate that word," one woman wrote) occupations, such as teaching and sales in retail stores. Though the pay was generally as low as in the other occupations, the work was less (only on a relative scale) humiliating and physically brutal.

Educational opportunities were as restricted as occupational ones. Women's intellectual, emotional and biological suitability for education was hotly contested. Prevented from entering most male institutions of higher learning (particularly the most prestigious), some *Revolution* writers argued in favor of women's own colleges. Even where women were allowed entrance into what were considered men's colleges, they were often prevented from taking the same courses of study as men. Few women were able to enter into the professions of law, medicine, university teaching or the ministry. Those who were able to enter programs of study faced ostracism and hostility from faculty and students. Those that finished their courses of study often were unable to find a position or find sufficient clients for a practice. A few – but important – exceptions were white women such as Antoinette Blackwell and Clemence Lozier and Black women such as Sarah Mapes Douglass and Rebecca Lee.

Writers in *The Revolution* advocated opening up both occupations and education for women. They exposed the terrible working and living conditions of needleworkers and blasted the pay differentials between women and men in teaching and other occupations (women generally made less than half or even a third of what men made), advocating "equal pay for equal work." They advised women to stay out of teaching and needlework and find better work in post offices, telegraph offices and printing offices. They suggested that women form their own businesses and institutions so that they could have good jobs and be independent of men's control.

Though sympathy for – and in some cases identification with – working-class women was apparent on the part of *The Revolution's* writers (Eleanor Kirk, for example, championed the worker in her fiction, and was supporting herself with her writing), it was Anthony who was the active labor organizer, her activities involving women who produced *The Revolution* and the content of *The Revolution* itself.

Before *The Revolution* entered the scene, women in some mills and industries (for example, the white workers in the Cocheco mill in Dover, New Hampshire, and in the Lowell mills in Massachusetts, and the Black launderers in Jackson, Mississippi) had already been involved in union organizing and had participated in several (usually unsuccessful) strikes. However, men's labor unions were neglectful of, if not outright hostile to, women workers. Working-class men who criticized women as strikebreakers driving down wages were often opposed to women working for wages at all. White unions generally barred Black men as well as Black and white women from becoming members, though the National Union of Cigar Makers admitted Black men and women in 1867 and the National Labor Union, a federal of unions, invited Blacks to join in 1866. The National Colored Labor Union invited women to join when it was organized in 1869 (see Wertheimer, 1977).

Though editorials in *The Revolution* championed both women and men of the working class against an oppressive economic system, women were exhorted to get jobs any way they could and to organize themselves into their own unions. In 1868, Anthony helped form the Working Women's Associations No. 1 and No. 2, which met in *The Revolution's* Woman's Bureau offices. Members of the first organization included Julia Brown and Elizabeth C. Brown, clerks in the *Revolution* office, and Augusta Lewis, a typesetter in the printing office of R. J. Johnston, the publisher of *The Revolution*. Lewis went on to become president of an offshoot of the Working Women's Association, the Women's Typographical Union.

Anthony did attempt to align the woman's movement with the men's labor movement through the National Labor Union. In 1868, Anthony, as a representative of the Working Women's Association, was seated as a delegate at the federation's national congress. In 1869, however, she was refused voting–delegate status on the grounds that she had advocated strikebreaking. In fact, during a strike of newspaper printers she had suggested employers establish training schools for women to teach them typesetting, justifying her action on the grounds that women needed to become skilled at typesetting in order to earn the same wages as men. No strong coalitions between men's labor interests and the woman's movement ever materialized. Berenice Carroll, however, has pointed out (in private correspondence) that (a) women's protective legislation and many aspects of labor legislation in the 1830s represented a coalition of US men's labor interests with "social feminist" women, and (b) some partial coalitions have been built around specific organizing in some industries or labor organizations (ILGWU, CLUW, farm workers and so forth).

Labor organizing did not – and probably could not have – become a major activity of the radical women involved with *The Revolution*. The Working Women's Associations merged and finally dissolved at the end of 1869, with few working-class women in membership. Working-class women, understandably, often preferred to put other priorities above suffrage. In addition, they may have been pressured against associating with the suffrage movement and woman's labor movement by their husbands, fathers and employers. Some working-class women, however, agreed there was a need for getting women the ballot that superseded the need for co-operating with the men's labor movement. Augusta Lewis, who had argued against the Working Women's Association involvement in suffrage when it was first organized, for example, concluded in 1871 that women's association with the typographical union had actually been a detriment to women. Women who were typographers and union members were kept out of union shops by men and out of non-union shops by employers. She went on to become a strong suffragist.

Bibliography

Butcher, Patricia Smith. 1986. "Education for Equality: Women's Rights Periodicals and Women's Higher Education, 1849–1920." *History of Higher Education Annual Vol. 6*. New York: University of Rochester Press: 63–79.

Clinton, Catherine. 1984. *The Other Civil War: American Women in the Nineteenth Century*. New York: Hill & Wang.

Flexner, Eleanor. 1959. *Century of Struggle: The Woman's Rights Movement in the United States*. Cambridge, Mass.: Belknap Press.

Foner, Philip S. 1979. *Women and the American Labor Movement: From Colonial Times to the Eve of World War I*. New York: The Free Press.

Janiewski, Dolores. 1976. "Making Common Cause: The Needlewomen of New York, 1831–69." *Signs* 1, No. 3: 777–86.

Jones, Jacqueline. *Labor of Love, Labor of Sorrow: Black Women, Work, and the Family from Slavery to the Present*. New York: Basic Books.

Seller, Maxine Schwartz, ed. 1981. *Immigrant Women*. Philadelphia: Temple University Press.

Stevens, George A. 1912. *New York Typographical Union No. 6: Study of a Modern Trade Union and Its Predecessors*. Albany, NY: J. B. Lyon.

Wertheimer, Barbara Mayer. 1977. *We Were There: The Story of Working Women in America*. New York: Pantheon.

The Bread Question

In glancing over the evening papers I saw it stated that there was a new sphere opening to woman. There was the usual sneer with the announcement, the little sarcasm, the small wit, which heralds every act of woman outside of the usual conventionalism. . . . Less than twenty years ago, Mrs. Swisshelm★ took her place in the reporters' gallery of the Senate of the United States to report for her own paper. She was ridiculed without measure, but she persisted, wrote spicy descriptions of men and subjects, and won the field. The next woman who took her seat there was almost unnoticed, and now women are seated at the reporters' tables and work with an easy familiarity that shows the field to be their own, and that the pay is sufficient for their *bread.*

. . . In the age of semi-barbarism and that period of civilization which preceded the era of steam as a mechanical power, manufacturing industry was to a large extent in the hands of women, and society depended so much upon their domestic industry, that however wretched the pecuniary remuneration which it afforded them, the family and the community awarded them useful and so far honorable employment. . . . Steam has engulfed a thousand household ' workshops, in every factory, and manu-facturers in like manner have departed from the fireside and the homestead, and installed themselves in vast workshops, where science directs and steam accomplishes the work of fabricating the food and clothing of the community.

It has been said by very high authority, "To my mind the Bread problem lies at the base of all the desirable and practical reforms which our age meditates." There is no question but it is the problem; but in what way it is to be solved is the next question of importance. Every avocation which belonged rightfully to woman, and in which she was honored, has been swept from her by the march of improvement. . . . In sweeping away the avocations by which bread was obtained honorably, our legal existence has remained still unrecognized, no political right or power has been accorded us as a compensation for the robbery of our employ-ments. The civil subjection of the past *was* bad enough, but it was mitigated by the social, domestic and industrial consequence of the period. Now we have genteel pauperism, dependence under pretty names, which in no wise conceals the contempt of their origin, much less our shame.

In striking out in any new sphere or any business avocation which will bring good pay, women must still longer expect to bring down on their devoted heads an avalanche of ridicule and opposition. . . .

Paulina Wright Davis★
September 23, 1869

[★ Jane Grey Swisshelm, an advocate of abolition and woman's rights, was a journalist and publisher who founded *The Pittsburgh Saturday Visiter* (her spelling), *The St. Cloud Visitor, The St. Cloud Democrat* and *The Reconstructionist.* In 1850, Vice President Millard Fillmore granted her request for a seat in the Senate Press Gallery. See the Appendix for biographical information on Paulina Wright Davis.]

Working Women Ill-Treated

. . . With the *"strong men,"* protected by "Trade Unions" and popular sympathy, we have little to do. Our mission is with that large, ill-treated, barely tolerated class, the working women of New York. It is not alone the limited fields of labor open to them of which women complain, but the stinted, grudging remuneration doled out for faithful service. It matters not that the pittance may be the only support of a wretched family, the laborer is a woman – God help her – and she must take whatever they give her. Until recently a woman was considered "out of her sphere," if she attempted any kind of work save with her needle. After the advent of the sewing machine, however, it was found that men could become operators and the poor victims were for a time still left at the old work of basting and finishing.

Poor, toiling sisterhood! they sang the "Song of the Shirt"* so long that their throats became parched, and the work hung limp and loose from their weary hands. When the war for the Union thinned the ranks, it was found that women could keep accounts, set type, write for the press, practice medicine, and do a thousand and one things requiring address, brains and energy.

Even here, however, is the great injustice practiced. Women are not admitted in equal numbers with men, and when admitted are paid inferior salaries. . . .

. . . An advertisement appeared in a city paper the other day, in which a lady copyist was wanted at – Chambers St. A lady friend who wrote a fine business hand answered the application. Upon stating her terms, the partners, highly respectable merchants, looked at her in amazement until finally one of them laughed outright, as he said, "Indeed, you must be from the country, Miss! *Ten dollars a week*; why, my dear young lady, *we could get a man for that!*"

February 19, 1868

[* "The Song of the Shirt" was a popular poem by Thomas Hood, used by needlewomen in their struggle.]

Highway Robbery

The Superintendent of Public Instruction gives the proportion of the average wages allowed to men and women for teaching in schools in this country since 1860: Maine, wages of male teachers per month, including board, $28.30; of female teachers, $10.50. New Hampshire, males $24.35; females, $14.12. Vermont, males, $27; females, $11. Massachusetts, males, $54.77; females $21.82. Connecticut, males, $28.19, including board; females, $15.80, including board. Ohio, males, $36.25; females, $21.55. Indiana, males, per day, $1.38; females, per day, $1.07. Illinois, males, per month, $30; females, $19. Wisconsin, males, per month, $36.45; females, $22.44. Iowa, males, per week, $7.91; females, $5.70. Kansas, males, per month, $36.74; females, $24.41. California, males, $74; females, $62.

Men call each other copperheads, but *brazencheek* should be one description if the above figures are set in judgment against them. The universal testimony of competent persons is that, other things being equal, women are the most competent teachers by far, both as to imparting instruction and exercising discipline. And yet it will be seen that they are paid *less than one-half the wages of men.* There would be uproar at once were there a proposal to tax women in the same proportion, and to administer all penalties and inflictions in the same degree. Robbery is not all committed in the night, nor on the highway. . . .

April 16, 1868

Help Your Working Sisters

. . . [W]omen should no more be ashamed to earn money than men should be. If money-making is honorable for the one it is for the other. . . . "*Genteel*" (I hate the word!) women, by their horror of useful, remunerative employment, do much to make more difficult the way for women who *must* work or starve, or do worse. If you would take a little pains to inquire and look into these things, you would soon find how truly the class known as "sewing women" are to be pitied, and would learn to search them out and give them the profits of their own labor, which now you put into the pockets of their employers.

If you have no occasion, or do not choose to earn money yourselves, do not, for humanity's sake, for God's sake, do not put a straw in the way of your striving sisters.

Miss H. M. Shepard
April 23, 1868

The Working-Woman Again

Not long ago there appeared in a daily paper an article taking ground against woman suffrage, and offering a crumb of comfort to women workers after this fashion: "The best we can say for a woman who is compelled to mingle daily with men on a working footing, is that we are sorry for her."

Now, in the first place, women as a class, or as individuals, are not on a footing with men in the work-day world. Either they are above them or far below. Custom has decided this, and the false education of the sexes must compel its continuance for a long time to come. The amount of meaningless sympathy extended to women who work has its beginning in this condition of things, and until genuine recognition and appreciation is awarded them in its place, their fate will not be brighter than at present.

Women, as a class, are poor, are divided in interests, and few in numbers compared to the great army of men who spend their lives in the workshop. And here let it be remarked that if the wealthy ladies of this and other cities would buy interests in business houses, and let the women workers have a voice in the matter of compensation, it would not be hard to find competent persons to fill positions and perform the same amount of labor that is required of men.

In truth, women have had enough of everything but the right kind of help. They have been surfeited with conventions and speeches, and tracts, and wholesale piety, and sympathy, and they would like a little *justice*. . . .

The poor, hard-working, long-suffering masses of working-women must toil on and toil unceasingly, and look to the future for relief. Not that it will come, for even of this we are not sure; but a vague kind of hope is better than none, and some natures feed upon this kind of food all their lives, and then accept death at last.

But who knows but that the last years of the century are to be its grandest; or that its closing decade will not mark the redemption of the working women from the thraldom of accursed customs?

Laura C. Holloway★

October 12, 1871

[★ Holloway was an editor and author who was editor of the *Home Library Magazine* and associate editor of the *Brooklyn Daily Eagle*. She published *Ladies of the White House* in 1870 and went on to write a number of other books.]

★★Literary Harassment★★

. . . [I am] utterly cast down when I think of the women who, in this enlightened nineteenth century, are dependent upon scamps, things called men – made in the image of God we are told; but it strikes me at the present writing that is a mistake! – for the means of support. Let me tell you of an instance which has lately come to my knowledge. A young lady, educated and talented, is compelled to earn her own bread and butter and be of some assistance in a relative's family of which she is a member. She attempts the path of literature, meets with fair success, and looks forward to a brilliant future. Several of her articles had been accepted and handsomely paid for at the house of one of our most respectable publishers; and finally, one of the editors proposes to pay the young lady the very handsome sum of $25 for a weekly article. The proposition is gladly accepted, and thus a little family are immediately lifted from pecuniary trouble. Then follows invitations from said editor to places of amusement, which she invariably declines. . . . Our editor makes a formal proposition – not for the lady's hand – a previous union renders that impossible – but asks the dumbfounded girl, in language which admitted of no misunderstanding, to become his mistress. Comprehending, at last, the dire intention of the smooth-tongued editor, she indignantly spurns the offer, and shows him the door; but continued to send MSS, as usual. Since then, each piece has been carefully returned, with a *printed* circular to this effect, that the articles were not exactly available for either of — periodicals.

Now, we ask, what can a woman do under such circumstances? Does she give the villain the publicity the case demands, she immediately places herself before the public in an unenviable position, and her name becomes a byword and a reproach. . . .

Eleanor Kirk★

July 30, 1868

[* See the Appendix for biographical information.]

Equal Pay for Equal Work

The New York *Atlas* said, last week, that there are 30,000 women in this city who labor night and day for a pittance upon which no tender-hearted philanthropist would attempt to support a favorite cat; yet in all progressive movements of the day, and all the revolutionary agitations touching the so-called rights of women, no one attempts to ameliorate the condition of these poor slaves of the needle. The *Atlas*, with the very best of intentions, no doubt, could not have been more mistaken. "*The Revolution*" was instituted pre-eminently for that very object. It exists for the one specific purpose, more than any other, of ameliorating the condition of *working* women.

. . . The *Atlas* adds, that the true way of benefiting these poor creatures is to devise a plan for increasing their pay to a rate comparatively equivalent to that given to male mechanics. That is exactly according to "*The Revolution*" Prospectus: "Equal Pay to Women for Equal Work."

August 20, 1868

Women's Double Duty

. . . We regretted but did not wonder that so few women were present [at the meeting of the Workingmen of New York], as they are not yet generally recognized as any part of the labor interest. It will be discovered, however, perhaps soon, that they are not only of the laboring class, but so terribly of it as to be beyond the reach of the eight hour law. For alas, how many of us must go supperless to bed, if woman shall attempt the benefit of that statute! . . .

Parker Pillsbury
August 20, 1868

Positions Wanted

The Herald of this morning contains nearly 1,500 advertisements; 413 females want situations; 171 people advertise for boarders and lodgers.

Probably the entire 171 advertising for boarders are women, too –

hence more than one-third of that vast number of advertisers were women, seeking work. And this, too, in a society based on the idea that every woman has some man to support and protect her. Where are the 585 men, whose duty it is to look after these women, so sadly out of their sphere?

October 1, 1868

Beware Insurance Companies**

The letter from a working woman we published last week, on the injustice of the "Hartford Insurance Company" to women, has drawn out many other communications on this subject. The proviso [in travel insurance] that "females will be insured against death only" (not accidents), is alike ludicrous and lamentable. . . .

Hath not a woman eyes, hands, organs, dimensions, senses, that men dare make such distinctions between themselves and us? Is not a damaged woman as great a loss to herself, the family, the church, the state, as a damaged man? Shall we ever get to the end of the absurdities into which men run on the supposed differences in sex. . . .

Moral – Let all women beware of Insurance Companies.

Elizabeth Cady Stanton
October 8, 1868

All Women are Working Women**

"But I am *not* a working woman!" says one. You are not a working woman; what, then, are you? *Every* woman whose soul has kept pace with, or even followed, however distantly, in the triumphant march of progress, must, of necessity, be a working woman. You have a husband? You are shielded? You have money, and, like the "ladies of the field," can be arrayed without toiling or spinning. Shame on a woman who, after confessing her time all leisure, also confesses no interest in the welfare of her suffering, scantily paid, down-trodden sisters! Every whole-souled, large-hearted woman is a working woman, and if necessity does not compel her to work exclusively for herself and family, duty and inclination will keep her employed for those who most require her assistance.

Eleanor Kirk
November 26, 1868

The Revolution in Words

Equal Opportunity Rag-Picking

From the best evidence [the Working Women's Association] committee has been able to gather, the number of rag-pickers in New York city is about 1,200 of all grades, a little more than one half being women. This is the only business, we believe, where women have equal opportunities with men.

Sarah F. Norton*

December 31, 1868

[* Sarah Norton, novelist and lecturer, became president of the Working Women's Association in 1869, shortly before it dissolved.]

Sewing and Teaching Don't Pay

Mrs. Stanton – *Dear Madam*: My friend —— and myself are very anxious to obtain some employment by which we can support ourselves. We are both able and willing to work. . . .

We receive many such letters from young girls, and we are always puzzled what to say; the employments for women are so few, and so poorly paid. If you and your friend can do so, try and get the Post Office in the place where you live, and let the man who sits there shoulder his axe, and go out West to fell the forests and cultivate the soil. If you have a telegraph office in your town, study that business and look for a place in some large city. If you have money, study medicine, or buy some land and raise fruit and vegetables for the New York market. Chickens and eggs pay well. Women have tried sewing and school teaching for nothing, long enough.

January 7, 1869

Wages for Housework

The following is from the *Weekly Mirror*; Mrs. Jane G. Swisshelm, associate editor:

The husband and wife are equal partners. The husband is out-door head of the firm, and the wife in-door member. Her work in the house is of as much importance to the welfare of the family as his work out of doors. No family can be well managed unless the wife and mother faithfully performs her part; and if she does this the husband and father does no more for the advancement of the interest of the family. This being the case, she is entitled to one-half of the income, to one-half of all that he and she accumulate. . . .

January 21, 1869

★★Matrimony a Blunder★★

Waterloo, Iowa

Dear Mrs. Stanton: Permit me to remind you of one quite important item you seem not to notice in your paper, that is, of women taking Homesteads, or buying government land and stand a chance to make a little money as well as men. I think of taking up a homestead this coming fall, but I am informed by my masculine friends that I cannot, because I am a woman. Now, I would like to ask, in the name of justice, how long are men going to monopolize all the money-making businesses of this earth?

Anna M. Caffrey

If you have not committed the unpardonable blunder of matrimony, that is, if you are a single woman or a widow, you can take possession of 160 acres of land. Why men desire to bring this divine institution into disrepute by disqualifying its feminine subjects from so many desireable rights, privileges and immunities, we cannot understand.

Matrimony under the happiest circumstances is so full of pitfalls and precipices, that all these artificial disabilities should be promptly set aside. When we hold the ballot, we shall have a word to say about these pre-emption laws, and see that they bear equally on men and women. A married man takes possession of 160 acres of government land. Why not a married woman?

July 15, 1869

★★Jobs Any Way We Can Get Them★★

. . . Talking of strikes; we heard a "male" compositor say the other day that "it was mean for women to step in and take work at the old price, when men had struck for higher wages; besides, it was degrading." "Mean," is it? well, we're agreed. We only wish to tell you one thing. Just as often as possible we shall step into new places, and then – get us out if you can. If you won't let us enter in any other way, we must enter in this; and, as to its being degrading, we beg leave to differ with you there. *Woman* is not degraded, but *man* is. Every time that a strike is made, and woman in consequence enters some new branch of business, she is elevated and man degraded. We think it will not be long ere the social scale will be balanced a little more evenly. Woman expects to be sneered at and scoffed at if she steps aside from the beaten track. If she edits a paper, man holds up his hands in holy terror. If she takes the speaker's chair he would blush, if he could. Does she write – she is a *blue* [bluestocking]. Does she take any prominent position – she is bold and masculine. If to be masculine is to be *smart*, do let her try; or are you afraid, if she has the chance, that a few of your laurels will droop? . . .

M. C. R.
March 19, 1868

★★Workingmen Don't Support Ballot★★

Resolved. That the low wages, long hours, and damaging service to which multitudes of working girls and women are doomed, destroy health, imperil virtue, and are a standing reproach to civilization; that we would urge them to learn trades, engage in business, join our labor Unions, or use any other honorable means to persuade or force men to render unto every woman according to her works.

The working men held their National Convention here last week, and among other resolutions passed the above, as the best they could do for woman. There was quite a spicy discussion in the Committee on resolutions on one demanding the ballot for woman, but it was voted down and the above substituted. Poor human nature always wants something to look down upon. These workingmen, struggling to throw off the chains of capitalists, bondholders and land monopolists, would forge new chains with their own hands for the women by their side. . . . A disfranchised class is always a degraded class, hence, they cheapen whatever labor they touch. When men strike, already you see capitalists substituting the cheap labor of women in their stead. But educate, elevate and enfranchise woman, and you raise the price of her labor at once. . . .

Elizabeth Cady Stanton
July 19, 1868

The bread question

★★Shut Out of Unions★★

Editors of the Revolution:

. . . I arrived [in San Francisco] five weeks ago, expecting to maintain myself and child by obtaining work as a compositor till I should establish myself as correspondent. I found the proprietors of all the offices quite willing to give me employment, but the Typographical Union refused to permit me to work, the members threatening to leave any office where a lady might be employed. . . . On making the particulars known, parties advanced the capital and a nice printing office is started under the head of Women's Co-operative Printing Union. . . .

However, we do not know anything about or wish to take any stand in politics, or want to vote, therefore you may have a contempt for our lack of strongmindedness. We all strongly sympathize with women who are unjustly oppressed and shut out from an opportunity of earning their living and will be willing to aid any way we can any who have been thrown in the same position as ourselves.

Very respectfully,
Agnes B. Peterson

P. S.   All the departments are to be filled by ladies.

September 10, 1868

The Working Women's Association

The Working Women's movement in this city is already assuming an importance unlooked for by the few who met together scarce one month since in the office of "*The Revolution*", to discuss the necessity of doing something for the protection of woman's labor. . . .

A Working Woman's Association was organized by Susan B. Anthony, which now numbers over two hundred members. They are to meet once a month to devise ways and means to open to themselves new and more profitable employments, that thus by decreasing the numbers in the few avocations now open to women, they can decrease the supply and raise the wages of those who remain. They propose, also, to demand an increase of wages in all those trades where they now work beside men for half pay. This can only be done by combination, for one person alone demanding higher wages can effect nothing, but 5,000 women in any one employment, striking for higher wages, would speedily bring their employers to terms. . . .

. . . One of Miss Anthony's most cherished plans is to have a magnificent printing establishment, and a daily paper, owned and controlled and all the work done by women, thus giving employment to hundreds and making the world ring with the new evangel for woman. . . .

Elizabeth Cady Stanton
November 5, 1868

★★Capital Strikes at Women★★

Dear Revolution: I thank you for the timely words uttered through your columns, in behalf of the eight hundred noble, but oppressed women who took part in what is termed the Dover strike.★

In this, capital struck at the women. In order to prove this, I must give you an idea of factory life thirty years ago. Then the work of a weaver was to attend to two looms. . . . Then they reduced their wages and added another loom. Again they cut down and added still another loom. Again and again this was repeated until now a girl's work is six and seven looms.

That was not the only outrage imposed upon them, but formerly a piece of cloth measured thirty yards, now there are twelve more added to it, making it in all forty-two yards at the same price. A short time ago this company purchased a machine to press warps for the looms at an enormous price, by which two hands can perform the labor of fifteen. In consequence of stock being low in the market, the stockholders issued a *regular prerogative* to reduce wages twelve cents on a dollar. . . .

. . . Fifteen years ago a similar strike took place in Manchester, N. H. They appointed a committee to wait on the agent. He refused to meet them, but instead, he sent the mayor out to read the riot act, but the women were afraid of the bullets from the cotton chilvary, so they went back. Fifteen years have elapsed, the working women have the platform and tongues to use, and no man now dares to come into an orderly meeting and read the riot act. We working women will wear fig-leaf dresses before we will patronize the Cocheco Company.

Heaven bless The Revolution and its two noble women. I thank you in behalf of the hundred thousand working women of Massachusetts.

Jennie Collins
January 13, 1870

The bread question

[* The Cocheco mills in Dover, NH had been the site of strikes by women on several occasions, beginning in 1828. Despite aid from *The Revolution* and the efforts of labor organizer Jennie Collins, this strike was lost.]

Alma Mater?

. . . Our colleges, and especially Harvard and Yale, are a disgrace to even American civilization. It is high time that at least half the students were girls, and half the professors women. . . .

August 6, 1868

Colored Women as Physicians

Our first white women who completed a regular Medical education had to go to Europe to do it. It is not strange therefore that colored women are compelled to do so too. We are glad to see by the *Anti-Slavery Standard*, which, by the way, is becoming valiant in the cause of impartial and equal rights, that our gifted country woman, Miss Sarah P. Remond has availed herself of a long visit abroad to acquire a medical course of education.*

Octoer 22, 1868

[* Remond, a prominent abolitionist and lecturer, got a medical degree in 1871 from a leading medical school in Florence, Italy.]

Girls Raised on Trash

Boys are twenty times as interesting as girls; for in their hands, strange as it may seem, rests the greatness of the coming time, the heroic action. The great deeds of the next generation will be their work; to them we shall owe the discoveries, the inventions which will yet astonish the World, while nineteen out of twenty of the girls will do nothing throughout life but look pretty until they are twenty five or thirty, and keep on looking uglier and uglier afterwards.

This is the sort of trash girls are educated on. Our newspapers and nearly all our magazine literature are made up of this doctrine. From our cradles we are taught that we are made to "look pretty" until we are married, and after the important event, in order to be genteel, we must be as helpless as possible. What encouragement do we receive in the cultivation of our intellectual faculties? If a woman

107

tries self-support instead of sitting with folded hands, and letting father toil away the best years of his life to support her, while she fritters away her precious womanhood over ribbons, laces and tawdry dresses, sighing —

> Uselessly, aimlessly drifting through life,
> What was I born for? *"For somebody's wife"*
> I am told by my mother.★★★
> But this is the question that puzzles my mind,
> Why am I not trained to work of some kind?

. . . Wouldn't it be quite as sensible to say all men must be laborers or mechanics as it is to pass the edict that all women must be housekeepers? . . .

Mrs "Pat Molloy"
January 28, 1869

★★Out of the Frying Pan★★

The Sorosis [a woman's club founded in 1868 in New York City] has abandoned its idea of a College for Cooks. *The Revolution* counseled its members to study the science of cookery themselves and teach their daughters and younger sisters at home. It would only be time and money lost to go and get up a College for Bridget.★ The moment she graduated she would be snatched into matrimony, for the very reason that so far, *she would be fit for it.* . . .

March 11, 1869

[★ Irish immigrant women were a major source of domestic servants, despite frequent complaints about their lack of training.]

Why Colleges for Women

At the late annual commencement of the Women's Medical College in Cleveland, Ohio, a most admirable address was delivered by Mrs. Dr. Cutler.★ *The Revolution* cannot copy it, but at the close, Rev. T. M. Forbush was introduced and made a few impromptu remarks. . . .

Speaking of diplomas, he said they were nothing except in name – his own had lain for years unseen. He closed by again protesting against women's colleges, as they tended to foster antagonism between the sexes, which must have a pernicious effect upon the happiness of society.

This speech brought Mrs. Cutler to her feet. She said Mr. Forbush had said some things rather broadly and she could not allow them to pass without explanation. He had not stated that this college was a *necessity*, rendered such by the action of his own sex in *shutting out women from other colleges*. Regarding the diploma, she said it *was* of some use to a doctor, although it might not be of any account to a clergyman. (Laughter.) Almost anybody may preach whether he has a diploma or not, but a doctor is not permitted to practice without that evidence of his qualifications. It might be a good thing if clergymen were brought up to a standard that they would be *required to show their diplomas*. (Prolonged applause.)

The worthy minister, it is added, was utterly discomfited and demoralized by this unexpected broadside, and seemed to feel as if he wanted to go home.

March 18, 1869

[* Hannah Marin Tracy Cutler was a significant figure in the struggle for married women's legal rights. She received her medical degree from the Women's Medical College in Cleveland in February 1869.]

Petticoats at the Bar

The other day, Mrs. Arabella Mansfield, a young lady of 24, was admitted to practice in the courts of Iowa.* We are heartily glad of it, for we dare say there are many functions of an attorney for which Mrs. Mansfield is admirably qualified. There is no reason in the world why the great bulk of what is known as office work in the legal profession should not be performed by women. . . . Mrs. Mansfield's husband was admitted to practice at the same time; and we presume the pair might make a very efficient firm under the title of "Mansfield & Husband" or "Mansfield and Wife," according to circumstances. . . . [I]f Mrs. Mansfield will mind the office while Mr. Mansfield attends to the courts, perhaps no two other lawyers in Iowa may be able to compete with them [*Tribune*]

. . . . Well, Horace [Greeley] says we may be lawyers, if we will only do the office business. Sit all day and copy saids and aforesaids, look up authorities, make abstracts, write briefs, wills and codicils [appendices to wills], thereto, tie up long papers with red tape, fold them up neatly and write some little lines across the top with a black mark under them. But we must not go into the court as judges, advocates or jurors, or visit prisoners in the Tombs, change our chignon for a horse-hair wig, or our rouge for the redness of animation, neither must we hector the judge, or flatter the jury. But, Horace, the work you assign us is not the most profitable or pleasant. The advocate is the one who makes the money, and then, you know, it is far easier to make the speech than to look up the authorities and write the briefs.

No doubt "Mansfield & Wife" would have the same office; and if Mansfield were a chivalrous gentleman, he would take on himself all the laborious part of the profession, and let his wife make the eloquent appeals to the jury. . . .

July 8, 1869

[★ Other women were not as successful. In the same year, Myra Bradwell was refused admittance to the Illinois bar and Belva Lockwood was turned down for admission to Columbia College Law School.]

Training Schools for Girls

Old England and New are determined to try them. They cannot make things worse. They may not much improve them. The present relation of maid and mistress savors far too much of the old slave quarters and kitchens. The only loveable or desireable qualities the mistress sees in the maid, are amiability and capability. If a maid have not these, she need expect no favor nor friendship of the mistress, and had better not apply. That only few girls, especially of foreign importation, possess both these, as understood in this country, need not be said. Every human ear is tired, stunned with complainings. Housekeeping is becoming infamous. . . .

. . . There is surely something needed more than schools to teach the poor how to work. How especially *to work for the rich*; for that after all is generally what is understood by such schools, as well in New England, as in Old. . . .

Parker Pillsbury
July 15, 1869

★★Clerkships Suitable for Women★★

937 Broadway, N.Y.
Susan B. Anthony, Proprietor of the Revolution:
As one result of our conversation to-day on educating women for

business I propose, if agreeable to you, to place in your hands *six* full course scholarships in the New York Business College, to be used by you in accordance with your judgement. . . .

There are thousands of good paying positions in this city and throughout the country, now filled by young men, which are far more suitable for women, and should be thus filled. In fact, if nine-tenths of the clerkships now held by young men should pass into the hands of capable women – thereby giving the former incumbents a chance to develop in more masculine proportions in the productive departments of life, the world would be made better by the change. What is wanted is a "revolution" in public sentiment on this subject and it is sure to come.

Mr. Packard
August 5, 1869

Women's Wages

. . .Working women, throw your needles to the winds; press yourselves into employments where you can get better pay; dress yourselves in costume, like daughters of the regiment, and be conductors in our cars and railroads, drive hacks. If your petticoats stand in the way of bread, virtue and freedom, cut them off. . . . Woman's dress keeps her out of a multitude of employments where she could make good wages. We heard of a family of daughters out West who, being left suddenly to depend on themselves decided to ignore all woman's work at low wages, so they donned male attire. One went to work in a lumber yard, one on a steamboat, one drove a hack in a Western city, and in a few years with economy they laid up enough to buy a handsome farm where they now live in comfort as women.

. . . If women are to have a place in this world they must get right out of the old grooves and do new and grand things. We have looked through the eye of a needle long enough. It is time for "THE REVOLUTION."

February 5, 1868

A New Work for Woman

The Boston *Traveller* says: "It is often the case when a person dies that there is much difficulty in finding any one of experience in such matters to 'lay out' the corpse. At the suggestion of undertakers and physicians, a woman of much experience gives

111

notice that she will hold herself in readiness to perform that duty
for the dead, in this city and surrounding towns. Her card is given
among special notices in that paper.

December 2, 1869

A Thousand Things to Do

. . . Among the new and untried fields ready for the occupation of
women is that of dwelling-house architecture. Every housekeeper
knows what enormous stupidity has generally been displayed in the
construction of the family dwelling. . . . Could any one, or a dozen
persons, compute the time, money and lives lost by unnecessary
labor of women owing to the miserable construction of dwelling
houses? . . .

Real Estate Agencies offer another excellent field for the activity
of women. It is a quiet, nice business, in which a lady would have
little to do but sit in her office and receive clients, boys being
employed, as they are now by men, to collect rents, show
dwellings, etc. . . .

There are a thousand things for women to do besides making
shirts and night-caps, though these are much better than doing
nothing; but the point is that they must do them. The entire
advertising agency business ought to be in their hands, and when
they have got some money to put in it they will want a bank – a
woman's savings bank – the president, directors and employees all
women. They will also want a Woman's Life Insurance Company,
but not until they have a vote, and their lives are worth insuring.

[Susan B. Anthony*]
April 7, 1870

[* This column was likely written by Anthony; her signature
appears on a column like this in another issue.]

Our Women Paupers

It would, perhaps, startle the most of us if suddenly in the midst of
a festive social occasion, or when seated in a crowded railway car,
or in church, at a lecture, or in some other assembly of people, a
whisper should reach our ears, "More than half these women
present are paupers!" And yet, startling as would be that
proposition, in most cases investigation would prove its truth.

"What, these well dressed women paupers!" you exclaim. Yes!

Probably nine-tenths of those gaily apparelled ladies could not dispose of even so small a sum of money as ten dollars without first asking for it from the purseholder of the family, and stating for what uses it was intended. And many of them would hesitate a good while before making the request, unless they were tolerably sure that their intended disposal of the sum would meet the wishes and ideas of the banker of the household.

The amount of poverty among women is something almost incredible. And it is not the wives and daughters of the poor who are the most straitened in money matters. One lady who resides in an elegant stone mansion in New York, surrounded by every elegance and ornament, who has fine dresses and plenty of servants, is yet more penniless than the lowest of her maids in her kitchen.

The display of wealth in the household is a part of the gratification of the pride of her husband.* Her dress serves the same purpose; these are the necessary expenses, but money for the indulgence of her own individual tastes and wishes she has none. Any charities, she must ask her husband to bestow, and the favorable or unfavorable reply to her request depends on his interest in the case, not on hers.

He is not an illiberal man, but it simply does not occur to him that his wife may like a little of the freedom with which he disburses money, for her own tastes, needs or benevolent schemes.

This is perhaps an exceptional case, but there are many women, the wives of men with respectable incomes, who would experience quite a novel sensation did they find ten, fifteen or twenty-dollars in their portemonnaises which they were at liberty to disburse without giving any account of its expenditure. . . .

No wonder that, worn and wearied by the constant pressure of household cares, [the wife] feels conscious that in the line of her duties, she has contributed as much to the family comforts as her husband in his capacity of the money-maker, and she is hurt when her work is treated as comparatively worthless.

For services such as hers, were she to be taken by death from her family, her husband would be obliged to pay a good salary, but he considers her food and necessary clothing an all-sufficient recompense for her life-long work. . . .

Among the happiest women we have known, we may reckon the writers, singers, artists, lecturers, milliners, and dressmakers, who have contributed to the maintenance of their families. They have been invariably the tenderest of wives and the most devoted of mothers – happy in the exercise of their talents, and in the pecuniary advantages which their families have reaped from their labors.

But all women cannot, nor should they desire to enter the arena of daily business with men – nor would they, were their home services regarded, as they deserve to be, of equal value with the out-door labors of the husband and father. . . .

July 14, 1870

[* Earlier writers had mentioned this same connection. One reminded women of their responsibilities to their husbands by declaring that a wife was to "dress for two" since she was an "investment for his vanities" ("Art of Dress," *Quarterly Review*, March 1847, p. 375).]

5
Man's sphere

Introduction

At a time when debate swirled over women's proper place and religious and scientific arguments were prescribing and circumscribing women's physical and intellectual movement, the women of *The Revolution* refused the terms of the argument. Instead of arguing for a different version of the sphere that was advocated for women, they rejected the notion of two spheres. To highlight the injustices being done to women by men, they focused on the power and privileges men had assumed for themselves, and turned the whole problem of "woman's sphere" on its head.

The nineteenth-century preoccupation with "woman's sphere" has been well-explored by feminist historians and scholars of literature. It was the means for and the rationale used to justify changing economic and social relations. As women's productive role in the family and community lessened with the spread of industrialism and as new values of competition and self-interest of the secular marketplace replaced the values of religion in public life, women and the home were designated as having a synonymous, private and moral character. The celebrated "individual" of the nineteenth century was a man, functioning in the public world. Women remained defined solely by their private, familial role.

The "cult of domesticity" or of "true womanhood," as scholars have discovered, was a public campaign to legitimate these new relations and gain their acceptance. The popular press and guidebooks for women on marriage and motherhood extolled the home as woman's proper sphere, praising her moral superiority and her function as wife and mother.

In fact, of course, many women remained economic producers throughout this period, but middle-class women became even more economically dependent upon their fathers and husbands. The philosophy of individualism and the power and independence that came with property rights gave men rights over their home and family that were not possible in the colonial days of community interest in the family. Women became more vulnerable to men's economic and physical control.

The women of *The Revolution* minced no words in attributing the blame to "the white male" for the injustices visited upon women and other subordinated groups, a fact that is probably responsible for the less than favorable evaluation the journal received from its critics. For one thing, *The Revolution* women argued, the division into separate spheres meant that the "man idea" was present everywhere – in marriage, in government, in religion, in the economy. The "man idea" meant competition, violence, greed and exploitation. Only when the male and female "principle" were united could the terrible conditions of society be corrected. This attention to the values of the public sphere contrasted sharply with the attention being directed to the values of the private sphere by everyone else.

The economic and physical abuses of women by men were also serious consequences of the power men had usurped for themselves, they argued. Contrary to popular claims, women could not count on men to take care of them, provide for them materially or protect them from danger. They were not women's "natural protectors." The writers cited case after case of women left to fend for themselves and their children, forced into the streets, verbally harassed on the sidewalks and physically beaten and assaulted. Men were not only responsible for these crimes, the writers pointed out, they made the laws that permitted them.

It is not surprising that following the Civil War violent crime increased dramatically, given the economic and geographic disloca-tions of war and the outpouring of hatred and violence that was fostered by it. What is unexpected was *The Revolution's* insistence that violence was a problem caused by men that victimized women. *The Revolution's* exposé of men's violence against women was one of its important contributions to the women's movement. Its focus was not on the drunken and abusive father and husband portrayed in earlier woman's rights publications, though this figure was present and commented upon. The abusive figure could be any husband, son, soldier or stranger – the point was that the power accorded to men because of popular and legal definition of their superiority to women gave them license to abuse women.

Though many states had laws by 1870 that prohibited wifebeat-ing, the laws seem to have been enforced only weakly. As *The Revolution* pointed out, it was not unusual for a woman to be

116

refused a divorce even if her husband beat her. Though public sentiment apparently did not support wifebeating, in fact, it seems that divorce was viewed as a more heinous crime than wifebeating. The infamous McFarland-Richardson case, well reported by *The Revolution*, illustrates how superficial public sentiment against abuse was at the time. Daniel McFarland, divorced from his wife, Abby Sage, whom he had abused, shot her new companion, Albert Richardson. Henry Ward Beecher married the two before Richardson died. Public sympathy ran strongly in McFarland's favor. He was acquitted on grounds of insanity, yet given custody of their child. *The Revolution's* defense of Abby Sage, and Anthony and Stanton's mass meeting of women to protest the double standard applied to women, brought even more controversy to this arm of the woman's movement.

In light of men's violence against women, *The Revolution* advocated that women arm themselves, that the streets be kept lit and that women serve as police officers. Instead of seeing another reason to keep women in the "safety" of the home, as others did, they recognized that the home was as much a site of men's abuse of women as the street. Anthony and Stanton were activists in a campaign to end men's violence against women. (Anthony had even earlier, in 1860, harbored a "fugitive wife" who was hiding with her child from an abusive husband, an act of support that abolitionists refused to condone.) It would not be until the contemporary women's movement, however, that sufficient public sentiment against wifebeating would be aroused to make it a major public policy issue.

Bibliography

Bauer, Carol, and Lawrence Ritt. 1983. " 'A Husband is a Beating Animal': Frances Power Cobbes Confronts the Wife-Abuse Problem in Victorian England." *International Journal of Women's Studies* 6 (March–April): 99–118.

Breines, Wini, and Linda Gordon. 1983. "The New Scholarship on Family Violence." *Signs* 8, No. 3: 490–531.

DuBois, Ellen. 1975. "The Radicalism of the Woman Suffrage Movement: Notes Toward the Reconstruction of Nineteenth-Century Feminism." *Feminist Studies* 3: 63–71.

Epstein, Barbara Leslie. 1981. *The Politics of Domesticity*. Middletown, Conn.: Wesleyan University Press.

Harris, Barbara J. 1978. *Beyond Her Sphere: Women and the Professions in American History*. Westport, Conn.: Greenwood Press.

Pleck, Elizabeth. 1970. "Wife Beating in Nineteenth-Century America." *Victimology* 4, No. 1: 60–74.

Pleck, Elizabeth. 1983. "Feminist Responses to 'Crimes Against Women,' 1868–1896." *Signs* 8, No. 3: 451–70.

Pleck, Elizabeth. 1987. *Domestic Tyranny: The Making of Social Policy Against Family Violence from Colonial Times to the Present*. New York: Oxford University Press.

Welter, Barbara. 1976. "The Cult of True Womanhood: 1800–1860." In *Dimity Convictions: The American Woman in the Nineteenth Century*, Barbara Welter, ed. Athens: Ohio University Press: 21–41.

★★The Sphere of Man★★

A few weeks since we offered Anna Dickinson's★ picture to *any one* (we meant any woman) who would send us an able article on the Sphere of Man. And, lo! in the simplicity of their hearts, at least a dozen "white males" have sent us essays on this important question.

This is truly amusing, as if we had the slightest idea of resting this matter on the decision of those who can only take a subjective view of the question.

On the same principle that man assumes to decide woman's sphere, we shall claim the right of deciding his sphere, though we shall not begin by shutting him up in a nut-shell, nor keep him six thousand years wandering without a purpose in the wilderness. We shall not veil his face, compress his ribs, put his feet in iron shoes, nor compel him to fight his way, inch by inch, into the world of work, art, science, or literature.

But we do propose to discuss his sphere thoroughly, just as our sphere has been discussed, from Father Gregory down to Dr. Todd, and we hope the brilliant *femmes covert* all over the country will rouse themselves for the work. Let our daily journals glow with "Man's Sphere," "Advice to Husbands," "Advice to Young Men," "Mrs. Sprague's Letters to her Sons," "The True Husband," "The Self-sacrifice of Man," etc., etc.

As to those essays already received, we shall give them a careful reading, publish the best one, and send the author the promised picture, though it is a work of supererogation for a being who has taken possession of the universe of matter and mind, explored the clouds, the North Pole and the bed of the ocean, put his name on every pyramid, spire and pinnacle, and written it in all the

118

constitutions from Alfred the Great to Ulysses the Small, to undertake to bound his own sphere. However, it will be amusing to see what these men say of themselves.

Elizabeth Cady Stanton
February 18, 1869

[* See the Appendix for biographical information on Anna Dickinson.]

Warning to White Males

. . . Let the "white male" get him to his sphere. A new day is dawning for women and negroes. . . .

May 14, 1868

Roam the Universe

. . . Nothing short of a right to roam through the whole universe of mind and matter will satisfy us. We ask the same right man has to go wherever we please, and do what we please, with the exception of three things. We do not wish to drink, smoke or make a voyage round the North Pole. . . .*

We have too much of the male element, which is violence and war, everywhere already.

May 14, 1868

[* There were several expeditions to the North Pole in the 1860s to find a faster route between Europe and North America.]

True Sphere of Man and Woman

The *Home Journal* of the 12th instant contains a communication from Rev. Dr. Deems of the Church of the Strangers in this City, which is so full of good sense on the question of Spheres of man and woman, that our readers must be glad to see it in "*The Revolution.*"

The sphere of every human being may be defined to be the position in which he can most readily do that thing which his nature and his acquirements enable him to do best. In this view, what is *women's* sphere? I confess I do not know, for the reason that I do not know of women what it is they can do best. There are, perhaps, a few things which most women have done better

119

than most men; some things that men, perhaps, have done better than most women. At least, there is a popular opinion to that effect. But whether there is anything that a woman can do better than man, or man than woman, is an open question. . . .

. . . There are men who can make fires, wash clothes, darn stockings, construct garments, keep house, set tables, ay, and even nurse babies, in a style which it was never given to any woman to surpass, and to very few to equal. Why should not *that* be the sphere of those men? On the other hand, if a woman can write a book, or manage a bank, or conduct a business, or preside over a railroad company, or do any other legitimate thing better than any man, who happens at the time to be free for this work, why should she not do it? . . .

. . . This division of the whole heaven of humanity into two spheres – a sphere for man and a sphere for woman – seems eminently absurd. . . .

August 27, 1868

Get Out of the Way!

The torrent of cheap logic which for years has been poured forth from all points of the intellectual compass by way of preventing woman from tumbling out of her sphere, not unnaturally suggests the question, one would think, as to whether *man* is always to be found in *his*. . . .

But her sphere! "She is rushing out of her sphere." Much you know about spheres, you great lubber, standing there, picking up little bits of metal with letters on the end, and arranging them in pretty rows [reference to printers], or dealing out haberdashery from behind the counter of a retail store. Don't talk about the damage to womanly qualities to come from doing what she is naturally best fitted for, until you have found some more manly employment yourself. You pitiful *hop-o'-my-thumb*, did you never feel the self-degradation of measuring laces and ribbons all day? . . .

. . . Your sphere, you nincompoop, if you did but know it, is in the realm of strength. It belongs to you to build the structure of civilization; the work of woman is to decorate it and *keep it clean*. So get out of her way. . . .

H.

February 18, 1869

★★Biggest Toad in the Puddle★★

DEAR *Revolution*:

. . . Man's Sphere is almost unbounded. . . .

[Men] hold it is strictly man's sphere to be the biggest toad in the puddle, and if any feminine toad dares to warble a note, to annihilate her on the spot. It is strictly in their sphere to take all the good things of this world and leave all that is of no account to women; to have not only the choice piece of meat at the table, but the choice of everything in the world of literature and art; and, according to Attilla, "all Heaven, too, when this little farce of life is over." It is not at all out of such an one's sphere to get drunk, swear, gamble, go to Congress, wear kid gloves at the expense of the government, ride fast horses, steal all he can from the public crib, insult decent women by encouraging prostitution; – in fact, these above things are strictly *manly*, and in accordance with the view of a majority of *man*kind. He should make speeches like the thrilling effort of Robt. Laird Collier, at the Woman's Convention in Chicago, whether he have anything to say or not. If he become convinced that he has not an ounce of brains and can't get into any other sphere, he may become a minister or doctor. If he fails to find his sphere in these he may go to the penitentiary, or – the legislature.

Mrs. Pat Molloy

P. S. – Pat desires me to state that he don't believe in *Man's* Sphere.

April 15, 1869

★★Mandom★★

Mandom, in all generations, exhausts wit and wisdom to find and fix the sphere of woman. All seasons and times come and go without such mean permission. Water finds its level and limit; smoke ascends; planets swing like pendulums in immeasurable space; earthquakes, thunder, tornado shake the land, rend the air and sweep the sea, asking no leave, begging no pardon; and man himself presupposes his commission and endowment equally free, and alike divine with theirs, but when he approaches woman it is with bit and bridle, if not whip and spur. In his opinion, God and nature decreed the sphere of all their created children, animate and inanimate, masculine, feminine and neuter, till woman came. Then that tremendous authority was delegated to him. And to determine the orbit of this mysterious luminary, has baffled all his powers for some thousands of years. That she is but a satellite to revolve about himself, shining only with his light, cheering only with heat borrowed from him, he assumed at the outset, and made his calculations accordingly. And the confusion, chaos and darkness which still brood over the earth, tell to what purpose. . . .

Parker Pillsbury
July 8, 1869

The Final Cause of Woman

Manchester

This is the title of Miss Cobbe's* Essay on *Woman's Work and Woman's Culture.* . . .

Miss Cobbe opens her subject by the somewhat obvious remark that "of all theories concerning women none are more curious than the theory that it is needful to make a theory about them." To which she wittily adds:

> That a woman is a domestic, a social, or a political creature; that she is a goddess, or a doll; the "angel in the house," or a drudge with the suckling of fools and the chronicling of small beer for her sole privileges; that she has, at all events, a "mission," or a "sphere," or a kingdom of some sort, if we would but agree on what it is. All this is taken for granted. But as no lady ever yet sat down and constructed analogous hypothesis about the other half of the human race, we are driven to conclude both that a woman is a more mysterious creature than a man, and also that it is the general impression that she is made of some more plastic material, which can be advantageously manipulated to fit our theory about her nature and office, whenever we have come to a conclusion as to what that nature and office may be. "Let us fix our own ideal in the first place," seems to be the popular notion, and then the real woman, in accordance thereto, will appear in course of time. We have nothing to do but make round holes, and women will grow round to fit them; or square holes, and they will grow square. Men grow like trees, the most we can do is to lop or chop them. . . .

In pursuance of her theme, the writer describes the generic types of feminine character, and classes them under two orders:

The first order of types or conceptions of female character, are those which are based on the theory that the final cause of the existence of woman is the service she can render to man. They may be described as the "Types of Woman considered as an Adjective."

The second order comprehends those conceptions which are based on the theory that woman was created for some end proper to herself. They may be called the "Types of Woman considered as a Noun." In the first order we find woman in her physical, her domestic, and her social capacity; or woman as man's wife and mother; woman as man's housewife; woman as man's companion, plaything, or idol. . . .

Rebecca Moore [English Correspondent]
October 21, 1869

[* Francis Power Cobbe was on the executive council of the London National Society for Women's Suffrage. She was an author of books and an editorial writer for London newspapers, specializing in suffrage, property rights for women and opposition to vivisection.]

Petticoats and Pantaloons, Principles and Prejudices

. . . Nature has decreed that Madame E. C. Stanton, of "*The Revolution*" of New York should wear petticoats, and, as says *Punch*, that she should stay at home and make the pot boil. But Madame Stanton believes that pantaloons and petticoats should hang on the same hook, without one having the right to surpass the other. . . . To mix the attributes of the two sexes would be contrary to the law of nature. It is in fact nature that created for them separate and distinct spheres, a separation which manners and laws have sanctioned and perpetuated for centuries. . . . – N. O. LesLibre.

Seeing, Messieur, that you are somewhat befogged on the comparative merits of petticoats and pantaloons, as well as the behests of Custom and Nature, we would suggest to you, that there is no real antagonism between suffrage and petticoats, nor necessary connection between the art of governing and pantaloons. . . . Custom has decreed that certain garments shall represent dignity, wisdom, and power, hence the mother of the race, popes, cardinals, bishops, chief-justices, judges, barristers, all wear the long, flowing robes, while the serfs of Russia, the peasantry of France and England, the African races in America,

millions of men everywhere wholly unrepresented in the government, wear pantaloons, showing that the style of dress has nothing
to do with this question, for pantaloons, as well as petticoats, are
under the ban of disfranchisement.

. . . If we reason from all man's failures for the last six thousand
years, it is fair to say, that the art of governing is not one of the
manly accomplishments; hence we propose to govern ourselves.

The sphere of women has been gradually widening and coming
nearer and nearer into the same orbit with that of man, and so far
from his respect decreasing, it steadily increases just in proportion
as they become equal companions in art, science, literature and their
interest in the government. . . .

June 25, 1868

Whose Pain is It?

. . . Let every woman be careful of whom she purchases [an
insurance] policy. Somebody writes us that not long since a man
and wife bought a joint policy against death and accident. The wife
was thrown out of the cars and broke her leg. The company refused
to pay anything, on the ground that husband and wife are one, and
that one the husband. Wonder if he bore the pain when the leg was
set.

October 22, 1868

First Strong-Minded Woman
. . . Eve took her destiny in her own hand. . . .

Elizabeth Cady Stanton
March 25, 1869

Women are Short-Changed

. . . We are amused with the vacillating magnanimity of masculine
writers on this question [of natural rights], who ever and anon
adopt the beautiful theory of "complements," "divided halves," and
then by their logic in five lines make woman nine-tenths of a
human being, or a negation.
For example, look at this:

We ask not if women are equal, inferior, or superior to men; for
the two sexes are different, and between things different in kind
there is no relation of equality or of inequality. . . .

124

Man's sphere

Now look on this.

> Of course, we hold that the woman was made for the man, not man for the woman, and that the husband is the head of the wife, even as Christ is the head of the church, not the wife of the husband.

> The women of the present day unfortunately no longer regard men in that light. I should think, that divided halves, complements must be equal, and when separated in any sphere incapable of harmonious action. How "divided halves, complements, beings that are neither superior or inferior to each other" can produce headships, is a question that man's reason must solve.

Elizabeth Cady Stanton
April 29, 1869

The Courtesy of Name Calling

A largely attended public meeting was this week held in the Corn Exchange at Crewe in Cheshire [England] to consider and support the bill of Mr. Jacob Bright for the purpose of extending the Parliamentary franchise to women householders and free-holders. . . .

To the fear that granting justice to women would destroy chivalry in men [Lydia E. Becker] replied by saying, "The politeness which men show towards women is nothing more than a return by man for the kindness, civility, and courtesy shown by women to men," and she asked if the epithets "strong-minded women," "blue stockings," etc., were specimens of the boasted courtesy of men. . . .

March 24, 1870

Strong-Minded Blue-Stockings

. . . People object to the demands of those they choose to call the "strong-minded," because they say, it will make the women "masculine." That is just the difficulty in which we are now involved, we have no women in the best sense, we have simply so many reflections and varieties of the masculine gender.

Men profess to have great fear lest women should become men, yet they are always ridiculing the womanly wherever they find it. With what contempt they speak of "woman's way." In fact what they seem to desire in the sex is, a lower order of subservient,

125

obedient men. Every woman that observes at all knows that she makes the men about her happy, just in proportion as she reflects their opinions and feelings, and is charitable towards their vices. They prefer that woman in the abstract shall be religious, but they do not wish her to mourn over their sins, they prefer that woman shall not smoke or chew snuff, but they do not wish her to be nauseated with the odor of the bitter weed when they approach her.

This would be a dreary wilderness to a pure-minded, loving, trusting woman; to keep her foothold here she must be as near like man as possible, reflect *his* virtues, *his* vices, *his* motives and prejudices. She must respect *his* statutes though they strip her of every inalienable right, and conflict with that "higher law" written on her soul by the finger of God. She must believe *his* theology, though it pave the highways of hell with the skulls of new-born infants, and make God a monster of vengeance and hypocricy [*sic*]. She must look at everything in its dollar and cent point of view, or she is a mere romancer. She must accept things as they are and make the best of them; to mourn over the miseries of others, the poverty of the poor, their hardships in jails, prisons, asylums, the horrors of war, cruelty and brutality in every form, all this would be sentimentalizing.

To object to the intrigue, bribery and corruption of public life, to desire that her sons might follow some business that did not involve lying, cheating, and a hard, grinding selfishness would be arrant nonsense. In this way men have been slowly moulding women to their ideas, and the better nature of both sexes has been subordinate to the lower. And to-day man stands appalled at the results of his own excess, and mourns in bitterness that falsehood, selfishness and violence are the law of life. Our daily journals are filled with murders, wives killing husbands, husbands wives, sons fathers, daughters mothers! Infanticide, homicide, poison, seduction, rape, arson, garroting, bribery and corruption meet the eye at every turn. The manly forces balanced by womanly forces would be the glory of the race; but either in excess is crime and evil, one ending in violence, the other in license, and both in death. What we need to-day is a new evangel of womanhood, and whoever does aught to restore woman to her throne, will help to usher in the new day of peace and rest for the race.

It was long supposed that woman had no soul, thought, or spiritual discernment, hence she was forbidden to read or write; but when in the progress of events she did put her foot into the world of letters, though she came on tip-toe, apologetically, as if to say, "I beg your pardon, gentlemen, for this intrusion on your time-honored exclusiveness," how the arrows of ridicule, of spite and spleen did fly around her ears, how grave and reverend seigneurs did council together of the danger of permitting woman one whiff of air outside the home sphere, how the holy Fathers, the statesmen, the poets, the philosophers, the men of letters, did rush to meet the invaders of what they had supposed to be their undisputed realm. With what haste and power they forged and hurled that ancient thunderbolt "blue stocking," carrying such wide-spread terror to every aspiring woman's soul and goose quill, and falling with the same paralyzing influence on all the sex, as has the modern Parrott gun "strong-minded" on the women of our times. But woman skilfully dodged the arrows, and quickly bid herself in labyrinthian windings that defied pursuit and wrote on.

And lo! what a change she wrought in literature, refining, elevating, spiritualizing every subject she touched.

As soon as woman began to read and think and write, such men as Fielding, Rousseau, Swift and Smollett went out of fashion, and were themselves the target for the poisoned arrows they had prepared for her. . . .

. . . Please remember that with women all things are possible. In entering the field of theology, they will not probably trouble themselves much about "the conflict of the ages," "the origin of evil," of any of the gloomy dogmas generated in a dyspeptic male brain, but believing in the expulsive power of a new affection, by cultivating a love of the good and true they will try to banish evil and falsehood from the earth, they will open the hearts of men and let the sun of love shine on the old theologies until their darkness and gloom are changed to light and rejoicing. . . .

Elizabeth Cady Stanton
December 31, 1868

A Really Good Woman

Macon, MO

Editors of the Revolution:

Is there such a thing as a *Dictionary of Familiar Phrases*? If there be, won't you, Mrs. Stanton, or Mr. Pillsbury, or anybody else who has time, please help me find it? Or, if there be not such a book, do please advertise for the correspondent of the *Advance* who ought to have made one, and may be he will tell us what "a really good woman" is.

Now, you are thinking me half a heathen to ask such a question – think it's queer I don't know. I think so too. But what's queerer yet, my husband (and he's the minister) doesn't either! Why I have heard him apply those very words to some in our church. "Really, good womon [sic]." And they are enough to deceive anybody. Keep the holes darned, the buttons on, the babies quiet (quiet as could be expected of prairie babies), *hardly ever talk* in meeting; *never* make stump speeches or muddy coffee, guide the house, (and the householder – somewhat more difficult, but equally essential); in short, do just as my husband – the minister, remember – has always thought and taught that good women should. But he has been mistaken; for (must I own it) *they do want to vote*. It sounds like slander to say so, now that *Advance* correspondent has told the world with what indifference "really good women" think (or refuse to think) of such things. *He* has "never seen one who had any desire for political rights." And you'd know by the way he says it, that if he hasn't seen one, it's plain enough nobody else has.

I feel woefully unsettled to find how my husband has been deceived about our members. He *had* been mistaken two or three times before, so that I had lost my moorings on just so many questions – my opinions being always anchored on his superior judgment – but they were small matters – beneath his comprehension, I suppose. Believed he could see the cardinal points of our mental and moral compass, through any fog of disputes. Now I flounder in a sea of doubt and darkness. Can't you, "Revolution," throw a rope to save me? What is "a really good woman?" Pray that *Advance* luminary to give us a definition. What does she do, and what doesn't she do?

These doubts are horrible. Everything seems attacked with chronic uncertainty. Is this the real alphabet I am using? I hope so; but maybe it isn't. How can I tell?

Yours teachably,

K. C. M.
July 30, 1868

The Degradation of Woman

. . . That American women do not realize their political degradation does not make it less a fact to-day. The true woman sees it, feels it in the very air she breathes, in the words of every man she meets, in every book and newspaper she reads, in the public sentiment of contempt for woman she hears at every turn, in the stereotyped sneers, "there's woman's work for you," "that's a woman's judgment," "that's a woman's way," "that's a woman's blunder," as if all incapacity and inefficiency were of the feminine gender. Male dolts, mules and cowards are uniformly called "Dame Partingtons," "Miss Nancys," and "Old Grannys," as if nothing ignoble, narrow or weak could be of the masculine gender! Yet the very men who use these phrases, at the mention of "woman's rights," go into raptures at once over the glory of womanhood, "too ethereal and exalted to come down to the polls." Ah! when women have the power to vote men in their places, they'll learn new phrases for their peers, just as they learned to spell "negro" with one "g," as soon as black men were free and held the ballot. . . .

Elizabeth Cady Stanton
January 15, 1868

Woman's Right to Cook

As to employment for woman, I hold that there is an immensity of work to be done that specially pertains to the sphere of woman, which goes undone or is done very badly and expensively because most women reject it. This country is in present, pressing need of a hundred thousand scientific, skilful, thoroughly qualified cooks; but very few American born young women are seeking to adapt themselves to this urgent national need. . . . – Horace Greeley

. . . Why should one hundred thousand cooks all be women! Many men have a taste and genius for cooking; in fact, the best cooks in the world are men. Men can stand heat and steam, and stews and grease with more calmness and philosophy than women. Women cooks are proverbially cross and ill-natured, and too often drown their sorrows by imbibing the wines intended for the pudding sauce, jelly, or venison. While men marshal round the stew-pans with an ease and good nature, licking instead of washing forks and spoons, and producing such exquisite combinations as proves them to the cook-stove born. If, after a girl has studied the science of navigation, or explored the planetary world, she would rather watch the evolutions of a boiling potato, or terrapin, than calculate eclipses, or take a ship round the world, why let her. But pray do not educate her for that occupation, when all her tastes may be in another direction. . . .

October 7, 1869

Partnership

. . . Woman was never placed above man's head, or under his feet, by our Creator – but side by side – coequal on earth – coequal in heaven. . . .

S. P. L.
February 17, 1870

Is Man the Natural Protector of Woman?

. . . Is man woman's "natural protector?" Let us see! How does he protect the sixteen thousand wretched girls found in houses of infamy, in the city of New York alone – saying nothing of the thousands in other places in this land of masculine protection and "Equal Rights?" Why, simply by paying starvation prices for honest labor, and offering for a sacrifice of woman's virtue a price that would keep her above actual necessity. . . .

But man *is* woman's natural protector: as a wife she is protected by him. Yes, the *rite* by which they were bound considered him her natural protector until they should be by death separated; but the civil law sets bounds to this obligation, this "protection." He is bound to protect her so long as she does not desert his "bed" and can eat the "bread" that he provides; but let her once desert his "bed" and the sacredness of the *rite* is no longer visible. Therefore, the sacredness of the marriage *rite* and the right to protection from woman's "natural protector" all depends upon her keeping his "bed" and eating his bread. He becomes her "protector" for a remuneration; nothing *natural* in this protection. . . . This masculine protection, this giving support to a "clinging vine" is all a play upon words, a farce, a picture of the imagination, that vanishes when you open your eyes to see the reality to the facts. . . .

The poet that wrote those lines ["clinging vine"] ought to be whipped around the standard of masculine protection as long as woman has been, for six thousand years, and we think a new song would be put into his mouth, even the right of self-protection to every intelligent human being. . . .

Marah
April 2, 1868

Men are Mean, not Manly

Editors of the Revolution:

Your types [typists?] make me use an expression I quite dislike

(See *Revolution* No. 16, page 249), and I am tempted to make it the occasion of a few words on the subject of this article. The expression is, "till then men will be men." This is just opposite the truth. The great trouble is, that men will *not* "be men." Not till woman is individualized, free, self-owned, will the mass of men exhibit true manliness. *Then* they will be *thrown upon their manhood.* The expression I used was, "till then (till woman asserts her individuality) men will be *mean.*"

It is not because men are men that they are so mean, tyrannical and unjust but because of their having arbitrary power. Any being who will accept arbitrary power will abuse it, or rather use it. Men, like most everything else, are well enough in their place. Women seem to me to show a very great weakness, who spend their time and breath berating "men." If I am not mistaken women are quite as much involved as men in sustaining those social arrangements which confer authority upon men, and heap outrage, and fault, and wrong of every sort upon woman. I never knew a man who recognized woman as the rightful owner of herself, who acknowledged woman's instincts, woman's judgment, woman's nature, as the true and only standard by which to settle questions of social relations and maternity, who did not at the same time insist upon her right to vote, her right to equal wages, etc. And is not the prejudice, the narrowness, the blindness and bigotry that sustains this false and corrupt and slavish social system, manifested quite as much by women as men? Are women any more ready than men to recognize in practical life woman's right to personal freedom? When women are no longer owned, when men are no longer slaveholders (and this will be when the *system* is abolished) then, and not till then, will men be manly and just, and women be recognized and treated as equals.

Francis Barry★
May 7, 1868

[★ Another letter from Francis Barry in the April 8, 1869, issue stated that Barry had started a newspaper, *The New Republic*, in Cleveland, Ohio that failed in six months "for want of support." Barry sent issues of *The Revolution* to pay out subscriptions.]

★★Pants Make the Man★★

In the conflict of the discussion on suffrage, the gravest aspect of the question is too often forgotten, and at this moment few people in this country do justice to the profound wisdom displayed by our law-givers in declaring that the all-important requisite for an election is a certain article of dress! This many seem a somewhat startling statement, but it is nevertheless true that at this moment, in this enlightened Republic, the one grand qualification which entitles a human being to a voice in the government, the right of choosing rulers, and all that gives civil liberty, is what may be delicately phrased as SARTORIAL BIFURCATION.

There was a time it was not so. At a remote period of our history property was held as the necessary basis upon which to place representation, and no man not possessing a certain stake in the wealth of the country had any voice in its government. At a later time education was deemed in many places important, and it was held that no one not able to read and write ought to control, even ever so remotely, the destinies of the nation. Again the idea was supported by a powerful party, that no person not native born should be empowered to vote in a country of whose necessities he could "know nothing," and lastly, for a long time, certain statesmen clung to the view that enlightenment was all important among citizens, and that degraded colored folks should have no right to the ballot.

One by one, all these prejudices have given way before the enlightened progress of modern thought, and the legislators of to-day have discovered at last the one, true, important and indispensible requisite for suffrage – GARMENTS!

They have said, "we must draw the line somewhere;" we cannot allow *quite* everybody to vote; we will let poor people vote, and ignorant people – "the halt, the lame, the blind, and impotent folk;" but there is one thing we must insist upon, they must wear masculine habiliments.

We have discovered now the sensible rule for regulating this matter when a person approaches the polls we will ask no more – Are you moral? Are you intelligent? Are you capable of defending your country in battle? We will simply look at him, and so he wear a certain garb we will admit him to the privilege he claims. The upper form may be clothed in woolen shirts, in short cloak, in fancy sack, or in well-fitting coat, we care not which, but upon one thing we insist, the attire of the lower form must be *bifurcated*.

Solved at last is the problem that has so long tormented the world. What restrictions shall there be on suffrage? The answer comes endorsed by a nation's verdict. The true restriction is sartorial. The tailor makes the voter, and thus stands the law.

132

No person wearing skirts shall be entitled to vote, no matter of what sex they are, how wealthy they may be, how moral, or how intelligent. But all persons wearing the usual masculine nether garments may vote, no matter which sex they belong, and howsoever poor, ignorant, and degraded.

Behold the grand motto of the party of to-day, which says proudly, "Our voters all wear trowsers!"

Great are the discoveries of modern thought; wonderful is the enlightenment of this latter part of the nineteenth century; we acknowledge with amazement its wisdom, and preach with enthusiasm under this new banner which waves its divided length majestically on the air.

Lillie Devereux Blake★
September 1, 1870

[★ See the appendix for biographical information.]

"A Strong-Minded Woman of a Gentlemanly Deportment"

To say a man is strong-minded, in common parlance, is high praise. To say a woman is strong-minded, in the same dialect, is like saying she has a beard. It is a reproach. . . .

Now, why should a woman be expected to be, not like the useful and noble things in life, in which strength is necessary and important, but only like dangerous substances – poisons, for example, which are safer weak than strong; or, like unimportant, as butter, in its perfection, sweet, soft and melting, and capable of moulding to any form. Butter is a pleasant addition to our meals, but not an essential piece de resistance, as meat and bread. This may be the true view of woman – pleasant, but not actually necessary. *Strong* butter is not good, we confess; but some firmness of substance and capacity for taking shape is better, even in butter.

Mrs. Emily E. Ford★
October 20, 1870

[★ See the Appendix for biographical information.]

★★Safer in Public★★

MRS. ELIZABETH CADY STANTON – Madam: I believe you first had the honor to make a *newsboy* out of a little girl. . . .

Now, madame, in all seriousness, is it well to expose young girls in this manner to be corrupted by our sex? Would it not be

133

The Revolution in Words

better to find some less public occupation for them? To see them mixing in crowds of men in bar-rooms and hotel parlors is heart-rending.

A FRIEND TO THE LITTLE GIRLS

Women and girls are much safer in a crowd against the insults of drunken men than in the privacy of home. . . .

. . . So long as men are drunken, brutal, vile, better far that girls should meet them in public places, where noble, virtuous men, stand ready to defend them with their strong right arms, than alone, where no eyes, save Omnipotence, takes cognizance of their wrongs. . . . If we had a company of noble, virtuous women as police, such men would be ordered to the station-house. Man has had the universe for his hunting-ground long enough. . . .

July 23, 1868

★★Worse than Mad Dogs★★

The French papers tell of a lady in a crowd of children who, being bitten by a mad dog, held on to the animal till he could be secured, and thus saved the lives of the others. For this bravery the government has given her a gold medal, her life happily being spared. Women may encounter mad dogs or wild beasts and be applauded as heroes, but men warn them not to approach them at the polls! "Beware of men."

December 10, 1868

Woman's Protectors

Springfield, Mass.

Nelson Spellman was arrested in this town today for an attempted rape on Mrs. Elizabeth Gibbons, an estimable lady, 55 years old, as she was going to church on Sunday. . . .

Memphis, Tenn.

Saturday night a negro, named Abe Vandberg . . . succeeded in outraging the person of Mrs. Smith. . . . On arriving in town with the prisoner it was with the greatest difficulty the marshal succeeded in keeping the negroes who had assembled from burning him.

134

Such are the outgrowths of laws, and religions, that teach men that women were made for their pleasure. In the face of such facts, we would suppose that fair-minded men would see the need of strengthening woman's power, and giving her every moral and material means for self-defense and protection; and yet we hear on all sides nothing but the cry of "Manhood Suffrage," while in Massachusetts and Tennessee, in her home and on her way to church, woman is alike the victim of man's lust. He to whom in nature she should look for protection is her destroyer, persecutor, tempter, seducer. Should he be her legislator, judge, juror, and representative? Do wise men ever think of the terrible slavery in which woman is held by her constant fear of man? Afraid to roam alone in green fields and forests, beside pleasant lakes and flowing rivers; afraid to walk alone in the streets of our cities, to cross a ferry after dark, to attend any public meeting or place of amusement; to go an errand of mercy; or to stay alone, even, in her own home?

The old proverb says, "a man's house is his castle, where no one has a right to follow him," but where is woman's tower of safety? . . .

Elizabeth Cady Stanton
January 21, 1869

Self-Defense

. . . Though we are a member of the Peace Society, yet we sometimes think that no young girl should ever leave the house without a bull dog, and a brace of pistols, to protect herself against her self-styled protectors.

January 21, 1869

Street Harassment

Anna Dickinson says the Philadelphia medical students are in the habit of insulting ladies in the principal streets of Philadelphia every evening, and in the most brutal manner. It is so in almost every large city. Even in Boston, the evil has become so prevalent, the Chief of Police recently dressed two or three trusty officers in woman's apparel, and sent them out to detect the ruffians who have been insulting ladies while quietly walking on the street. One of the officers reported that more than twenty-seven men accosted him.

Some of these shameless fellows move in the most respectable society.

March 11, 1869

Safety of Soldiery

The peace is always supposed kept, where the military are stationed. And yet the universal testimony in all times and in all countries is, that nothing is safe in its presence, from female chastity to the fruits of the orchard and garden. The telegraph brings word that a militia soldier stationed near Pulaska, Tenn., committed a gross outrage upon the person of a young negro girl. The father and other negroes caught him, and beat him so terribly with their muskets, that he is reported to be in a dying condition; but even the military commander justified them in their terrible revenge.

March 11, 1869

Who Needs Enemies?

From the Morning Star, Wil., N.C.:

A young scoundrel in Indiana, recently knocked his mother down and kicked her to death, because she reproved him for spilling his coffee on the tablecloth.

Do not your Fathers, Husbands, Brothers and Sons represent you. Are they not your *natural* protectors?

April 29, 1869

Not to be Trusted

. . . At the close of my lecture, one man arose and asked if when women vote they would light up the streets with gas or leave that to the moon, on whatever side of the earth it might be. Though not prepared for a question on that point, I replied no, we should always keep the streets light so as to watch the men. . . .

Elizabeth Cady Stanton
January 13, 1870

Have Women Any Right in a Hotel?

. . . A single woman shrinks from presenting herself at one of these temporary sojourns; for if she does not receive insult in words, she

136

has to pass a critical survey from the officials, who scan her from head to foot, in attempting to decide for themselves whether she is or is not a responsible woman, while her blood tingles in every vein with her shame and indignation at this mute investigation of her moral character.

No single man has to pass this crucial test of immaculate purity before a room is assigned him, nor can we believe that it is the high standard of morality of hotel-proprietors which leads to this scrutiny of single women. There is little investigation of the character of a woman accompanied by a man who visits a hotel, even if her appearance and manners are of a suspicious sort; and many of our large hotels have an unenviable reputation of sheltering fast women with their paramours.

But women of stainless character – ladies in every respect – have suffered from this strange unwillingness on the part of hotel proprietors to receive a woman traveling alone. . . .

Is it not a disgrace to our cities that women should receive such treatment in our public houses, which, as their name indicates, should be the homes for all travelers, without distinction of race or sex?

November 3, 1870

Sweating is Men's Curse

. . . "But how do you dispose of the curse pronounced upon woman," a gentleman asked us a few days since in all seriousness, "It seems to me," said he, "that woman's degradation is ordained of Heaven." A curse, we replied, was also pronounced on man: "In the sweat of thy brow shalt thou eat thy bread," and yet we find all men trying to get rid of that curse "ordained of Heaven." Our politicians do not sweat much except just before election. Our lawyers, doctors, merchants, clergymen, professors, teachers do not sweat a great deal, and even our mechanics and farmers, by the aid of science, have much of their sweating done by machinery. . . .

Elizabeth Cady Stanton
April 2, 1868

Small Man, Small Argument

. . . A Rev. Mr. England [at the Woman's Convention in Milwaukee] profanely claimed the Bible on the side of tyranny, and seemed to think with George W. Downing, that "Nature intended

137

that the male should dominate over the female everywhere." As Mr. E. is a small, thin, shadowy man, without much blood, muscle, or a very remarkable cerebral development, we would advise him always to avoid the branch of the argument he stumbled upon in the Milwaukee Convention, "the *physical* superiority of man." Unfortunately for him, the platform illustrated the opposite, and the audience manifested, ever and anon, by suppressed laughter, that they saw the contrast between the large, well-developed brains and muscles of the women who sat there, and that of the speaker. Either Madame [Mathilde] Anneke, Mrs. [Mary] Livermore, Dr. [Laura] Ross, or Susan B. Anthony,★ could have taken the Rev. gentleman up in her arms and run off with him. Now, I mean nothing invidious towards small men, for some of the greatest men the world has known have been physically inferior, for example, Lord Nelson, Napoleon, our own Grant and Sheridan, and ex-Secretary Seward. All I mean to say is, that it is not politic or in good taste for a small man to come before an audience and claim physical superiority; that branch of the argument should be left for the great, burly fellows six feet high and well-proportioned, who illustrate the assertion by their overpowering presence.

Elizabeth Cady Stanton
March 18, 1869

[★ See the Appendix for biographical information on Mathilde Anneke. Mary Livermore was editor of *The Agitator*; Laura Ross was instrumental in organizing the Milwaukee convention.]

The Weaker Sex

. . . [M]an is the weaker sex. . . .

Any one who has had experience can testify to the truth of the assertion that women show greater fortitude under affliction than men. . . .

Ask any surgeon, who bear pain with the greater fortitude? and they will tell you, women. . . .

. . . Sydney Smith asserts, as an indisputable fact, the equality of the minds of both sexes, which a great many at the present day are loath to admit. He says, "that there is a difference in the understandings of the men and women we every day meet with. . . If you catch up one-half of these creatures, and train them to a particular set of actions and opinions, and the other half to a perfectly opposite set, of course their understandings will differ, as one or the other sort of occupations has called this or that talent into action."

G.
February 10, 1870

The Fourth and Its Questions

Out here in the "Garden of the West," celebrations of Independence day have been conducted on a grand scale. Whether they exceed in largeness of gatherings and variety of amusements those of any preceding Fourth, and if so, why? are *not* the questions that interest me.

But as a woman, deeply interested in the development and elevation of my sisterhood, I search the records of addresses delivered by "eminent men" upon that one day of the year devoted to a national jubilee.

Through long columns of fine type, forgetting, occasionally, the object of my search in patriotic, eloquent, and well rounded periods, but remembering and renewing it again as I stumble over some glaring absurdity and evident contradiction – through whole pages of this trying newspaper print I labor, and seek in vain for any recognition of woman's right to equality before the law, or *her* inalienable right to life, *liberty*, and the pursuit of happiness.

In some of the orations the existence of woman is entirely ignored (which is quite as well under the circumstances, and less aggravating); only man's equality, man's happiness, man's glory, and his right to self-government, are considered. Why, a stranger from another (if a better) sphere, would suppose this to be a nation of *men* exclusively – black, brown, and white, debased, ignorant, and educated, all in one confused jumble – a mass of *mankind*, claiming and *securing* equality for *themselves*, and would never imagine *woman* to be a human being, a citizen, with a soul as immortal as man's. She would appear to such a celestial visitant as a sort of upper servant,

"A little better than his horse,

A little dearer than his dog;"

created expressly to minister to man's happiness and glory, and freedom. . . .

Lewise
August 3, 1871

6
Going to unfashionable lengths

Introduction

Men have, through the years, shown an intense interest in women's clothing. The women of *The Revolution* were conscious of men's critiques of women's forms and fashions because many of them had tried in the 1850s and 1860s to change to more comfortable and healthy clothing. Many consequently experienced street harassment and ridicule from newspaper and magazine editors; some were denied admission to schools because of their new clothing styles.

For a time, "the strong-minded women" (as they named themselves) thought that the logic of their arguments would silence their critics. In *The Revolution* and elsewhere women described the effects on a woman's health and energy of wearing a long, heavy (as much as 12 lb) dress, and tightly laced corsets (which constricted the diaphram and forced the wearer to breathe from the upper part of her chest). They wore and recommended a dress with a shorter skirt and loose waist, worn with trousers. Their concern for a much healthier and safer costume accompanied their interest in fresh air and exercise for girls and women.

In 1852 in *The Lily* (a periodical "Devoted to the Interests of Women"), editor Amelia Bloomer carried illustrations and a pattern for the "new Costume." Bloomer had seen the comfortable, convenient costume worn by Elizabeth Smith Miller (a cousin of Elizabeth Cady Stanton and a supporter of *The Revolution* sixteen years later). Because of Bloomer's publicity, use and advocacy of the costume, others labeled the costume "bloomers." Other names used during the second half of the nineteenth century for the combination of tunics and trousers were Turkish dress, reform dress, Bloomer dress, neuter dress, American costume, rational dress, gymnastic dress, shorts, hygenic costume and bifurcated garment.

Most women wore the reform dress for convenience and health. Lucy Stone, a lecturer on abolition of slavery and woman's rights in the early 1850s who wore the new costume, later wrote:

Those who wore the Bloomer costume put it on in the hope that a dress at once comfortable and useful, in which you could walk up stairs and not step on your clothes, and down stairs and not be stepped on, a dress that was still clean after the longest mud and slush, with no endless yards of cloth to brush, would commend itself (quoted in Blackwell, 1930: 112).

Some women wore "men's" attire in order to get "men's" jobs and pay, and in order to walk more safely on the streets at night. In doing this they were subverting the established identity system. Women's clothing was expected to exaggerate the rather minimal differences in male and female anatomy by decreasing the waist and enlarging the bust and hips, and was used to define women as frivolous, ornamental, inactive and delicate.

Many women activists found that persistent attention to and ridicule of their new dress overwhelmed their efforts to bring about other social and legal reforms, and many reluctantly went back to the trailing skirts of "fashionable" length. Elizabeth Cady Stanton had once hoped that if enough women were willing to endure the insults, that the "great national petticoat" could be cut off for good, but after several years she decided that while the dress gave her more physical freedom, the additional ridicule gave her too much "mental bondage."

Others persisted. Lydia Sayer Hasbrouck began wearing a knee-length dress with pantaloons in 1849 and was denied admission to a school because of her costume. She lectured and wrote for dress reform and the related reforms of temperance, medical training for women, woman's suffrage, greater occupational freedom and good diets. She edited *The Sibyl*, "A Journal of Reforms" (1856–64), to "advocate a Reform in Dress, as well as all needed reforms in every department of life, and to exhibit to the public gaze the evils as well as the folly of Fashion, not only in dress, but in all other health-destroying usages of society." She was president of the National Dress Reform Association in 1863–4. Her refusal to pay local taxes (to protest against laws prohibiting women from voting) once prompted a tax collector to steal a bloomer costume from her house and advertise it for sale. (See the companion volume, *Radical Womens Press of the 1850s*, eds Russo and Kramarae, for additional material on the early dress reform movement.)

Harriet Tubman was another activist who found her work during the Civil War demanded the reform costume. In June, 1863, she dictated a letter that indicated her need:

I want . . . a *bloomer* dress, made of some coarse, strong material, to wear on *expeditions* [guerilla forays in which she carried a musket, canteen and haversack]. In our late expedition up the river, in coming on board the boat, I was carrying *two pigs* for a poor sick woman, who had a child to carry, and the order "double quick" was given, and I started to run, stepped on my dress, it being rather long, and fell and tore it almost off, so that when I got on board the boat there was hardly anything left of it by shreds. I made up my mind then that I would never wear a long dress on another expedition of the kind, but would have a *bloomer* as soon as I could get it (quoted in Dorothy Sterling, 1984: 260).

The women's trousers most mentioned in *The Revolution* were those worn by Dr Mary Edwards Walker. In the exerpts which follow, women comment on the meaning of her reform dress for the general society and for the woman's movement. Because her activities were both expanded and constrained by the reform dress and women's and men's responses to it, Walker's actions deserve some special attention. She began wearing the costume when it was introduced in the early 1850s. After medical training, she was married in a bloomer costume. Besides working against anti-abortion laws and being involved in campaigns for equal education and equal pay for equal work, she also tried to become an official army surgeon at the beginning of the Civil War. Eventually appointed an assistant army surgeon she wore a gold-striped trousers, felt hat and jacket as she cared for wounded Union soldiers and crossed Confederate lines to care for civilians. Arrested in New York City for disturbing the peace (for wearing pants in public), she was acquitted, winning for women in New York City the right to wear trousers on the street. She continued wearing "masculine attire" for the rest of her life, which upset the more moderate reformers who worried that Walker's presence on woman's rights platforms and on public streets would bring additional ridicule to the woman's movement.

In 1869 Amelia Bloomer wrote to *The Agitator* (a woman's rights paper published for a short time by Mary Livermore), defending Dr Walker's right to wear the short skirt and pants but advising her that "it would be well, in the present state of public opinion, if Dr. Walker could conform to the fashionable style, or else make herself less conspicuous. . . " Bloomer suggested that it might be best to sacrifice comfort and preference for the sake of the greater cause.

These women had learned that for all men's jokes about the silliness of women's fashions, women were not to be allowed easily to change the design of their clothing in order to move more freely. Yet the dress reform movement continued through the century, with advocates protesting against tightly laced corsets, tight and thin-soled shoes and heavy skirts. In the 1880s and 1890s more women abandoned stays in order to engage in more active careers and to participate in exercise and sports, and more women put on bloomers or divided skirts to ride the bicycle.

Today, women's fashions are still very different from men's, and the women's clothing industry is big business. Meanwhile, women in homes, in factories and in the sweatshops of the Third World, have had the primary responsibility for sewing all clothing, women's and men's. In the mid-nineteenth century, some strong-minded women hailed the invention and production of the sewing machine which they thought might free women from endless hours of eye-straining work. They were also enthusiastic about the development of dress patterns to make dressmaking easier, a development led by women. (For example, Ellen Louise Demorest owned a pattern company and co-edited with June Croly *Demorest's Monthly*. Both Demorest and Croly were members of the Freedom of Dress Committee of the women's club, Sorosis.) But through the years women discovered that fashion standards and the clothing industry would be designed and organized for profit and exploitation, rather than for women's comfort, safety and change of status.

Bibliography

Blackwell, Alice Stone. 1930. *Lucy Stone: Pioneer of Woman's Rights.* Boston: Little, Brown & Co.

Russo, Ann, and Cheris Kramarae, eds. 1990. *Radical Women's Press of the 1850s.* London: Routledge.

Kreamer, K. A. 1985. "A Study of the Impact of Women's Movements on the Emergence of Women's Athletics and Sports in the United States." Thesis in Education. University of Kansas, Lawrence.

Lee, Mabel. 1977. *Memories of a Bloomer Girl.* Washington, DC: American Alliance for Health, Physical Education and Recreation.

Oliphant, Mrs Margaret. 1879(?). *Dress.* Philadelphia: Porter & Coats.

Roberts, Helene E. 1977. "The Exquisite Slave: The Role of Clothes in the Making of the Victorian Woman." *Signs* 2, No. 3 (Spring): 554–69.

The Revolution in Words

Sterling, Dorothy, ed. 1984. *We Are Your Sisters: Black Women in the Nineteenth Century.* New York: Norton.

A Female Sailor

A rather romantic incident has occurred on board the Flying Venus, now in the harbor of Bombay. The captain shipped a young fellow at Liverpool, under the name of Thomas Brown, as a seaman, and after serving a considerable time on board the ship, it was only yesterday discovered that he was a woman. She stated that she left her home at Aberdeen at fourteen years of age, through the ill treatment of a stepmother, and having procured boy's clothing, went to sea. She contrived to preserve the secret of her sex for five years, and performed the duty of a seaman remarkably well. . . . On this account, and seeing that she is far from home and from friends, it is proposed to find her a moderate wardrobe, and such a purse as will give her a chance of a new career in honor, having regard to her capabilities and station in life. – *Bombay (India) Times*, Dec. 28.

This fact shows two things: 1st, That it is easier to earn a living in the employments of men than women. 2nd, That woman's dress is a constant barrier in the way of her advancement. . . .

Seeing that the girl led a virtuous life, was a skilled sailor, and had kept her secret five years, it would have been more honorable and humane in Mr. Sitter to have retained her in his employ, and helped her keep her secret by promoting her in the service. We wonder if these gentlemen, so desirous to protect young "Brown" from the danger of male attire, thought of the greater danger of turning a young girl out of an employment in which she was skilled. . . . So much for man's protecting care. He not only prescribes woman's sphere but how she shall dress in that sphere. Now one of the rights we claim for women is to wear a bifurcated garment and be sailors and soldiers and whatever they choose.

June 11, 1868

New and Important Law Question

The papers say a young woman of New York, who has worn male attire for five years, without being detected, is determined to test in Court the right of any person to decide what she shall wear – if anything.

August 27, 1868

144

Arrest of a Feminine Pedestrian

"Madame Moore" arrived in Rochester on Saturday afternoon and in the theatre in the evening created no little sensation. After the close of the theatrical entertainment she visited a gambling hell [*sic*] in St. Paul street, and was there taken into custody. On Monday morning in court, she said that she had been six months engaged in the walking business, and described herself as Mrs. Anna Fitzgibbon, a native of England, aged 22 years. She wore blue pantaloons and waistcoat, check shirt, sack coat, jockey hat, and her neck was tastily dressed with a stand up paper collar and fashionable necktie. Her hair was cut short and combed behind her ears. She says that she can beat Weston★ walking, and that she has made money in some places and lost in others. Her home is in New York city. She has been an actress in Buffalo. The Justice committed her to the penitentiary. – *Rochester Paper.*

Men make the laws! We should like to know, so long as the price of labor is regulated by dress, why woman should be compelled to wear that dress which commands the lowest wages. What is Madame Moore's crime, for which she is sent to the penitentiary? gambling, walking, or wearing the male attire?

November 19, 1868

[★ In 1867, Edward Payson Weston walked 1,326 miles from Portland, Maine, to Chicago, in fewer than twenty-six days.]

★★The Neuter Dress★★

Lake Constance, Wright Co., Minnesota
To E. C. Stanton and Susan B. Anthony: . . . It is *cowardice* to not wear the neuter dress. If, in some places, a few policemen do not know better than to arrest a woman for wearing a rational dress, they will soon learn it. No real gentlemen will ever insult a lady for wearing such a dress; and no vagabond or blackguard can. In Washington, I accompanied Dr. Mary E. Walker about half a mile on the streets, and she was not insulted by anybody. One or two boys said only, "See the lady doctor," or something like that, which was more a compliment than an insult. Let the first thing the women's leagues do, be to adopt the neuter dress and fix a certain day when all at the same time will adopt it. This is easier

145

accomplished than voting, only a little moral courage is needed. *All* depends on the women *themselves*. Do not shirk your duties.

Yours respectfully, if you wear the neuter dress,

Frans H. Widstrand
December 24, 1868

Grace Greenwood and Dress Reform

"Eden Home," Cable, Ohio

Editors of the Revolution:

In a late number of your journal I noticed an account of the National Suffrage Convention in Washington, by Grace Greenwood [Sarah Lippincott Clarke, writer], in which she wandered away from her subject, to discuss the propriety of Dr. Mary Walker's costume; and characterized it as "fearfully hybrid," an "idiotic eccentricity," "indecent," etc., and denounced all wearing it as "anomalous creatures," devoid of mental and moral culture, and "thirsting for vulgar notoriety." My dear "*Grace*," are you aware of the fact that it is the easiest thing in the world to apply bitter epithets and sarcastic comments to persons, or things, that differ from *our* prescribed ideas of right and propriety? . . . No individual can represent any other individual, or class of individuals. In the sight of God, if not in the sight of man, every person has an individuality of his or her own. Therefore, to assert that *all* who wear the reform dress (or American costume) are deficient in intellectual ability, and moral force, desirous or notoriety, etc., is not only palpably unjust, but evinces a spirit of wicked prejudice, and a bigoted, unchristian illiberality. . . .

Grace Greenwood, like many others, denounces the reform dress, not from any true physiological or philosophical reason, but because it is in defiance of "social laws" and "Proprieties." This, being rightly interpreted, simply means, it isn't *fashionable*. . . .

. . . [H]as not *every* reform been in direct defiance of "social laws," an innovation upon effete proprieties? Was not this very Suffrage Convention, and its object, which Grace Greenwood eulogizes, and claims a deep sympathy with, in defiance of "social laws," in defiance of social "proprieties," and even "decencies?" Were it not for innovations upon "social laws" and customs there would be no progressions and the world would settle down in one great cesspool of mental, moral, and political stagnation. The object

146

of all true reforms is to bring "social laws" and customs up to a right and just standard. . . .

Yours for reform,

Mrs. M. Stephenson Organ, M.D.
March 11, 1869

Garb of Sex

A Washington dispatch says:

Dr. Mary E. Walker, a seeker after notoriety, of the feminine gender, who wears a nondescript costume, has endeavored to secure an interview with President Grant, but it is said that he has declined to receive her unless she appears in the garb of her sex.

The Boston Commercial *Bulletin* wonders, and so do many others, "what is the garb of the sex?" Broadway presents many garbs, but to what sex, race, or nation most of them belong, none can truly tell. Not to the human race, it is to be hoped, many of them at any rate. The *Bulletin* wonders whether the garb is a silk trail sweeping a yard or more into the mire; boots with heels under the instep, deforming the ankles and giving the whole figure an awkward stoop forward; hair combed back from the face so as to expose the roots to the searching of the air; and head crowned by a ridiculous little ornament of the size of a tea-saucer, and backed by a great ball of false hair? The cool impudence with which beings thus attired pretend to rebuke and reprove "Dr. Mary Walker," or anybody else, who commits no greater offense than to walk the streets in cleanly, comely Bloomer costume, is the best argument which can be given in support either of total depravity, or total stolidity. And this is said without any wish to encourage the style of Dr. Walker, or any others.

Parker Pillsbury
April 22, 1869

Girls and Gowns

Mrs. Dr. Major Mary Walker has recently been walking the streets of Cincinnati in what is described as "semi-male attire." This did so excite, stimulate and arouse the ambition of a young woman named Ida Price, that she made an appearance in complete trousers, unmitigated vest, and an absolute coat. Whereupon, we grieve to say a stony-hearted and highly

147

inconsistent policeman, who had permitted Mrs. Walker to walk without interference, seized the unfortunate Miss Price and carried her to the station-house, in which, at the last accounts, she was howling at the despotism of man. We always told the ladies emulous of our raiment, that their great danger would be from the policemen. And here is proof of the propriety of our good-natured warning. – *Tribune.*

We should like to know under what statute women are persecuted for wearing a convenient dress, that may chance to bear some resemblance to male attire? Priests and Judges and our Chief-Justice Chase all wear gowns in the discharge of their highest duties, why are they not arrested for their infringements on female attire.

In discussing this point some time ago, we mentioned that women had been arrested for presuming thus to imitate their sires and sons. A New York lawyer wrote us that such a thing could not be done because there was no law to warrant it. Let some one now commence a suit for Miss Price in Cincinnati, that the women of Ohio may test the question whether a woman in that state can dress as she sees fit, with out the interference of the police.

October 7, 1869

A Woman's a Woman for A' That*

It is a great trial to many of the new converts to our cause, that a woman arrayed in Bloomer costume occasionally graces the platform in our conventions.

Mary Walker arose in the late St. Louis convention, merely to give notice of a meeting, whereupon the convention was summarily adjourned, and the dear sisters fled from the platform. This was neither wise, humane, or well-bred.

Good Lucretia Mott, once presiding in a convention at Washington, under a similar visitation, promptly quieted the agitation on the platform, and protected the speaker in her right to be heard, until she wandered so far from the question before the convention that she was obliged to call her to order and dispose of her in a parliamentary way.

With the many wrongs and oppressions that our sex suffers to-day, we need not wonder at any peculiarities, idiosyncracies, or mental aberrations in women, and when any such, through great tribulation, come to our platform, let us treat them as tenderly as we best can. If thereby a little ridicule fall on us and our cause, no matter, let us sacredly protect the rights of the humblest, and always manifest some *esprit de corps* for our own sex under all circumstances. Mary Walker's dress is far more sensible and convenient than the style usually adopted by women, and was gracefully worn years ago by Lucy Stone, and others, both on the Anti-Slavery and Woman's Rights platform. . . .

Abolitionists used to treat all men and women who came to their platform with a divine patience, and the poorest, scarred, jaded, runaway slave who came there, with broken English and bad grammar, to tell of his wrongs, was welcomed with a tenderness and consideration that might with profit be imitated by women in their treatment of their own sex to-day.

We regret to hear so much said just now about the importance of keeping our platform clear of all humble, plain-spoken, uncultivated people, as this is always the class that most gladly accepts the gospel of reform, and labors most self-sacrificingly for its success. . . .

October 21, 1869

[★ The title refers to a line in Robert Burns' poem, "For A' That and A' That," but Burns was referring to the equality of men.]

★★When Women Judge Men's Beauty★★

The *World*, in an editorial under the head of "Mrs. Stanton's Standard," deplores that, in a recent visit to Washington, we [E. C. S.] viewed our representatives through an opera-glass, and pronounced our New York Senator "the ablest and handsomest man in that body." Now, a little pride in this direction is pardonable when we remember how feebly the Empire State has been represented since Mr. Seward's day, and how seldom "the gentleman from New York," has been so "handsome" as to be worthy of remark. Women have been looked at through opera-glasses six thousand years – their faces, forms and fashions been the invariable subject of comment by all men, great and small. What are brains compared with beauty? No matter what women think, or say, or do the only question is, are they "handsome?" . . .

The *World*, in its reports of our "woman's conventions" has always mourned the lack of "handsome" women on the platform: and having been a faithful reader of that journal, under its new dynasty, and learned its hates, we kindly reported for its benefit the "handsome" men at the Capitol. We wish the *World*, however, to

149

take notice that "ablest" is our first adjective; "handsome" is merely thrown in to heighten, not lead the admiration of the women. But our real object in using the "opera-glass" was to find a kernel of wheat in the reconstruction chaff that has been accumulating in the Senate Chamber for the last four years. Being disappointed in our search, we analyzed the coming man to see if there was hope in that direction.

Elizabeth Cady Stanton
February 19, 1868

Men Should Try Wearing Dress

Rev. Dr. Todd would have us believe that *all* women who dare to wear a convenient, healthful, physiological dress are "semi-men." Dr. Todd can know nothing of the motives and principles that govern most of the women that wear "bloomers," or else he cannot appreciate true womanhood. Hundreds of women to-day owe their health – aye, their lives – to the change from long, tight dresses to "bloomers," "American costume" or the "gymnastic dress." . . .

If any *man* thinks woman's dress is what it should be, let him array his own body in the most approved style of any "fashionable dressmaker" for only one week – meantime attending to daily duties – then give his views on paper. . . .

J. H. B.
February 26, 1868

Something Against The Ladies

According to the *Atlantic Monthly*, "Men say, in reply to those who object to their clubs, their men's dinner parties, and their smoking rooms: 'Women overwhelm society with superfluous dry goods. The moment ladies are invited, the whole affair becomes a mere question of costume. A party at which ladies assist is little more than an exhibition of wearing apparel. . . .'"

Time for Revolution! The remedy for all this, gentlemen, is to give women something to do, something better to think about. All human beings must have some outlet for their forces. If you make dolls of women, and shut them up in palaces without a voice or interest in the great outer world of struggle and suffering, all the intensity of their feelings will be expended in fashion and frivolity, in gay dress and gorgeous furniture. It is too true that what is called society, is nothing now but senseless display. Our most intelligent

150

women, who would be an ornament to any circle, avoid altogether what is called society, because they have no time, money or thought to waste on these elaborate toilets. To those who have daughters growing up, there is something appalling in the thought they, too, may be victims to these abominations.

April 9, 1868

Long Dresses

Oliver Wendell Holmes has a keen eye for the beautiful, none clearer, but he says, "Confound the make-believe women we have turned loose in our streets; where do they come from? Why, there isn't a beast or a bird that would drag its tail through the dirt in the way these creatures do their dresses. Because a queen or duchess wears long robes on great occasions, a maid of all work or a factory girl thinks she must make herself a nuisance by trailing through the street, picking up and carrying about with her – bah! that's what I call getting vulgarity into your bones and marrow." But Doctor, why do you designate the "factory girl and maid of all work?"

May 14, 1868

★★Dangerous Fashion Journals★★

Arthur's Home Magazine . . . This journal is now in its 33d volume, but is still given rather too much to dress and ornament for earnest, momentous times like these. Neither of the ten commandments says exactly, thou shalt love the latest fashion with all thy heart, and with all thy soul, and with all thy mind. Such a commandment as that, when kept, soon deprives its devotee of heart, soul and mind altogether. . . . [I]t must be said in behalf of womankind, that most of this class of periodicals are not only useless and worthless, but of absolutely hurtful and dangerous tendency.

March 25, 1869

Woman's Dress

. . . No one feels the importance of a radical change in woman's dress more than we do.★ We could neither wear nor recommend the costume called "the American dress," worn at Dansville and here and there throughout the country, once known as the "Bloomer dress," because, though convenient, it is neither artistic nor attractive.

151

The true idea is for the sexes to dress as nearly alike as possible. We have seen several ladies dressed precisely like gentlemen, who appeared far more elegant and graceful than any real man we ever saw. A young lady in Fifth avenue dressed in male costume for years, travelling all over Europe and this country. She says it would have been impossible to have seen and known as much of life in woman's attire, and to have felt the independence and security she did, had her sex been proclaimed before all Israel and the sun.

There are many good reasons for adopting male costume. 1st. It is the most convenient dress that can be invented. 2d. In it woman could secure equal wages with man for the same work. 3d. A concealment of sex would protect our young girls from these terrible outrages from brutal men, reported in all our daily papers. . . .

. . . When we have a voice in legislation, we shall dress as we please, and if, by concealing our sex, we find that we too, can roam up and down the earth in safety (not seeking whom we may devour), we shall keep our womanhood a profound secret.

This is our right and duty, in view of the fearful increase of the outrages on women, owing to the terribly demoralized condition in which war always leaves the men of a nation, and the infamous proposition of "manhood suffrage" which makes every woman the inferior of every man, and degrades her in the eyes of all mankind.

Elizabeth Cady Stanton
July 22, 1869

[* Stanton adopted the bloomer costume (created by her cousin Elizabeth Smith Miller) in 1851. While allowing her to climb stairs and run more easily, it was rather difficult to sit in, and showed more pant leg than many considered proper. After two years of ridicule Stanton stopped wearing the bloomers in public. It was called the "Turkish dress" until 1852, when Amelia Bloomer published a sketch of it and advocated its adoption in her women's rights newspaper *The Lily*.]

More About Dress

Howard, Steuben Co., N.Y.

Editor of the Revolution:

Having been a constant reader of your valuable paper from the first, I have found much to admire in its columns, and was not a little surprised to find sentiments expressed, so devoid of common sense, or reason, as were found in an article in No. 22 [July 3, 1869], entitled, "A word about Dress," by Olive Logan; in which she says: "that *Fashion* is what constitutes the test of modesty or immodesty, decency or indecency." This may be true as regards certain ideas of what is so considered, but *true* modesty is an abiding element in the *nature* of a true woman, and is just as apparent whether the style of her dress is cut after a fashionable pattern or not, or the material is cotton or velvet, linen or satin.

If a woman's dress must be cut after a fashionable model, no matter how much in opposition to the laws of life and health to the wearer, to make the subject of her discourses acceptable to the "ladies" of the "Woman's Rights movement," it would seem that Fashion was Queen, instead of reason, truth, purity or principle.

If a dress made in harmony with Hygenic law, so as to give to the wearer freedom, convenience and comfort is *so* objectionable, I scarcely know what might not, in truth, be said, in regard to the present fashionable style of dress. . . .

The motto of *The Revolution* is "Principle not Policy," and its editor has complained because certain Abolitionists would not join her ranks; but the conscientious and therefore practical Dress Reformer, has received a little sympathy from them and downright opposition and persecution from others; even when you say "that no woman could be healthy and wear a fashionable style of dress." Although like your "weak-minded" sisters, you hug your chains, and practically acknowledge yourself a slave to the tyrant custom, and a worshipper at Fashion's shrine, O how weak for one so strong! Where can a place be found large enough, on which to found a hope for any improvement in the health of the women of the nation, while our best minds remain such slaves to Fashion? And why is it that reporters describe the dress of Ladies only!

I doubt not, but there are many readers of *The Revolution* who would be as much interested in reading a description of the dress of Parker Pillsbury as that of Mrs. Stanton, Miss Anthony, Anna E. Dickinson and Olive Logan.⋆ And I would suggest that when members of the "Women's Rights Association" again meet in convention, if we must have a description of dress, it shall be confined to the gentlemen; for the readers of *The Revolution* are getting pretty well posted as to what the ladies wardrobes contain, and a change would give variety and possibly flatter the vanity of such men as Ralph Waldo Emerson, A. Bronson Alcott, William Lloyd Garrison, Wendell Phillips, Henry Ward Beecher, and others;

notwithstanding it is said, that "mind makes the man" if Fashion does make the Woman ("Ladies"), according to Miss Logan's idea. The style and material of a speaker's dress, if made to meet the demands of comfort and convenience, and did not violate the laws of life and health to the wearer, make very little difference to either the men or women of Principle. To such it matters but little, whether Mrs. Stanton's "imperial eloquence," Miss Anthony's irresistible logic, or Anna Dickinson's captivating oratory, reach the ear through an atmosphere breathed by the devotees of fashion or otherwise, or rustled by silk and satin, cotton or wollen.

For genuine, practical reform, until "Mind" shall make both men and women, instead of Fashion, Position or Bullion.

Yours,

Julia C. Franklin
July 22, 1869

[* See the appendix for biographical information on Anna Dickinson and Olive Logan.]

Dress Reform Picnic

So. Newbury, Ohio
Dear Revolution: I herewith send you a brief account of our Dress Reform Pic-Nic. It was announced to come off the 8th inst., but was postponed to the 10th, on account of a protracted rain storm. Notwithstanding the unavoidable postponement, we had a company variously estimated at 2,000 to 4,000 people. Had the weather been good on the 8th, it is universally admitted that at least 10,000 to 12,000 persons would have been present. . . .

. . . If the votaries [worshippers] of fashion think we hold these annual gatherings only to have a good time, they greatly mistake, not only the genius of the movement, but the character of those engaged in it.

The active workers in this reform see in it a principle, broad and deep as the needs of the [human] race, and they do not propose to cease their efforts until some radical change is effected in the style of woman's apparel.

These annual gatherings of Dress Reformers have become a fixed fact, and we invite all who feel an interest in the matter to unite with us in the good work.

D. M. Allen
November 4, 1869

Going to unfashionable lengths

Costume

The *Tribune* asks, "What is to be the costume of the emancipated woman?" The fastidious young editor of the *Tribune* asks this question with all the earnestness the most devoted votary of fashion could show asking her modiste [designer] the style of trains.

We the strong-minded have been so busy with the real interest of women, which we are seeking first to understand, and then to labor for, that we have not had time to read up all those "manuals of good society," and so must thus make answer to our young, friend: First, to thank him for the wide and deep interest he feels in all that pertains to us – gloves, chignons, yarn mittens, long trains, scarfs, and all the little nothings that go to make up a lady's toilet.

Second, to remind him that we have always worn clothes, and that we wear them at other places besides conventions.

. . . [W]e have always advised women to dress as they choose, only regarding the health and ease of the body. We are lovers of beauty and fine fabrics as well as our aesthetic friend, but, unlike him, cannot feel competent to decide for others upon matters of taste.

Will he pardon a little motherly advice given in love: Speak respectfully of a gentle, lady-like woman, even if she dress with good taste on the platform, and the tasteful notice it.

W.
November 18, 1869

Home Truths

Woman's want of muscle is a crying shame and a sin. In truth, this want of harmonious muscular development is the one need of the whole American nation. . . . Women sacrifice health, usefulness, happiness life even, to the one insane desire for "*delicate* beauty." Delicate beauty may do for heaven, but something more than that is wanted to bring up children in this world. You want bone and blood and muscle to do your duty here below. . . .

January 15, 1868

Flabby Old Woman – Cause and Effect

Whence comes the general idea, that the majority of old women must necessarily be objects of endurances and charity?

"He is nothing but an old woman." "What an old granny!" This

155

not only means that one's mind has become flabby and imbecile, but that even the muscles of his face and body have become generally flabby, and his walk and occupation also.

Well! what produces this desirable stagnation of body and soul? A want of proper exercise of the mind; change and variety of occupation.

In one class of society, what is the general occupation of women? Get breakfast, wash the dishes; get dinner, wash the dishes; get tea, wash the dishes. Day in, day out; year in, year out; life in, life out. And is the remainder of their time entirely occupied in sewing and patching? No indeed! The woman is young, and naturally must be interested in something. Does she read the newspapers; post herself in politics, or in the current interests of the day? Does she interest herself in her husband's or her father's business? Does she know what was the cause of the war? This is not to be expected. It is unfeminine, and what is more monstrous than a would-be literary woman? But I say she is young and must interest herself in something, so her mind runs only in the narrow channel of her neighbor's affairs.

It is the same in a so called higher class (By the way, it is difficult to know, if intellect, or ignorance, money, or *what*, constitutes the standard *higher class* in the feminine world.) It has been said of the French women, their sole occupation is to "habile, babile, and dishabile."

Well! to be sure, my "higher class" do not wash the dishes. It would be well perhaps, if they might take the amount of exercise.

But it is

> Dress, dress, dress,
> Simper, simper, simper,
> Novels, novels, novels,
> Whimper, whimper, whimper.

(They are quite as sensible and sublime as my poetry.)

Men! I have no patience with your unreasonable prejudices. To what does the occupation of your idols tend? To stagnation of body and mind – to final disgust, and contempt. . . .

Can you not tell the difference between a strong minded!!! old woman, and a tolerated old woman of *society*? In one the eye is still bright with the glowing spark of intellect; the exercise of strength. . . .

Adele Summers
October 29, 1868

Going to unfashionable lengths

Pale, Novel-Devouring Daughters

The following from the lectures of Mrs. Ellis will suit any meridian: "My pretty little dears, you are no more fit for matrimony than a pullet is to look after a family of fourteen chickens. The truth is, you want, my dear girls, generally speaking, more liberty and less fashionable restraint; more kitchen and less parlor; more exercise and less sofa; more making puddings and less piano; more frankness and less mock modesty. I like a buxom, bright-eyed, rosy-cheeked, bouncing lass, who can darn stockings, make her own frocks, mend trowsers, command a regiment of pots, and shoot a wild duck as well as the Duchess of Marlborough or the Queen of Spain, and be a lady, withal, in the drawing room. But as for your pining, moping, screwed up, wasp-waisted, putty-faced, music-murdering, novel-devouring daughters of fashion and idleness, with your consumption-soled shoes and silk stockings, you won't do for wives and mothers."

January 15, 1868

Brain and Body Power

. . . We understand perfectly that mind depends far more on nervous force than muscular power (hence the superiority of women?)

It will be time to contrast the physical power of the two sexes when both have the same advantages of physical education. After girls play ball, skate, are trained in gymnasiums, swim, row boats, and have all their clothing hung *loosely* on their shoulders like boys, for a generation; after girls are taught that they have the same rights on the earth, to go wherever they choose, and do whatever they can, just like boys, enjoying full mental and bodily freedom, we shall then be able to make some just comparison, but not now.

April 15, 1869

Concerning Delicate Women

. . . That miserable misanthrope, Lord Byron, wrote "there is a sweetness in woman's decay," and who can tell the amount of sentimental, sickly young ladyism that has resulted from it. A school of novelists, that, happily, is fast passing away, always represent the angelic young woman who is heroine of the tale, as slender, fragile, pale, fainting away upon the slightest provocation, exhausted by the smallest exertion. It seems to be the aim of many young women of the present day to imitate her. . . .

Helen Ekin Starrett★
September 9, 1869

[★ See the Appendix for biographical information.]

Woman's Pet Virtue

John Stuart Mill says that when public sentiment demanded "delicacy" of woman as her most charming characteristic, women felt called upon to have turns of fainting or hysteria on all those sudden occasions, when clear thought or prompt action would have been more available, but in the progress of civilization, as greater vigor of mind and body was called for, by an improved manly taste, these graceful weaknesses went quite out of fashion. . . .

The next feminine weakness he suggests for serious consideration is the womanly passion for "self-sacrifice." This has been theoretically presented to woman so long by crafty, selfish teachings as the acme of her virtues, and so patiently practiced, that all women have fallen into a kind of inane apathy over their slavish condition. . . . The religious faith of woman has been so perverted and played upon, that she has really come to think that the chains that hold the mothers of the race slaves to their own sons, were forged by the hand of the living God, and that there is no human sacrifice He so much enjoys as this annual holocaust of womanhood, from weakness, weariness and vice; from overwork, unhappy marriages, excessive maternity, prostitution, and from a humiliating dependence on man for her daily bread. The mass of women sacrifice themselves to their cloths [*sic*], houses, children, fashion, custom, and their fathers, brothers or husbands at home. . . .

September 16, 1869

★★Physical Exposure★★

[At] the Medical University of Edinburgh . . . regulations require that women shall only attend classes entirely composed of females. This discrimination should, to be consistent, exclude male students not only from all examinations where women are patients or subjects, but also from all lectures where allusions to woman's organization make it improper that the sexes should attend together. Strange that exposure of woman in the lecture room, to whatever extent, has never shocked the delicate sensibilities of men, and does not now appear to paralyze them! . . .

Parker Pillsbury
November 25, 1869

A Word to My American Sisters

No matter who I am. The sisterhood includes me, but whether a spinster of doubtful age, or a "girl of the period," or yet a happy matron, you are at liberty to speculate at your leisure. That is not at all to the point here. I want to talk to *you*, to put a plain question to each daughter of the nineteenth century. It is this. What are you living for? What is the *object* of your life? Yes, *you*, of the chignon and pannier – *you*, belle of your aristocratic "set" – and *you*, pretty country girl, take the question home to your heart, and ponder it well. . . . Don't fear the appellation "strong-minded," and think with that term must come "bloomers" and gaunt, ungainly manners. Your mind can be strong, while you maintain the sweet womanly ways, which everybody – man or woman – admires. . . . You don't know what you might be if you would look beyond the ball, the opera, the fashion-plate – and right over the heads of the perfumed, mustached *bipeds* who *call themselves men* and worship at your feet. . . .

Mattie Chappelle
April 28, 1870

What a Woman Did to Please her Husband

HOW BLONDES ARE MANUFACTURED
A Long Beach correspondent of the Springfield *Republican* writes:

"I have heard some interesting details of blonde manufacture. I heard much this summer of manufactured blondes, and one was pointed out to me as unquestionably a manufactured article. I believed it vaguely, but my interest in the matter was aroused one day recently when I called on a friend in the city, and saw the most wonderful change in her. Her hair, a week ago a dark-brown, was almost light with a decided tinge of red in it. I asked explanations, and they were frankly given; she was undergoing the process of being changed into a blonde. . . . My friend, logically and good-humoredly, replies to remonstrances, that her hair is her own, and her husband likes light hair, and that she is

159

assured by the highest authority among hair-dressers, that the application is not injurious to the hair or health. . . .

"And her husband likes light hair." Why did not he think of this when he married her? How far are men, with their endless longings for variety, responsible for the changes of fashion? Who dictates these changes? And they oftentimes affect to grumble at the folly of their wives; yet who is prouder of an elegantly dressed woman than her own nearest male relations? Certainly not the female portion of her household, or her coterie of lady friends, who are dying with envy because she has outdressed them. Who manufactures hoop-skirts, devises endless varieties of corsets, establishes large business firms that *must* be supported? Who is it that *creates new wants* by publishing long articles on fashions, which appeal to female vanity by recommending elegant toilettes, and ridiculing those who don't come up to the style, etc., etc.? Who does this but our intelligent and shrewd male members of society? And having done this, do they not emulate Adam by charging all this vanity and pride at the doors of the innocent and irresponsible Eves of society.

Harriet I. Brooks
October 13, 1870

7

Man/dated language

Introduction

The women of *The Revolution* considered English words and the standard rules for their use as man-made problems of their lives. They drew attention to many of the problems: false generics (such as "man" for "humans"; "his" for "her and his"); the constant labeling (in cartoon, proverb, joke and academic treatise) of women's speech as different and inferior to men's; men's attacks on women's writing as aesthetically and morally unacceptable; the use of terms of endearment ("honey," "doll," "angel" and so on) to place girls and women outside the realm of human rights; men's renaming of the women they marry; restrictions on women's voices in "public" ("men's") places; the exclusive language (like "brethren," "our Father") of churches.

These are also topics which feminists in the 1960s, 1970s and 1980s have been discovering as important to our analysis of women's lives. They seemed to be new topics – certainly they were not in our textbooks or in our mass media, the places where issues of importance to our culture are supposedly discussed.

But as the following excerpts make very clear, these nineteenth-century feminists had experienced and written similar critiques of sexism, sexual harassment, male chauvinism and racism (which they called by such terms as Alma Pater, Noodledom, and negrophobia or colorphobia). The issues and the analyses are not, of course, exactly the same; the laws and customs supporting sexism and racism are somewhat changed. Yet what many twentieth-century women find at once exhilarating and depressing are the strength of the earlier women's anger and arguments – and the similarities to feminist work more than a hundred years ago.

They coined terms and redefined existing words. (An "old maid," one contributor suggested, takes care of herself, looks and feels well, works for wages and for independence.) They discussed the shadow titles (such as "Mrs Ralph Smith") used by most married women which disguise the women's own history and identity. The matter of names for married women received attention even in the men's press when, in 1855, Lucy Stone, a woman's rights activist, kept her name through a marriage ceremony and thereafter. *The Revolution* advised other women to do the same. The discussions about "married names" (a term which, significantly, is always used to refer to married *women's* names) has continued in every decade since. (See Stannard, 1977, for part of this record.) And "Lucy Stone" continues to be a principled name. In 1921 Jane Grant, co-founder of *The New Yorker* magazine, and Ruth Hale founded the Lucy Stone League dedicated to the right of a woman to retain her own name after marriage. In 1951 Grant revived and expanded the league's goals to support women's rights in marriage, education and politics, as Lucy Stone had a hundred years earlier.

The women and (few) men associated with *The Revolution* were often given unwanted names by the press. Parker Pillsbury was called "Mrs Stanton" because of his editorial association with that "unsexed" and "unsexing" Mrs Elizabeth Cady Stanton, one of those "noisy scolds," "monsters," "non-women" and "perverts."

In the mid-nineteenth century, as in succeeding years, many women dared not identify too closely with the woman's movement, for fear of being called whatever the current label used for discouraging women activists. Today some of the favorite epithets used to try to frighten and divide women are "man-hater," "strident feminist," and "lesbian." Today many women who want to avoid those labels while still speaking their minds preface their remarks with "I'm not a feminist but. . ." In the 1860s one of the qualifiers was "do not mistake me for a woman's rights woman, but. . .," a strategy used to avoid being labeled as one of those lunatic, unattractive, unhappy, mannish women as described by the men's press.

Women had to watch their speech in other ways. Stanton, who in the 1850s gave up wearing "bloomers" in public because of the ridicule she received on the street and in the men's press, resisted swearing in public or on the pages of *The Revolution*, to avoid the certain censoring which would follow. Once in an editorial she wrote that she had been so angry she had felt like saying "damn it." The New York *Tribune* was critical of her for this. Her published retort was that *Tribune* editor Horace Greeley and other "good men" make free use of this expletive (April 28, 1870). To her cousin she wrote, "A friend of mine, a professor and a wise man, says our movement will never come to anything until the women are mad enough to swear."

However, she and the other women had constantly to decide what restrictions on women's behavior they could break at any time and still attract many women to the movement and convince the voting men. The columns of *The Revolution* contain many supportive notices describing the women speaking in public – their topics, their styles, and public response to them. Many of even the most committed of the woman's rights activists were initially hesitant to speak in public; in the first half of the century the few women who gave public talks – even those who spoke to support men's policies and causes – were considered radical women indeed, and often shocked newspaper editors' sensibilities. In the 1860s a woman speaking in public was still a curiosity (and, to some, an "unnatural" woman, "a hen trying to crow like a rooster"). The women, who had received no speaking training, also often encountered opposition from the fathers and husbands upon whom they were economically dependent.

In general the editors of *The Revolution* were very supportive of women's expansion of their speaking and writing. However, Stanton did not think literate women working for voting rights should have to plead with Black or immigrant men who could not read or write English. She later became a strong advocate of educated suffrage, recommending a "just" literacy requirement for all voters – Black, white, foreign, native, men and women.

When women dared to speak out at anti-slavery or woman's rights conventions, their voices (as described in *The History of Woman Suffrage* and other accounts) were initially often tremulous, and inaudible to many. *The Revolution* not only contained encouragment and praise for women speakers, it also contained analyses of the opposition of the clergy to women speakers or preachers and news about the few courageous women who persevered to the pulpit. (Throughout the nineteenth century the clergy were a major force criticizing and restraining woman's rights activities.)

All these issues of language, and men's restrictions on where, when and how women could use language, were concerns of *The Revolution*. The editors and contributors *used* the ridicule they received (often quoting their critics) to open discussions. Anthony and Stanton later wrote of their enjoyment of these hectic *Revolution* years when they were opening their columns to many other women's words and activities, as well as their own. The contributions of *The Revolution* include the editors' and contributors' own creative use of language, their expression of unsolicited (by men) opinions on numerous topics previously off limits to women, and their critique of the form and content of men's talk.

Bibliography

Conrad, Susan Phinney. 1976. *Perish The Thought: Intellectual Women in Romantic America, 1830–1860.* New York: Oxford University Press.

Farwell, Marilyn. *Jane Grant: A Biographical Essay.* Working Paper No. 2. Center for the Study of Women in Society. University of Oregon, Eugene.

Stannard, Una. 1977. *Mrs. Man.* San Francisco: Germainbooks.

Stanton, Theodore, and Harriot Stanton Blatch, eds. 1922, 1969. *Elizabeth Cady Stanton,* Vol. 2. New York: Arno Press and *The New York Times.*

★★Sororific★★

. . . Accept my sororific greetings,

H. L. Louis.

The gentlemen have adopted for themselves the word *fraternal,* what prevents our using for *ourselves* the word sororific?

June 11, 1868

Alma Pater

Crawfordsville, Indiana

Editors of the Revolution:

The little city of Crawfordsville, Ind., is situated upon the New Albany, Evansville and Crawfordsville railroad, and is surrounded by beautiful scenery, fertile and well-cultivated farms. . . . In the western part of the town, in the midst of a magnificent park of about forty acres, stand the buildings that constitute Wabash College, one of the oldest and best institutions of learning in the West. It is exclusively for males, as will be seen, its doors being closed against members of the opposite sex. . . .

[The trustees] refused to educate us, not because the laws of the college forbade, not because our moral characters were such as would contaminate those of the male students, not because we were mentally their inferiors, not because we were incapable of learning, but because God had seen fit, and most unfortunately, to create us women instead of men.

The only excuse they could give was that "they had no room!" – an excuse denied by the students themselves. Such an excuse as that, to give women who are eager and starving for knowledge which most of their students view as a small matter.

Had twenty-three young men applied for admittance, the doors would have been thrown wide, and the Faculty, in the holy name of the Alma Mater, bid them "welcome!" Just here, allow us to suggest that the proper title, according to the proof the Faculty has just given us, would be Alma Pater. If they cannot admit us, we positively refuse them to fasten our sex to the name of their jealously guarded institution. . . .

M. H. K.
October 15, 1868

Men's Twaddle About "Unsexing"

. . . In these countries where women are the mere tools, toys or drudges of men, there is no talk of "unsexing," but in England, France and America where the best type of women know too much to be either, men are sounding the alarm, but they do not understand the movement. Instead of unsexing we are asserting the sex as it never has been before.

This phrase, "unsexing," is quite as absurd for those who pretend to believe in fixed laws as to express a fear lest the birds should lay aside their wings or the fish their fins. It is far more philosophical to believe that what women are doing to-day is in the line of their sex, than that they are working outside of it. . . .

Elizabeth Cady Stanton
June 10, 1869

Noodledom

A year or two ago Mrs. Stanton brought down the laugh of all Noodledom, an immense multitude, for suggesting in an address on woman's rights to labor, that she might drive a coach or street car as well as a man. . . .

August 13, 1868

165

Its Favorite Victim

Blackstone says woman has ever been "the favorite of the English law."

November 19, 1868

★★New Words for the Cause★★

We have just received from Merriam and Co., Springfield, Massachusetts, a copy of Webster's Pictorial Dictionary. If, from time to time, our readers perceive that the language of *The Revolution* is more copious and varied, let them thank Mr. Merriam. In the volume before us we have five thousand new words with which to plead our cause. . . .

The poor "white male," in view of the fresh showers that must inevitably fall upon his head . . . will, no doubt, exclaim, "five thousand new words!! And, alas! those strong-minded women have got hold of it."

October 28, 1869

★★Incomplete Dictionaries★★

The citizens of Janesville, Wisconsin, have elected Miss Angie King, Post Mistress of that city, and now it is said *at least a dozen men* (so called, by courtesy,) are in the field all in eager greyhound chase, as her competitors. THE REVOLUTION believes in Dictionaries, and has plenty of them, but they contain no words to describe a strife so mean as that.

March 4, 1869

The Modern Old Maid

. . . The modern "old maid" is round and jolly and has her full complement of hair and teeth, and two dimples in her cheek, and has a laugh as musical as a bobolink's song . . . and she goes to concerts and parties and suppers, and lectures and matinees, and she don't go alone either; and she lives in a nice house, earned by herself, and gives jolly little tea's in it. She don't care whether she is married or not, nor need she. . . .

Ah! the modern old maid has her eye-teeth out. She takes care of

166

herself, instead of her sister's nine children through mumps, and measles, and croup, and chicken-pox, and lung-fever, and leprosy, and what not.

She don't work that way for no wages and bare toleration day and night. No, sir! If she no money, she teaches, or she lectures, or she writes books or poems, or she is a bookkeeper, or she sets type, or she does anything but hang on to the skirts of somebody's else husband, and she feels well and independent in consequence, and holds up her head with the best and asks no favors, and "*Woman's Rights*" has done it! . . .

She carries a dainty parasol, and a natty little umbrella, and wears killing bonnets, and has live poets and sages and philosophers in her train, and knows how to use her eyes, and don't care if she never sees a cat, and couldn't tell a snuff-box from a patent reaper, and has a bankbook and dividends; yes, sir! and her name is Phoebe or Alice [Cary]★ and Woman's Rights has done it. [from the *Ledger*]

Fanny Fern★
September 2, 1869

[★ See the Appendix for biographical information on Phoebe and Alice Cary. Under the pseudonym "Fanny Fern" Sara Payson Willis Parton published children's books and wrote weekly articles for the New York *Ledger* from 1856 to 1872.]

★★Cock-Pecked Wife★★

. . . How few sneer now at strong-minded women, since I started the satirical cry of "Three cheers for *weak*-minded women." "All those in favor of weak-minded woman, say aye." These twists on the human mind cut into the bone. . . . Men are sensual, women intellectual. Men tell bawdy stories, women do not. Men are human, women have more dignity. Men are brutes, women are human beings. "The Revolution" is coining a new vocabulary.

It is time that woman should be plaintiff. She has been defendant too long. Having killed several proverbs, texts and sayings which men used to keep women down, I may as well coin a new word for "The Revolution." A man who pays any attention to his wife is called henpecked – to sneer him down.

The term is as old as Adam. Now, then, for a new word. Let us call the woman that is a drudge, a slave, a shadow of the husband, "a cock-pecked wife." We can thus shame her into independence. She will no longer say through fear of the ridicule of her husband,

167

that "she don't want to vote." When we hear that phrase from a woman, you may know she is "a cock-pecked wife." When you see a woman sneer at "The Revolution," say, "Oh, I see, you belong to the cock-pecked brigade." When some young girl turns up her nose at a woman lecturer, shut her up with, "Ah, miss, what a cock-pecked wife" you will make. When a clergyman lectures you about woman voting, rest assured that man has a "cock-pecked consort." . . .

George Francis Train
October 8, 1868

Lucy Stone

A woman was divorced in Chicago last week, left the court room with the privilege of choosing between five names, to all of which she had an equal right – Warren, Greendyke, French, Conners, and Grant. The last was her maiden name: the rest were the names of four husbands, the last of whom had just been legally disposed of.

Let all women do like "Lucy Stone,"★ honor her own name, and then keep it. As men are liable to disgrace their names, and run away from their clinging vines, it is better for every woman to maintain an individual existence and a life-long name to represent it. There is no more reason in every wife taking a husband's name than in his taking hers.

In slavery, the black man was Cuffy Davis or Cuffy Lee, just whose Cuffy he might chance to be, but the moment he reached the land of freedom, he took a name of his own, and maintains it.

March 25, 1869

[★ Lucy Stone, abolitionist and suffragist, retained her own name after marriage in 1855.]

★★Can a Married Woman Have a Name?★★

Editors of the Revolution:

Can a married woman have a name? My parents, as is the custom, gave me my father's name. When we were married, husband and myself retained our own names. As many persons cannot comprehend any change from the old custom, frequently

Man/dated language

I am called Mrs. D——, my husband's name. I let that pass, but when called upon to sign a legal document, I am told my name is not lawful without it has my husband's attached. Is it true? Please help me, and you will oblige one who cannot see why she should be obliged to change her name.

No. All you have to do is to sign your name; then say, wife of Richard Roe.

May 8, 1869

★★Blissful Independence★★

The Revolution advises women to honor their own names and then keep them; in other words, it wants them, married or unmarried, to hold fast to the cognomens of their maidenhood, lest, taking the name of another, by marriage or otherwise, they be disgraced by it, as has been the case thousands of times. Lucy Stone did this, regarding her relations with one Mr. Blackwell, and Lucy is quoted as a shining example. It seems to us that *The Revolution* does not talk with its usual wisdom in this particular. We can imagine nothing more awkward than such a rule would be – no matter more calculated to bring the marriage rite into disrespect. It ought to be assumed that no woman will consent to marry a man until she is convinced that he will not disgrace her; or if she has doubts about the matter and still marries him, she is not a woman in the true sense of the term unless she is prepared to share whatever disgrace may chance to fall on his shoulders. *The Revolution*'s doctrines are gradually but surely becoming objectionable. It is coming to ignore all that is noble in woman, all that is self-sacrificing, all of the great characteristics which have made the newly married and the middle-aged of the sex lovely in the eyes of men. Its logic is making it selfish, not to say unreasonable. . . . If Miss Anthony is going to follow her logic to the bitter end, she might as well reach that point at once. It is, that marriage means a struggle between the parties to the contract, to last as long as they live, as to which shall be the superior of the other; that weddings shall become things of the past with all classes of people not absolutely fools. [*The Rochester Chronicle*]

Oh! no, dear *Chronicle*, we wish to end that struggle now going on everywhere, by declaring the divine principle of equality. Instead of

169

ending weddings, we intend to make the whole married life as happy as the wedding day.

. . . Our chief reason for recommending women to keep their own names, is to express the right to an individual character. "Womanhood" is more dignified than "wifehood" or "motherhood," and as the greater includes the less, it can never be merged in either. Every woman has an individual existence, and must have a name to represent it. . . .

April 29, 1869

Mrs. Man

. . . [Horace Greeley, editor of the *New York Tribune*]* is so tenacious of the old idea of the common law, that husbands and wives are one and that one the husband, insisting that every woman shall be called by the name of her husband, that we fear he might shock ears polite by speaking of Queen Victoria as Mrs. Albert-Franz-August-Kart-Emmanuel-Laxe-Coburg-Gotha.

November 26, 1868

[* Greeley apparently had seen to it that Elizabeth Cady Stanton would be referred to as "Mrs. Henry Stanton" in the *Tribune* after she publicly embarrassed him. When Greeley, who was supporting Black male suffrage before universal or women's suffrage, was chairing the New York Constitutional Suffrage Committee in 1867, Stanton appeared before the committee reading the names of women petitioning for the vote, including the name "Mrs. Horace Greeley," in this case deliberately using this name form.]

Relicts of Husbands

. . . If maiden life, or widowhood were respected, and equal honor shown to the woman who earned her own livelihood as is shown to the man who earns his livelihood, thousands and thousands of women would remain single in preference to entering a state which takes from them their personal identity, even to christian name, and places them before the world as Mrs. John So and So, or Mrs. Isaac Somebody – which in most states "confiscates their property," denies them any legal control of their own children, governs them by another's will, and speaks of them after death – if, like Hindoo women, unfortunate enough to survive their husbands – as the *relicts*, or fragmentary portions of the previously deceased husbands. . . .

Joslyn
June 11, 1868

A Lifetime Name

Geneva

Mrs. Stanton: . . . [W]hat I want to know now is, if, as you propose, she retains her maiden name after marriage, what name is she to give her children, should she be so fortunate as to have any? . . .

A.

The whole point about the name is, that an individual being should be known by one name from the cradle to the grave. Mrs. Lucy Stone calls her daughter Alice Stone Blackwell, and as she is a girl of much force and originality of character, she will probably retain her own name as long as she lives.

June 3, 1869

A Bad Word

The Belleville (Ill.) *Advocate* says the word *white* is one of the most mischievous words in the language when used in constitutions and legal enactments. It is of the same class as the word "male" used in the same connections. Both are utterly obnoxious to the truly radical and progressive mind. The *Advocate* adds, we are glad to see an effort made to strike the word "white" out of our Illinois school laws. When our convention meets to revise the State constitution we want to see both these discriminating words *white* and *male* left out.

February 25, 1869

Slave System Language

. . . There is, in Washington, a Bureau that has named itself "The Union Land Company": "formed for the purchase and sale of southern lands, and for the encouragement of emigration to the south." . . . In a lengthy Circular addressed to the people of the south, the Company say they have for months past been directing their energies towards turning the tide of European emigration southward. . . . "We have reasons to believe that within the next year, many thousands of valuable *white servants* can be added to your population." . . .

> What we now require is your practical assistance in remitting to us *orders for servants*, with a precise description of the kind of servants desired, *and the amount of compensation to be given in each case*. The low wages hitherto offered in the south is the chief difficulty to be met. A *white domestic* at $10 or $12 per month, is of more profit to her employer than a *negress* at $6; the same is true of *field-hands*, mechanics, etc.; the increase of pay is more than equalized by the greater amount of work done and the superior manner of its performance.

Those who are familiar with the language and usage of the old slave system must fancy we are rapidly turning back to it and to all the most revolting features of the domestic slave trade, to boot. . . .

. . . A "negress" (mark the elegant word!) now gets, it is intimated, six dollars a month. It is not true in half the instances, nor a tenth part of the instances where they are now employed. . . .

Parker Pillsbury
December 9, 1869

A Striking English Language

A lady in Charleston writes . . .

. . . Woman is a slave, and must feel so every day of her life, unless her sensibilities are already blunted and benumbed by her condition. Of what use is it to be called an "angel" and then to be endowed with nothing but "instincts" in common with the brute creation? Or what use is it to woman to hear herself lauded as the only human being who possesses sensibility, tenderness, sympathy for others' woes – patience – a quick perception – and the most practical mind, when, according to the laws, she cannot hold in her hand *one penny* that she can call her own, to bestow for the fulfillment of her beneficent ideas. . . . Well, I forbear and shrink again into helpless silence! The English language would flash like burning, electric wires if I expressed all I think and know! . . .

December 16, 1869

Man/dated language

Negrophobia

. . . The *Post* of [Philadelphia] gives sad account of the management of the Academy of Music there. It seems that application was made recently by responsible gentlemen who wished to rent the building for a lecture to be delivered by Senator Revels of Mississippi. Surely, the *Post* says, a Senator of the United States might be allowed to speak in our Academy of Music. But Mr. Revels is a colored man, and this respectable Board has the negrophobia. It has it the *worst* kind. It has repeatedly refused Frederick Douglass [Black reformer who had escaped from white slavery] the privilege of lecturing in the Academy, though he has alone more brains than almost any six members of the Board together. . . .

April 14, 1870

Dr. or Doctress?

Dr. Gregory has given the world a tract of eight pages to answer that question. He might have been worse employed, for until women are no longer an exception in the profession, it will be at least convenient to have some designation. The Doctor argues that Doctress, Drss., should be the title, because it is neater and more convenient; because Doctor is appropriate to male physicians; because the use of Doctress avoids all ambiguity, and it makes it evident at once who is meant; because it accords with good usage. Worcester and Webster both sanctioning it, and many of the most cultivated ladies of the country and scholars, whose opinions are worthy of high regard, approving it; and finally, because it is the title which the Trustees of the Boston Female Medical College prefer.* So then, we shall go in for Doctress. The Boston *Traveller* sides with Dr. Gregory, and so does this Editor.

November 19, 1868

[* The Boston Female Medical College was the first medical school for women, opened in 1848.]

A.B. is Belle of Arts

As the learned ladies of the state are now to have college degrees granted to them by the "Institutes" in which they have been educated, it is a botheration to consider that, grammatically, a woman can be neither a *Bachelor* of Arts nor a *Master* of Arts. The various reforms of the century promise, indeed, to make a

173

hopeless jumble of gender. "A.[M.]" may well enough signify in English "Mistress of Arts," but it will be impossible to give "A.B." anything like a feminine twist. "A.V." might stand for "Virgin of Arts," but suppose that the graduating fair happens to be married? "A.M." might equally answer for "Miss of Arts," or "Matron of Arts," but it would be, we fear, as the lawyers say, "Void for uncertainty." – *Tribune*.

Profound, logical minds, never see what lays in the surface. The feminine twist for A.B. is Belle of Arts. Now, thank woman's intuition, Horace [Greeley, *Tribune* editor], for suggesting what you could not discover. Have no fears, oh! faithless *Tribune* that there is the least *uncertainty* that woman is to fill the dreadful *void* you men have made in the world of thought and action. Give us the places and honors, and we will soon teach you how to address us.

July 8, 1869

Lady Versus Woman

A correspondent signing himself *Lady's man* is desirous to revise the dictionary so as to make the word *lady* more easily comprehended. . . .

. . . I venture to assert that *no* man, irrespective of age or class, would hesitate one instant in offering to a "lady" anything in his power likely to contribute to her comfort or convenience; but unfortunately, when that title of highest nobility, which can neither be bought nor bartered, is applied, indiscriminately, to every female entering the vehicle, whether a colored washerwoman, an Irish cook, or one in higher social circumstances, it need not cause surprise if the occupant of the seat consider the applicant, in many cases, as well able to stand as himself, and hence, declines to yield in public that recognition of social equality which he would most assuredly refuse at home. . . .

LADY'S MAN

Sorry enough to differ with Lady's man, but really we cannot help it. An honest but tired "colored washerwoman," or hard worked "Irish cook," with her heavy market basket on her arm is just the kind of "lady" to whom we would give our seat in car or anywhere, or any other kindly attention or favor.

Parker Pillsbury
October 22, 1868

★★What *is* a Lady?★★

. . . I was much pleased with Theodore Tilton's speech★ . . . His
definition of a lady is capital; lest you may have overlooked it, I
enclose it for our readers. . . .

What, then, *is* a lady? Herne Tooke, who once chased a lady so
far as to hunt her etymology – I cannot say how much further –
wrote that by unimpeachable Anglo-Saxon derivation a lady is a
woman who is "the equal of her lord." Gentlemen, that's the
definition for me! A lady the equal of her lord! Freed not from
her duty to him, but freed from her *subjection* to him. A lady is a
wife, equal with a husband; a sister, equal with a brother; a
woman, equal with a man. Now, sir, I want to make every
woman in this land a lady – a lady not by the obsequious verdict
of fashion and society; a lady not by reason of her grand house
and gay attire; a lady not because of her daily phaeton in Central
Park; a lady not merely as the ornamental appendage of a rich
man's estate; a lady not even by the nobler title of beautiful
manners and cultivated tastes; but a lady in the grand old Anglo-
Saxon sense – a lady proven and acknowledged such because she
is an equal with her lord – his equal in the family, his equal in
society; his equal in the church, his equal in the state – his equal
in every rank, in every sphere, in every place. That, sir, is my
own idea of a lady. . . .

. . . Man is but half a being, with half an idea on every subject, and
must always be fragmentary until he is complimented by a noble,
full-developed womanhood. . . .

Elizabeth Cady Stanton
December 2, 1869

[★ Tilton was editor of the *Independent* and a supporter of woman's
suffrage.]

Lady to Woman

We have a lady in New York, it is said, aged twenty-five, who
now enjoys the privilege of a fourth husband, having been three
times divorced since she was eighteen. When the said *lady* becomes
a woman she will be wiser than all this.

April 30, 1868

A Reign-*Bow*

Naples, N. Y.

A bow of promise has appeared in the heavens for woman, by her admission into the Labor Congress, and receiving a "pledge of their individual and undivided support to the daughters of toil in this land." I hope it will not prove a mere mouthing and mockery. . . .

. . . But let it never again be said, after the mass meetings, with their processions, that have been so numerously attended by *women* (I adhere to the good old Saxon word, women, because *ladies* are generally too *obsequious* or fastidious to know what *they* do want), that it is indelicate for them to go to the polls and signify by the ballot their choice between the candidates who are to administer the laws. . . .

E. M. A.
November 12, 1868

★★Gentlemen and Ladies★★

. . . The Rev. Gilbert Haven, editor of *Zion's Herald*, was introduced [at the 1869 Annual Meeting of the American Equal Rights Association]. He said: Ladies and gentlemen – As I believe that is the way to address you, or shall I merge you into one and call you fellow-citizens ——

Miss Anthony [said] – Let me tell you how to say it. It is perfectly right for a gentlemen to say, "ladies and gentlemen," but a lady should say, "gentlemen and ladies." (Great applause.) You mention your friend's name first before you do your own. (Applause.) I always feel like rebuking any lady who says, "ladies and gentlemen." It is a lack of good manners to say so. (Laughter and great applause.) . . .

May 27, 1869

★★Female or Woman★★

The Manhattan (Kansas) *Standard* does not like the word *female* as applied to woman. It says, "a cow or a sow is female as much as a woman is, and no woman calls herself a *female* without sharing the distinction with the brutes." The *Standard* is right, and its application is worth giving in full, as below:

Some of our exchanges talk about *female* voters, and the rejection of *female* voters; and ministers announce *female* prayer meetings,

176

and somewhere we have seen mention made of a *Female* Medical College; and in the office of "The Revolution", lately, a *Female* Typographical Union was formed, according to the report of the New York *Tribune*. In fact this indiscriminate application of the term female, is something almost disgusting, and the sooner we attempt to correct ourselves in this particular, the better.

But according to the *fact* in the *Revolution* office, "The Women's Typographical Union" was formed, which now numbers over thirty of the best women compositors of New York city.

January 7, 1869

Woman Vs Female

The term "female" as a synonyme [*sic*] for woman, is a vulgarism that ought to be scourged out of good society. As it is equally applicable to one half of the brute creation, its use instead of woman, lady, or girl, tends to lower the dignity and position of womanhood. When it is used without the proper substantive, one is sometimes provoked to inquire whether it is the female sheep, or bear, or swine, that is intended. Those who have a true respect for woman would never employ a term so indelicate and objectionable as this, if they realized how bad it is.

There may be occasions when its use is correct and unavoidable; but to speak of schools for young women as female seminaries, or female colleges, is not only ungrammatical, but essentially vulgar. Gail Hamilton, in one of her "spasms of sense" in the *Independent*, holds up a young lady to ridicule because she objects to being called a female teacher. The objection is reasonable and just. We do not say "male" teachers, "male" schools, "male" colleges, "male" clubs; certainly the great army of patient, hard working, underpaid women, should have the privilege of being called "women," and not set down as "females." How absurd it would seem to hear people say Harvard Male University? Yet is that any more ridiculous than to say Rutger's Female Institute, or Troy Female Seminary? How often we hear men speak of meeting "females" in the street. Would they feel complimented or insulted were ladies to pass them by as "males?"

Jane O. De Forest★
July 27, 1871

[★ De Forest, from Ohio, was a lyceum lecturer on woman's suffrage.]

177

All Mankind Women?

The Manchester (England) women, to the number of almost six thousand, demanded to be registered as voters, and appeared by Counsel, Mr. Cobbett, before the registry Board. Mr. Cobbett made one point in favor of his clients that is both new and strong. The word *man*, he said, must have one of two meanings in the reform act. It is used either in the sense of man in the most common acceptation, as distinguished from woman, or in the sense of mankind. If the former, it clearly imported the masculine gender, and if it imported the masculine gender, then Lord Romilly's act of 1850 distinctly said that being a term importing the masculine gender, it shall be held to include the feminine also. Give it the other sense. Let it mean mankind, and it is still more clear that it means both man and woman.

October 29, 1868

Woman a Preemptress

It has been a question whether woman could preempt with men the public lands [i.e., occupy to establish claim]. The question being raised, whether "an unmarried woman, over twenty-one years of age, not the head of a family," had the right to preempt, the law extending that priviliege [*sic*] to: 1. "Every person being the head of a family;" 2. "A widow;" 3. "A single man over the age of twenty-one years," a decision was rendered that, in the spirit of the law, the "unmarried woman" was "a single man."

The argument through which this just conclusion was reached, it is said, was this:

The Anglo-Saxon word "mag-an" means to be able, or strong; this, by elision, naturally glides into the word "man," a generic term, applying to both sexes, the original Saxon, from which the English word is derived, having been used in a sense so comprehensive as to mean "mankind," man, woman; a vassal, also any one like the French "*on*," Gothic "manna" – the Hebrew, meaning species or kind. "That's woman's ripe age, as full as thou art, at one and twenty." Understanding the terms of the law in their wider sense the office decided that an unmarried or single woman over the age of twenty-one years, not the head of a family, but able to meet all the requirments of the preemption law, has a right to claim its benefits.

February 4, 1869

Man/dated language

★★Womanliness★★

. . . What *is* real womanliness? Every true heart believes that there is such a thing. It is something inherent in woman's nature. *You* did not create it, brother. It will not depart from woman if you *take off your hands* and allow her to arise and be *free*. That is all we ask – just *take off your hands*. . . .

Faith Rochester
March 17, 1870

Womanish

Oakland, Cal.

To The Editor of the Revolution:

Our minister told us last Sunday, in regard to a certain matter, that we were becoming "womanish." I have been studying over this word for a day or two. I ask, is there any such quality as that embraced in the term "womanish" belonging to a womanly woman? "Womanish", you know, in the everyday rendering of the word, implies a shrinking and shrieking at rats, mice, cows, dark nights and spiders. It means simply a silly cowardice. The dictionary doesn't say this exactly, but there are words which have one meaning in the dictionary and another out. Of these "womanish" is one.

Our mothers, wives, daughters and sisters may be womanly, but shall they be "womanish? It is no part of the womanly woman. She is no coward. She has courage, nor does that courage one whit lessen her feminine delicacy and refinement. Is she not as composed in the face of danger and death as the man? Does she not as well bear pain – if not better? Has she not walked straight from her home into the battle hospital, with wine, lint and bandages, among groans, shrieks and warm, flowing blood dabbled over face and form – among gashes, dreadful mutilation, shattered and splintered bones – and though her cheek may have paled, have not her nerves braced themselves as strongly as the man's?

Has she not in time past, disguised in male apparel, stood in the battle's front while musket, rifle and cannon puffed their flame, and smoke, and iron and lead in her face, while the invisible death pellets struck down to the right and left, and still her nerves were steel, and she has stood while others fled.

I object *in toto* to this term "womanish." It is an insult to the female nature. Courage, as well as intellect, is no special attribute of any one sex. Dictionaries, as well as men, need revolutionizing,

179

that justice be done woman. Let us drive the word from the language, from press, from pulpit. Let it be "womanly," not "womanish."

Truly yours,

Prentice Mulford
January 26, 1871

Concerning the Names of Women

To women who hold the theory that they are independent, thoughtful beings, able to support themselves, and something more than the pets and playthings of men, I have a suggestion to offer.

It would be more dignified, and sound much better in coming before the public, if women would give their christian names in full, without disfiguring them with any of the diminutives that are so fashionable and common. Elizabeth is a stately name; but Lizzie is suggestive of one who is weak and dependent, however lovely she may be. Catharine is beautiful and strong but Katie or Kittie! – what a burlesque on the original name. So with all pet or nick names. Who could imagine Miss Anthony doing so ridiculous a thing as to call herself Susie? Think of Hattie Stowe or Maggie Fuller! One Kansas paper had the hardihood to nick name Mrs. Stanton, Liz., but it produced a tremendous recoil on the editor's [h]ead. How ridiculous would men appear in public or in business life with their names thus belittled? Wouldn't Sandy T. Stewart sound well as a merchant prince? or Johnny C. Green or Willie E. Dodge? True, we can say Andy Johnson and feel that it is appropriate, but think of Lyssie Grant or Cumpy Sherman, or Phillie Sheridan or Sammy Chase! Men don't want their names minced or belittled as if they were babies. So give us your full names, ladies; it will add dignity and strength to all you say or do. One of the correspondents of "The Revolution" signs herself Lizzie Leavenworth, M.D. Now I shall never take any of her medicines – not one single homoeopathic pill of it – till she calls herself Elizabeth. I feel relieved now, and remain yours sincerely,

Helen
November 19, 1868

A Church in Trouble

Mt. Pleasant, Iowa, seems to be in great affliction by reason of a woman who refuses to keep silence in the church, thereby, as the elders affirm and believe, "endangering the peace and purity of the aforesaid church."

Mrs. McGuigan, the offender, was, it seems, expelled from the Presbyterian Church of Mt. Pleasant, on October 5th, 1868, for "speakin' in meetin'." Mrs. McGuigan, despairing of a hearing in the church, makes an appeal to the public, of which the following is an extract:

". . . I claim that I have the right to speak or pray as the spirit of God may direct or inspire me, for in the spiritual church, or in Christ, there is neither male nor female, but all are one in Him. And, in conclusion, I am determined, by God's grace, to continue to speak in public as power is given me."

September 23, 1869

Thank Heavens

. . . To sing in the choir and play on the organ are privileges [women] have long enjoyed, as Paul never chanced to say, "I suffer not a woman to *sing* in the churches." . . .

Elizabeth Cady Stanton
May 12, 1870

Our Mother who Art in Heaven

Our mother educates us. Rears us to boyhood. Our father seldom sees us. Our mother is always with us till we are ten years old. Our mother teaches us to pray – to say, "Now I lay me down to sleep," "Lord, what if I this night should die?" and "Our Father, who art in Heaven." Why not pray to our mothers as well? The Virgin Mary saved the Catholic Church. Yet the Pope is down on woman! Celibacy, carried to its length, would stop the Church and end the world in one century! Let us swear by our mother. Let us say our Mother, who art in Heaven. Our mother would not "lead us into temptation." How odd that we should pray to our Father not to lead us into temptation? The Catholics pray to our Mother. My religion, also, opens the door to both sexes. If created in His image, can we not compare the earthly with the spiritual Father?

George Francis Train
December 3, 1868

181

The Revolution in Words

Brethren?

Louisville, KY

Dear "Revolution": Do you know of any reason why ministers always address their congregation as "*Brethren?*" Said congregations are invariably composed principally of women, and I don't know why their presence should be totally ignored.

I don't think any form of address is necessary, but if something is needed to fill up a pause, why can't they say, "Friends," or "Christian Friends?"

Please mention the subject in your next issue, if you think it of sufficient importance. I hope you will not become discouraged in your endeavors to rouse the women of the land from the apathetic state into which they seem to have taken. Many of them talk in a very trying manner.

Mrs. Stanton ought to have thrown that negro over the graveyard fence, that tried to assert his superiority to white *women*. She might have had any amount of help.

Very respectfully,

Mrs. F. J. Dibble

. . . We remember once going into a cathedral in England with some ladies. It was a week day and during the morning service. We were the only persons present, and when the curate addressed as "dearly beloved brethren," the mischievous girl by our side quietly remarked, "is the man blind that he takes us for whiskerandoes?"

December 17, 1868

Man's Chivalry to Woman

. . . Christianity and chivalry, it is often remarked, have placed woman on a throne. Let those who boast of the royal position which civilization has given to woman, look for additional light in the very use of the words man and woman. While her name has become the synonym of fraility, fickleness, and levity; a little word of only three letters has been made to embrace in its signification every human being that has ever lived on the planet. In science, literature, and art, *man* is the central word around which the word woman revolves as a mere nebulous satellite. In Holy Writ, also, man is all in all. Genealogies begin with father and end with the son. Eve never had any descendants! Moses, though careful to give both the names and histories of the sons of Adam, forgot to

182

mention even the names of the daughters. It is man that fell and man that is to be redeemed, but who ever heard of the fall of woman! Earth, heaven, and hell are the three spheres assigned to man; but neither philosophers, divines, nor prophets have been able to determine even one for woman. How is all this explained? Is it that man and woman are one? Unfortunate for women, man is always the *one*. . . .

September 16, 1869

★★It's All in the Telling★★

. . . When lions paint pictures men will not always be represented as conquerors. When women translate laws, constitutions, bibles and philosophies, man will not always be the declared head of the church, the state, and the home. . . .

Elizabeth Cady Stanton
August 13, 1868

★★A Superior Idea★★

. . . When woman is commanded submission to any human authority, it presupposes in all cases something superior to herself. In harmony with this higher idea, the Methodist Church has lately struck the word *obey* from its marriage services.

Elizabeth Cady Stanton
August 6, 1868

To "The World," Foolishness

. . . Perhaps when women generally begin to read and think and write, they will have a style peculiarly their own and reject altogether the grammar, rhetoric and logic of those old male worthies to whom the *World* so tenderly refers. . . .

September 16, 1869

Facts in Social Life

"Mrs. K——, I have a little criticism to make on your last article, which I hope you will receive kindly," said a bland publisher to me the other day. "It was *entirely* too broad, or, rather" – clearing his throat confusedly, aware of his mistake – "you take the wrong view of the case. Now, women are not half so much abused as you

183

endeavor to make out here;" tapping the MSS. with his little fat forefinger quite suggestively.

"Very well, sir; if you are not pleased with the article, I will take it again with pleasure. It was certainly a piece of stupidity on my part to have brought facts like these to such an institution;" and I held out my hand for the obnoxious story.

"Oh, by no means, by no means, Mrs. K. I will not consider such a proposition for a moment; but I simply thought if you would strike out a few of these strong epithets, and substitute expressions more appropriate, something softer, more womanly, you would oblige me very much. This is so different from your usual felicitous, easy vain, that I can scarcely reconcile the two styles."

"Not an erasure, not an addition, no alterations," I replied firmly. "If it does not meet with your approval, I can dispose of it elsewhere. That, sir, is a leaf from my own individual experience, and every fact was baptized with my heart's blood before it was committed to paper. That heroine was myself, and those men who so grossly misconstrued, insulted, and abused the poor, struggling, heart-broken women, were men who opposed the truth, trod upon principle, and only united to see if hunger, cold, and the wail of starving infants would not drive to crime and prostitution the poor, poverty-striken creature – and a dozen pairs of arms were extended, anxiously awaiting my first fall. The light easy style you appear to admire so much, I adopted, because I knew it would please the majority, and thus secure pecuniary recompense; but now that success has in a measure attended my efforts, I shall whenever and wherever I am able, lift up my voice for the truth; shall write if I please for "Woman's Rights," or Woman's Wrongs; and if an account of my own terrible trials can be of any service to other struggling, tempted women, they can all have it for the asking.*

I left my auditor in a state of stupid astonishment. The transition from meek to bold, from the tired employee, trembling lest her little stories might be rejected, to the earnest, fearless woman, was too much for my gentleman's nerves. I fell to thinking as I went out of the lives of some of these individuals. The man I had just left was a successful publisher, and had established a first-class literary position by paying starvation prices to all who wrote for him. An article carefully constructed, requiring considerable talent and time, received just about half its actual worth, that is, if written by a woman. A masculine [writer] was considered sufficiently capable to set a price on his own work. It was no use to protest against such unfairness. "If you are not suited, Madame, there are plenty of ladies as able as yourself, who would be glad of the position." And that was the truth, the miserable, heart-aching truth. . . .

Eleanor Kirk
March 26, 1868

[* Eleanor Kirk was an active member of the Working Women's Association. In her articles she specialized in descriptions of the economic hardships and subsequent prostitution of many New York City women. See the Appendix for more biographical information.]

Us

(Olive Logan has an article with the above title in *Packard's Monthly* for October, from which we make the following extracts as pertinent to the objects of *US* of "The Revolution.")

By Us I mean ourselves, of course – women. It is the fashion to write about Us, and it is the fashion for Us to write about ourselves, but is it the fashion for other people to read what we write or what others write about Us? I mean, of course, on the *Great Subject* – our political, mental, moral, social, physical and general advancement. Anything else that is written about women, particularly if it be anything scandalous or disgraceful, is eagerly perused. I have watched men narrowly at all sorts of places – in the railway cars, the omnibuses and on the boats – and I have generally observed that when there is an article in a paper about Women's Rights, men skip it quickly, and turn the newspaper inside out. But if it is some trifling story, derogatory to the dignity of woman, or some stupid talk about a flirtation, or some hideous relation of conjugal shame, they pore over it as if the reading of it were one of the chief duties of the day. . . .

Olive Logan*
October 15, 1868

[* See the Appendix for biographical information.]

The Wonder Is . . .

. . . Men can never weigh all the depressing influences that work against woman's development. Such has been the crushing effect of public sentiment, that women feel almost like apologizing for being on the earth at all. Having been taught that her highest honor was to make a pudding or darn a stocking, why wonder that she should not excel in writing a book or making a speech? In the face of all the adverse influences, the wonder is she should ever attempt either.

Elizabeth Cady Stanton
November 5, 1868

Neither Virile nor Feminine Style

Dear *Revolution*: You are aware that about the 1st of September *L'Amerique*, a new paper, published in the French language, commenced its existence in Chicago, with Madam D'Hericourt as leading editor. Her articles have been written with her usual thoughtfulness and were far in advance of most newspaper writings, Madame D'Hericourt finding that the proprietors hesitated to espouse openly the cause of Woman's Rights, has resigned her position . . .

Madame D'Hericourt takes exceptions to the use of the word *virile* as applied to the productions of a woman's pen, and has prepared a "Reclamation." . . .

Messrs. Geroult & Pinta – *Gentlemen*: In the very complimentary words with which you accept my resignation as editor-in-chief of your paper, there is an adjective which repels the pen on which you bestow such praises. This pen most earnestly protests against being *virile*. It has denied the existence of sex in minds, because she who holds it, has known too many vigorous minds among women, and too many mediocre and weak ones among men, to admit what is contrary to the truth. There is neither virile style nor feminine style. . . . To-day strong women do not wish to be compared to men. They understand that they owe themselves to their sex, and if anything about them is honored, this honor should reflect on their whole sex because this is justice, and it is one of the means of destroying an absurd prejudice lying in the path of progress in all that relates to laws and customs.

It is because my opinion is their's that my keen and unaccountable pen refuses positively to accept the epithet *virile*; it is simply the pen of human conscience which has reflected much and has had time for self-culture, and which has compelled itself to acquire those qualities of style which clearly reflect its owner's thought – thus permitting it to serve its sisters and brother in humanity. . . .

Jenny P. D'Hericourt★
October 28, 1869

[*See the Appendix for biographical information.]

A Revolution in Table Talk

. . . The birthday-festivities were kept up several days, and as we decided to have speeches and toasts at the dinners, the mornings were passed in the preparation of something to say (instead of to wear). We counselled the gentlemen to toast the ladies on their common sense, intellectual vigor, executive ability, their equestrian skill, etc., and not to mention physical grace or beauty; while we counselled the ladies to do just the opposite. The result was, a Revolution in table talk. . . .

Elizabeth Cady Stanton
February 26, 1868

Man Cannot Keep a Secret – Woman Can

George Francis Train dares openly assert what he *knows* to be true. Although it has been handed down since that "little affair in the garden" as a maxim of four-fold importance, "that woman could not keep a secret, and was not to be trusted." And how often do you hear men imparting profound secrets to a fellow-man, with the injunction, "don't say anything about this to your wife! I would not have *my wife* get hold of it for a sum. You know there's no end to a woman's tongue." But Train has "hit the nail on the head" – men talk. . . . And often has a woman's fair name been sullied by some masculine absurdity, who in his anxiety to relate something marvellous, oversteps the bounds of veracity. . . .

"You never hear woman boasting of her conquests." . . . It is a secret "buried in the grave with her." Again, a "woman cannot keep a secret." How many women live on year after year of married life, with a brutal husband, from whose lips the only words of kindness ever received are in the presence of strangers. . . .

Eva Field
August 19, 1869

Brazen Hoydens! Noisy Scolds

That fastidious newspaper, the Boston *Daily Advertiser* speaks very kindly of a lecture just delivered by Mrs. Lucy Stone in that city. "She never," says the critic, "puts off the robe of her womanly refinement." "It is much to be regretted for the sake of decency," adds the *Advertiser*, that not all the women who strut their brief hour on the lecture platform are made after this pattern. For Mrs. Lucy Stone will make five converts in an evening where a dozen are lost to her cause by the brazen hoyden or noisy scold who delights in flaunting her unwomanliness in the face of astonished audiences." Brazen hoydens! Noisy scolds! To whom can the *Advertiser* thus ungallantly refer? – *Tribune*.

To answer this honest inquiry of the *Tribune*, I presume that this fastidious editor refers to those pictures of women with words coming out of their mouths which we see in the comic papers, edited by other fastidious gentlemen.

For twenty years we have been hearing about "noisy scolds," who stunt their brief hour on the platform. The brazen hoyden, we confess, is a new acquaintance. She belongs to the select circle of the editor of the Boston *Daily Advertiser*. But as one after another of these "noisy scolds" have strutted their brief hour before an audience, some fastidious editor has said of them in the morning paper, "If all the women who lecture on Woman's Rights were as womanly as Mrs. Stanton, Mrs. [Julia Ward] Howe, Mrs. [Mary] Livermore, Miss Anthony, Mrs. [Isabella Beecher] Hooker, Mrs. [Caroline] Severance, Mrs. [Celia] Burleigh, Mrs. [Charlotte] Wilbour, Mrs. [Phebe] Hanaford, Miss [Lily] Peckham, Miss [Phebe] Cozzens [Couzins], Miss [Anna] Dickinson, then we should have nothing to say against them." ★

But yet our Boston *Daily Advertiser* still leads the van of the fastidious, for he is the first man who has demanded that "for the sake of decency," all the women should be cut to one "pattern." . . .

W.

November 18, 1869

[★ See the Appendix for biographical information on the women who were affiliated with *The Revolution*.]

"Damn It"

The New York *Tribune* publishes rather severe comments on the wickedness of women ever allowing themselves to be in so unhappy a frame of mind as to feel like saying "damn it," and reads us quite a lecture for confessing to such weakness on one occasion.

At the time referred to, good *Tribune*, please note, we did not swear, but nobly resisted the sore temptation, though in that tempest-tossed condition of mind in which we had observed 'that great and good men make free use of this popular expletive. In a long acquaintance with Mr. Greeley, the distinguished editor of the *Tribune*, we have noticed that in those dire emergencies, when nothing else could be said or done, he invariably said, "damn it," and evidently felt better.

On one occasion, in Music Hall, Boston, even the silver-tongued orator, Wendell Phillips, wound up one of his glowing periods in denounciation of the cruelty and injustice of Massachusetts to the colored race, with the profane climax, "God damn the Commonwealth of Massachusetts!" . . .

With such associations and examples in the leading minds of the republic, was it an unpardonable sin, that in the most perplexing situation imaginable, the thought of "damn it" should have crossed *our* mind.

April 28, 1870

The Grammar of the Husband

. . . The Husband of To-Day ever considers his wife but as a portion of his my-ship.

Nominative I.
Possessive My, or Mine.
Objective Me.
This is the grammar known to the Husband of To-Day. . . .

June 24, 1869

His or Her

The following letter was written to Horace Greeley for the *Tribune*. . . .

When the slaveholders talked of the will of the majority, the *Tribune* was trying to make them see that there could be no fair majority, where one half the males were not allowed a voice. Are you not as blind in regard to women? When you talk of securing to each the "ownership and enjoyment of *his* rightful gains," will you please amend and say *his* or *her*?

C. S. Middlebrook
July 15, 1869

189

8
"What about the babies?"

Introduction

When women talked about expansion of their activities – through, for example, voting and other political activities – their critics asked: "What will happen to the babies? Who will take care of the babies?" The women answered their critics in several ways. First, they pointed out that the critics weren't actually concerned about the babies as much as about whether women would continue to work as housekeepers and household nurses, and stay out of lawmaking. As *The Revolution* editors say: "We never hear men say that washing, ironing, cooking, blacking their boots, splitting kindling wood, building fires, or any other menial service conflicts with maternity." Why then all the alarm about women obtaining political rights? "There is something very suspicious, to say the least, in all the anxiety men express on this point" (February 17, 1870).

Second, if men think that motherhood is woman's noblest mission and that motherhood means the devotion of a whole lifetime to children, why don't men also think fatherhood a high office worth lifelong attention? And if men were really worried about the babies, wouldn't the men want to give the women caretakers more control over the laws which affect the economic and physical security of themselves and their children?

Further, some of the women suggested the question should rather be "What *has* happened to the babies" in a system which keeps women basically economically dependent upon men. A woman deprived of means of support – through a husband's death, cruelty, financial difficulties, ill health or alcoholism – cannot take care of her children. The writers pointed out that many women were resorting to abortion because of their inability to care for their children. Eleanor Kirk, who herself suffered a deplorable marriage and had great difficulty trying to support her children after she finally left her husband, writes that those people, seemingly so concerned about what will happen to the babies if women become more self-reliant, were ignoring the reasons for, and large numbers of, abortions (May 28, 1868). Many women were obtaining planned abortions for unwanted pregnancies, but many abortions were spontaneous. Just as many slave women had miscarried because they were overworked and badly clothed and fed (Sterling, 1984), similarly other poor and sick women also had a high rate of spontaneous abortions. (See section 3 for further discussion of abortion and infanticide.)

The blame for problems within families should not be placed on activist women, the writers stated, but on those men who supported "man-marriage," an institution maintained through men's religion and law which makes women the toys of men, to be given from one man to another, and used in perpetual servitude.

These discussions were a continuation of those in the woman's rights newspapers of the 1850s where marriage was called a social mechanism that produced many unwanted children and made a woman an unpaid housekeeper, cook, nurse and sexual partner, even in situations where she loathed her husband (see Russo and Kramarae, 1990). In 1853, Elizabeth Cady Stanton, who was a contributor to the earlier women's papers, wrote to her new friend Susan B. Anthony that "The right idea of marriage is at the foundation of all reforms." If laws and public sentiment allowed, a woman would no longer live as wife with a "cruel, bestial drunkard," for example (Stanton and Stanton Blatch, 1969: 48). In 1857, she wrote, "A man in marrying gives up no right; but a woman every right, even the most sacred of all – the right to her own person" (Stanton and Stanton Blatch, 1969: 70).

A *Revolution* article (March 24, 1870) suggested that the traditional promise to "obey" in marriage ceremonies was a violation of the Thirteenth Amendment of the Constitution which states "there shall be no slavery or involuntary servitude in the United States." It was argued that in a society where many women believe they must marry for economic support and survival, the vows they speak cannot be considered to be voluntary. Other articles reported on efforts to remove the word from religious ceremonies. Even earlier, in the much publicized, praised and ridiculed 1855 marriage ceremony of Lucy Stone and Henry Blackwell, Stone omitted the traditional promise to "obey." Blackwell agreed at that time that he had no right to the "custody of the wife's person" and he would not attempt to impose his sexual desires upon his wife. More than 120 years before the contemporary discussion of what is now called "marital rape," feminists were discussing and defending a married woman's right to abstain from sexual intercourse, as a means of controlling her body and her pregnancies. One contributor to *The Revolution* wrote that many so-called "devoted husbands" were devoted to self-gratification, not recognizing that forcing intercourse on their wives is "the very vilest prostitution." Infanticide ("child murder") is one of the unsurprising results, the writer continued (July 8, 1869).

Wifebeating is another result of "man-marriage." Then, as now, many women dependent upon men (through social pressure, economic insecurity, fear of losing custody of children and psychological and physical ill-treatment) continued to live with men who tormented them. One writer referred to this situation as "Wed-Lock" (July 23, 1868). Others called it "legalized prostitution," a term women have used as one definition of marriage in several countries for many years (see definitions in Kramarae and Treichler with Russo, 1985).

That these articles and reports on the misery caused by marriage laws appear in *The Revolution* is not surprising given that Elizabeth Cady Stanton was one of the few woman's rights activists who, in the face of much hostility from press and pulpit, dared publicly to advocate not only woman's legal equality in marriage but also the option of divorce as a safety valve – to enable the institution of family to continue. Under an oppressive domestic system, with most economic alternatives to marriage closed to women, a "home" is a present or potential place of "violence, discord, debauchery" (Stanton, December 17, 1868) for any married woman and her children.

The laws and customs which result in forced intercourse and childbirth, husbands' beatings of their wives, and women's servant status in their "own" homes – these were the actual issues which these *Revolution* writers thought were behind men's cries of "But what about the children."

Bibliography

Davis, Angela Y. 1986. "Racism, Birth Control and Reproductive Rights." In *All American Women: Lines That Divide, Ties That Bind*, Johnetta B. Cole, ed. New York: Collier Macmillan: 239–55.
DuBois, Ellen Carol, ed. 1981. *Elizabeth Cady Stanton/Susan B. Anthony: Correspondence, Writings, Speeches*. New York: Schocken.

Kramarae, Cheris, and Paula Treichler with Ann Russo. 1985. *A Feminist Dictionary*. Pandora Press/Methuen.

Russo, Ann, and Cheris Kramarae, eds. 1990. *Radical Women's Press of the 1850s*. London: Routledge.

Stanton, Theodore, and Harriet Stanton Blatch, eds. 1969. *Elizabeth Cady Stanton, as Revealed in Her Letters, Diary and Reminiscences*. New York: Harper.

Sterling, Dorothy, ed. 1984. *We Are Your Sisters: Black Women in the Nineteenth Century*. New York: Norton.

Who Will Then Take Care of the Babies

New Bremen, Md.

Mrs. E. C. Stanton: I have been a reader of your paper since the first number. Living remote from town, it has not been my good fortune to hear any of the popular lecturers on "Woman's Rights;" while the papers of our State when they speak of such questions, usually it is to but sneer. Thinking it best to hear both sides of all questions, I subscribed for *"The Revolution"* as soon as I knew of its publication. I find much in it to admire; its earnestness, its plain manner of denouncing wrong and oppression in high places and among high officials is worthy of all commendation. I have distributed several numbers of the paper among my more intellectual lady friends. Their comments on the paper and the cause which it advocates are various; although they all find much in it to commend. My most intelligent lady friend, after reading one of your articles urging the right of woman, not only to vote, but to hold any office of honor or trust, suddenly inquired, "Who, then, will take care of the babies when that good time comes?" Not being able to give my friend a satisfactory answer, as one of your subscribers, I ask you to insert this, and also to answer my friend's question in *"The Revolution."*

J. G. M.

We have taken care of seven babies; yet have worked in the cause of women twenty years or more. We have addressed our Legislature many times, spoken on education, temperance, slavery and written many articles for the press. When we went to Albany to address the Legislature we took our nurse and babies to the Delavan House, left them safe there in a room, went to the Capitol, found it filled with ladies, and made our speech. It takes no longer to speak than listen. When we finished, we shook hands all round, and went home to our babies, and the rest of the women to theirs. If we were a member of the Legislature we could spend the few hours every day at the Capitol which other women spend in fashionable calls, shopping, gossiping, dining, dressing, and idling. . . . It is because we love babies that we long to see healthy, happy, common sense mothers, and true fathers who neither smoke, drink, nor swear nor gamble, sit down together and make laws for the government of their children both in the family and the nation.

Elizabeth Cady Stanton
May 14, 1868

What Will Become of the Babies

From every quarter is wafted this cry – and wherefore? . . .

What will become of *your* babies, madam, should you be suddenly deprived of the means of their support? Have you the courage, stamina, ay, *ability*, to fight the world single-handed? . . . We have been there, thank you, and know about it. Every heart-throb, every blush of indignation, every dastardly attempt to change the wages of labor for the wages of sin, we are familiar with; and it makes us *sick* when we see an intelligent female looking at so great a subject through so small a glass, and dirty at that. What will become of the babies? Why don't somebody ask – what *has* become of the babies? Ask Restelle [an abortionist] and thousands of physicians, male and female, who have been engaged in their work of destruction for years. Physicians who have graduated from our first medical colleges, physicians with high sounding diplomas, whose elegant equipages stand in front of Fifth avenue mansions, who pocket a big fee and a little bundle of flesh at the same time, and nobody's the wiser! not even the *husband* in hosts of instances. What will become of the babies – did you ask – and you? Can you not see that the idea is to educate women that they may be self-reliant, self sustaining, self-respected? . . . Then marriages of convenience will not be necessary; men and women will come together, attracted by mutual respect; namby-pamby, doll-faced, wishy-washy, milk-and-water feminine bundles will be unmarketable. God speed the time, for the sake of the babies. . . . My dear fellows, this is quite as much for your benefit as ours. What we propose to do, is so to arrange things that should you ever become sick or poor, we can put our hands to the plough and run

194

the machine, nursing, sympathizing, attending to the finances, and loving you to distraction at the same time. How do you like the picture?

Eleanor Kirk★
May 28, 1868

[★ See the Appendix for biographical information.]

Babies

Was there ever anything that so stuck in the throats of the enemies of "Woman's Rights" as *the Babies*? "But the babies! who'll take care of the babies? what will be done with the babies?" is repeated by them over and over again with distended nostrils and eyes wild with apprehension. Don't be frightened, my poor deluded, but answer me. Who took care of Queen Victoria's babies of whom there were quite a number? Who takes care of the babies on Fifth avenue! Surely not the mothers of the innocents. Now, there are more babies neglected by mothers with nothing else to do in the labor line but to care for them, than by mothers who work to support them. . . . I don't see but the babies of Harriet B. Stowe, Lucy Stone, Elizabeth C. Stanton and Francis D. Gage have fared as well as any babies, and they surely have cause to be proud of their mothers. Why, babies are not at all in the way of Woman Suffrage, but rather their existence is a great reason why their mothers should have a right to assist in making the laws that these little ones must grow up under and obey. There is nothing that looks so sweet to me as a baby; and my deep interest in them is one great reason why I am so desirous that their mothers should have their full rights, and stand side by side with their fathers. I feel ashamed to have the boys grow up and have more rights than their mothers. . . .

Julia Crouch
October 29, 1868

Bread and Babies

We are constantly asked, if women vote, what will become of the bread and babies?

In view of the heavy bread, and badly cooked food we find on most tables, and the shocking mortality among infants, we contemplate with wonder and pity the blind faith of man in the maternal and culinary intelligence of "the weak minded" who have

195

no aspirations beyond Hecker's flour, Mrs. Winslow's soothing syrup, and Wheeler and Wilson's sewing machine. . . .

. . . We have seen children a year old that had never tasted water, when they should have it half a dozen times every day from the hour of their birth. We have found fathers who worked hard all day complain bitterly of being disturbed at night by crying children, hence the common use of Mrs. Winslow's soothing syrup, which only tends to increase the irritable condition of the nervous system, and permanently weaken the brain.★

Young mothers no doubt imagine that this Mrs. Winslow is some experienced, humane old lady, who loves little children, knows just how to soothe them to sleep and pilot them through all the pitfalls of infancy, when, in fact, this abominable syrup is compounded by some ignorant man, in whiskers, broadcloth and boots, who lives and fattens on his ill-gotten gains, while babies are sent by the hundreds to untimely graves or made idiots and lunatics for life.

Elizabeth Cady Stanton
November 26, 1868

[★ Ironically, the *Revolution* was sold, in May 1870, to Laura Curtis Bullard, a woman's rights supporter whose family fortune had come from sales of Dr. Winslow's Soothing Syrup. (See Elisabeth Griffith, *In Her Own Right: The Life of Elizabeth Cady Stanton*. New York: Oxford University Press, 1984, p. 133.)]

★★Men's Maternal Concerns★★

Albany, Oregon

Editor of the Revolution: It is with no little gratification that I notice an editorial in your sprightly and sensible weekly, in which you deign to answer, with irresistible argument, the flat and stale inquiry of some frightened Oregonian, who – doubtless he is a bachelor – sends out a wail from our valleys, asking, in the bitterness of his anguish, "who will stay at home with the babies while women go to the polls?"

You have answered the question so ably that I trust the poor fellow's fears will be allayed; but lest he should relapse into another spasm of maternal tenderness – pity for the babies he was not born a woman – let me here assure him that Oregon mothers can manage to get their cradles tended on election days without difficulty. . . .

"What about the babies?"

Be comforted, good Oregon brother, women are fertile in expedients. . . .

I am the mother of six children, own and carry on a millinery establishment of no mean proportions, write sketches and "squibs" for half a dozen newspapers, talk human rights on appropriate occasions, keep pretty well posted in politics, have a life insurance agency, and still have plenty of time to vote without neglecting the baby, who will, I'll venture a prognostication, grow to be a woman's rights man, and wonder at the benighted days of his infancy, when some frightened Oregonian wailed in his anguish, "who will stay with the baby while his mother goes a-voting?"

Abigail Jane Duniway★
October 6, 1870

[★ Abigail Jane Duniway's own weekly woman's rights newspaper *The New Northwest* first appeared on May 5, 1871.]

★★Child Bearing Not Noble★★

Rev. Mr. Hammond of Chicago says, "One great objection to the extension of Suffrage to woman is, that it will interfere with the rights of infants. They have a right to be born and to be cared for by their mothers."

It is interesting to observe how suddenly men have awakened to an interest in infants; to a fear they will be abused or abolished. For six thousand years, women have been giving birth to children, nursing them, devoting their whole lives to them. Men have shirked not only the care but the training of their own children, throwing the responsibility upon over-burdened wives, and the wives have done the best their cramped lives would permit; have done nobly, if the present race lays any claim to nobility. But suddenly a set of men have taken alarm lest infants will be neglected or destroyed. . . . Mr. Hammond's assertion that "it is woman's especial mission to bear children," I resent as an insult to our highest womanhood. Is it man's special mission in this world to become a father? . . . The mere bearing of children is not noble though a million men should declare it so. . . .

Mrs. H. P. Jenkins★
March 11, 1869

[★ Helen Jenkins was an author and speaker who lectured on woman's rights in Pennsylvania. She wrote a series of newspaper articles called "A Mother's Letters."]

197

Outraged Motherhood

We heard the other day of a young mother who was converted to the woman cause by reading a pamphlet which had been placed in her hands, and which startled her into the knowledge that by the laws of the State where she lived she did not own her baby.

It is amazing that this bare, unvarnished fact does not of itself alone bring into our ranks all the mothers in the land. So long as the atrocious laws standing upon our statute books make the child the property of the father, motherhood is everywhere outraged. How can mothers, while clasping their babies to their bosoms, scorn the woman movement, when it seeks, before all things, to give them the control and ownership of their own offspring. They would not scorn it if they knew all the iniquity of the laws. An effort has been organized in Connecticut to lay the black record of the statute book before every mother in that State. It will be strange if it does not bear fruit, and raise up an army of mothers ready to fight for the ballot, that they may repeal the enactments which do them such deadly harm. . . .

December 1, 1870

Glorious Daughters

. . . [I]f there is any degree of glory in a woman's crown of motherhood, is it not in the bearing of daughters?

We have men enough for the present – judging from the specimens before the public. The world needs a whole generation of daughters, so many that all the offices of wife and motherhood could be filled, and an overwhelming majority be left to take possession and "clean house" in the places that men have rendered vile. . . .

Let women, then, be ambitious to become the mothers of daughters. . . .

March 18, 1869

Nursery Tales

Washington, D.C.
May 11, 1869

Dear Mrs. Stanton and Susan B. Anthony:

. . . May you both live until children will wonder what *ever could*

198

"What about the babies?"

have been the *necessity* of a meeting like this [American Equal Rights Association], and you still have strength and memory enough to relate to them the doings of the old days of barbarisms, and hear the ring of their merry voices as they cry, "Good! good! tell us more of the funny people who used to think mothers would go away and neglect their baby if they let her vote. Did women go *to church then*, Mrs. Stanton?" And you, looking archly over your spectacles, your deep voice and snowy curls both trembling a little, reply, "Yes, my dear, *three times a day (but the babies were dreadfully neglected")*.

Clara Barton
May 20, 1869★

[★ This was the year Barton became involved with the international Red Cross movement.]

Maternity

One of the most common objections to the political rights of woman is her motherhood.

If all women became mothers, periodically, on the same day that elections occurred in the several states, there might be some force in the objection, but . . . it is as absurd to say that for this reason all women shall be denied the suffrage, as it would be to deny all men the suffrage, because some are liable, periodically, to inflammatory rheumatism, delirium tremens, or financial failure. . . .

We never hear men say that washing, ironing, cooking, blacking their boots, splitting kindling wood, building fires, or any other menial service conflicts with maternity. Then, why should they always start up with alarm lest the honors and privileges of life should be detrimental to such relations? There is something very suspicious, to say the least, in all the tender anxiety men express on this point. We think its germ lies in selfishness rather than generosity, something like the solicitude the slaveholder felt lest the negro could not take care of himself in freedom.

February 17, 1870

Husbands Not Wanted

. . . One of man's chronic taunts of woman has been her desire to marry. "Managing mama's," "husband-seeking daughters," "widows bewitched," are epithets that have run the rounds of newspapers, magazines and books. Men have been represented as wary fish and women as anxious anglers equipped with the paraphernalia of rods, lines and all the variety of bait needed to secure the shyest trout. Of late an additional cry has been raised; woman is *so* extravagant that young men are forced to remain single. A young husband would not be able to indulge! his wife in ribbons and lace and at the same time keep himself in tobacco and pay his club fees.

Let me whisper a secret into these men's ears. Tenfold more men marry for love, *i.e.*, because they are anxious to marry, than women. What those women desire who "angle for husbands," is money, not matrimony. In the present condition of society the wife is mainly dependant for position and wealth on the man's position and wealth whom she marries. . . .

Joslyn
June 11, 1868

Old Maids

That there should exist a necessity for the vindication of Old Maids is one proof of the imperfectly developed civilization of this progressive century. To close our eyes against an unpleasing fact and try to persuade ourselves that we do not recognize it as a fact, is foolish and cowardly. The fact which we would face just now, is that the condition of the unmarried woman, who is far enough past the bloom of youth to be reckoned beyond the probability of matrimony, is not respected, nay, is held in the veriest contempt, notwithstanding what the press, the pulpit, law, literature, society, and the world at large may occasionally pretend to the contrary. She is, at best, a something to be only tolerated; a cipher in creation, whose sole use, if she have any, is to fill up the vacant places of existence and, like the arithmetical naught, impart to the significant figures of humanity a value which she can never attain.

Let the world attempt for once to render a fair reason why it regards this class of women as special objects of reproach. What is the only show of a rational answer that it is able to make? "Since she has never been chosen as a life companion, we infer that she lacks the charms and virtues which attract man to woman." A hasty, wholesale inference this; one which takes for granted the infallibility of man's discrimination. When we consider the multitude of imbeciles, termagants, unscrupulous intriguers, heartless, selfish, worse than worthless women, who enter the lists of matrimony, we have not the conscience to affirm the old maid just possibily worse than these. . . . She may have remained unmarried because she had no appreciation of, or faith in, the virtues of the voting sex. Worse and worse! that she should presume to turn the tables and bring to bear against you, gentlemen, your allegation against her. Man might forgive her undeservingness of him, but her depreciation of him, never! With this excuse for her offending, she need expect no mercy. Pass on! She may once have had her heart's choice and lost him early; perhaps by death, perhaps by opposing circumstances, perhaps by his own treachery or inconstancy. None of those hypotheses are disparaging to her. "But stop," says her opposer; "might not the loss proceed from misconduct on her part? how then?" Why in that case she had at least principle enough left to keep her a penitent old maid; so do not impute as a crime her one solitary virtue. Again: a woman may be so situated in life, so environed with cares claiming her exclusive regard, that the opportunity of marriage is far removed from her, and she chooses to pursue the line of duty marked out straight before her rather than forsake it to attain a new object, preferring the lot of a conscientious maid to that of a wedded lady of a style we leave you to depict.

I come now to the last possibility: she may have made her ideal choice, and set up in her soul her model of the man who alone could keep it company, and never on her way through life finding the real of her ideal, she cleaves with constancy to that ideal as better than an uncongenial real. . . .

. . . Why should [man] seek to remove the stigma from the woman whose very condition implies a slight which his vanity cannot forgive? The earth is man's and the fulness thereof: is it to be expected, however modest his self-appreciation, that he will concede to woman, aside from himself, any right or mission upon *his* earth? Was she not created for *me*?" he argues: "and failing *me*, what use in life can she claim?" . . .

Let woman's native talent lead her where it will, it is the prompting of the God within, and, left free, never makes mistakes. Whether the chosen path be literature, legislation, science, the professions, the useful or the beautiful arts, let her follow, and it will crown her brow with the dignity of purpose, and make strong her soul in the calm consciousness of selfhood. Then only will the phrase old maid, applied to her, cease to be a synonym for contempt; she can see her early youth depart, leaving her unmated in the flesh, and will not be tempted into falsehood and deceit to persuade the world that she is not yet under its interdict. When you, ye persecutors, censure a woman for her folly and weakness in concealing her age, think of this and blame yourselves: repent, do her justice, and she will be truthful. Who has not the instinct to shrink from and put off an evil day? Cease to make an evil day of the noontide of her life and she will greet it as cheerfully as if it were her girlhood's hopeful dawn.

E. M. H.
August 20, 1868

Slattern Genius

. . . How many times I have heard a woman called a slattern, because she could not keep a house in order, when had she been allowed to write out her sublime thoughts, which were all in another direction, she would have astonished the world with her genius. Talk about women getting out of their sphere; can they do so any more than they are now. Look at the thousands of women who are not fit to be mothers, and yet are constantly bringing children into existence, children which will rise up to curse them for that very existence; and why is this? because society is forcing women into marriage, before they have any knowledge of what they are fitted for and what they might excel in. We want better wives, mothers and children, and before we can have this, we must have better women.

Lizzie Leavenworth
September 17, 1868

Educating Girls into Wives

. . . It seems to be assumed, with the narrowest sort of views of what human soul in a feminine body is, that the only reason for educating a girl is to make her a better mother, wife, sister and perhaps cousin. We might say that the office of mother being the highest in the world, one cannot be too highly educated for it. But we will not press the point. We only note that schools for girls being only a kind of domestic nursery to turn out complete wives, etc., after the standard mentioned, we are not aware of any schools

202

where boys are sent to learn of their duties as husbands, fathers and brothers.

February 26, 1868

Bridal Presents – A Letter to My Girl Friends

. . . One of our girl friends is about to leave us, to go from her childhood's home a bride. We cluster around her with parting gifts. Gifts that we hope will serve to remind her of us during the years of separation; and what are these gifts? Nine times in ten, they are either *something to eat with or something to wear*. Spoons, forks, castors, cake-baskets, fish-knives, berry-dishes, or lace collars, or handkerchiefs, jewelry, or other ornaments; now, owing to the usage of modern civilization, spoons, knives, etc., are indispensible to housekeepers, and they will in some manner be provided. . . . Better a suggestive picture on the wall, or a book filled with elevating thoughts in the library. . . .

Lizzie M. Boynton★
November 25, 1869

[★ See the Appendix for biographical information.]

★★Woman the Toy of Man★★

. . . Thus far, we have had the man-marriage, and nothing more. From the beginning, man has had the whole and sole regulation of the matter. He has spoken in Scripture, and he has spoken in law. As an individual, he has decided the time and cause for putting away a wife; and as a judge and legislator, he still holds the entire control. In all history, sacred and profane, woman is regarded and spoken of, simply, as the toy of man. She is taken or put away, given or received, bought or sold, just as the interests of the parties might dictate. But the woman has been no more recognized in all these transactions, through all the different periods and conditions of the race, than if she had had no part or lot in the whole matter. . . .

October 29, 1868

The Man Marriage

In reply to many letters asking if *The Revolution* is opposed to marriage, I desire to state my objections as briefly as possible to our

203

present system, which I call the "man marriage," because to the creeds and codes and customs which govern the present institution woman has never given her consent.

1st. I object to the teachings of the church on this question. Its interpretation of the Bible, making man the head of woman, and its forms of marriage, by which she is given away as an article of merchandise, and made to vow obedience as a slave to a master, are all alike degrading to my sex. . . .

Hitherto we have had the "white male" interpretation of the Bible, making it wise and just and good to enslave the black man to his avarice, and the woman to his lust. The late war gave a new interpretation to the Bible on slavery, and we shall hear no more of sending back Onesimus [a disciple of St. Paul]. But the negro is not the only class set free by the discussions of the last century.

Women have been listening, thinking, studying Philosophy, Hebrew, Greek, first principles, and when they translate the Bible for themselves we shall have a new evangel of womanhood, wifehood and motherhood. When woman understands the science of life, she will see the wisdom of the command. "Be ye not unequally yoked," and of the solemn warnings, given mid the thunders of Mount Sinai, "The sins of the fathers shall be visited upon the children." If the Bible teaches one lesson, it is a pure and holy marriage, in which weakness and vice, rum, tobacco, disease and lust can have no part whatsoever. . . .

2d. The position of the State on this question is quite as objectionable as that of the church. . . .

There is not a man in this nation, who, knowing what the laws are, but would repudiate for himself a relation that would so wholly merge his individual existence in that of another human being. Suppose the law should say, "The husband and wife are one, and that one the wife." How many men would go to the hymenial [marriage] alter and vow obedience to that idea? Here and there one might do so for a fortune, but most men would choose freedom and equality to gilded slavery. No sensible man would put his head into a noose that stripped him of personal and property rights, of children, wages, name, moral responsibility and the right of locomotion.

The laws for married women in some states are exactly parallel with those of the slave code on the southern plantations. Husbands, as well as slaveholders, have availed themselves of this absolute power of the old common law. To-day hundreds of wives in their right minds are shut up in insane asylums, or dragging out

"What about the babies?"

miserable, dependent lives in those living sepulchres called home, where the light of love has all gone out. . . .

April 8, 1869

Marriages and Mistresses

I frankly admit that to be a "mistress" is less dishonorable than to be a "wife;" for while the mistress may leave her degradation if she will, public sentiment and the law hold the "wife" in hers; and while the man is obliged to render compensation (poor I admit for the sacrifice) to his "mistress," he may *demand* of his "wife" that she perform his drudgery, submit to his blows, and (worse) live the uncomplaining victim of his rapacity.

Francis Barry
October 15, 1868

Marriage and Divorce

. . . If marriage is a human institution, about which man may legislate, it seems but just that he should treat this branch of his legislation with the same common sense that he applies to all others. If it is a mere legal contract, then should it be subject to the restraints and privileges of all other contracts. A contract, to be valid in law, must be formed between parties of mature age, with an honest intention in said parties to do what they agree. The least concealment, fraud or intention to deceive, if proved, annuls the contract. A boy cannot contract for an acre of land, or a horse, until he is twenty-one, but he may contract for a wife at fourteen. If a man sell a horse, and the purchaser find in him "great incompatibility of temper" – a disposition to stand still when the owner is in haste to go – the sale is null and void; the man and his horse part company. But in marriage, no matter how much fraud and deception are practised, nor how cruelly one or both parties have been misled; no matter how young or inexperienced or thoughtless the parties, nor how unequal their condition and position in life, the contract cannot be annulled. Think of a husband telling a young and trusting girl, but one short month his wife, that he married her for her money. . . .

. . . You all know our marriage is, in many cases, a mere outward tie, impelled by custom, policy, interest, necessity; founded not

205

even in friendship, to say nothing of love; with every possible inequality of condition and development. . . .

Elizabeth Cady Stanton
October 22, 1868

Extra Warning

The Pawtucket (R. I.) *Gazette* and *Chronicle* published the following advertisements, last week:

"NOTICE. – Whereas, my wife, Sarah A. Sheldon, has left my bed and board without due cause or provocation, this is to give notice that I shall pay no debts contracted by her from this day. LOWELL SHELDON."

"NOTICE EXTRA.– Whereas, my husband, Lowell Sheldon, has posted me without just cause or provocation, this is to give notice that he never had any bed or board for me to leave; and that I could not live with a man that would drink a quart bottle full of Richardson's bitters, sweetened with a pint of Opodeloc* in five hours. All persons are cautioned against trusting said Lowell Sheldon, as I shall pay no bills of his contracting after this date. SARAH A. SHELDON."

Sarah has not read *The Revolution* in vain. The rapid growth of womanly independence, purity and dignity is refreshing to our waiting soul. We hope there will be a general stampede from bitters, opodeldoc and tobacco. None but pure, healthy, moral men should become husbands and fathers. "Paternity" is a subject to which we would direct national thought and consideration.

April 29, 1869

[* Opodeloc was a preparation which might contain alcohol, camphor and oils of marjoram and rosemary.]

Marriage as Only Vocation

. . . Other vocations mainly closed against her, the throng of womanhood has, for centuries past, flocked through the open door of marriage. Not that all would so have done could they have forced a passage into some new thoroughfare; for all did not enter thereinto as upon an ideal of happiness, but with a passive acceptance of the sole portion proffered by a parsimonious fate.

Hence arose rivalries, jealousies, contentions, and their long retinue of feminine arts and intrigues. . . .

January 20, 1870

Marriage – Its Sacredness and Security

Florida

. . . When you take love, confidence, and respect out of marriage, in the name of Heaven, what remains to be desecrated? Surely nothing but the lives of the parties consenting to such a life of degradation, for which there is no name save that of legalized prostitution. The old idea that "marriages are made in heaven," is obsolete. Few have the hardihood to place all the miserable copartnerships existing under the name of marriage, at the door of the Lord! . . .

Esther H. Hawks, M.D.
February 10, 1870

"Obey" in the Marriage Service Unconstitutional

. . . We think that all these reverend gentlemen who insist on these humiliating ceremonies, that place all wives in the light of slaves, should be impeached in the Supreme Court of the United States, for a direct and positive violation of the Thirteenth Amendment of the Federal Constitution, which says, "there shall be no slavery or involuntary servitude in the United States."

In the meantime let all brides who have any true dignity or self-respect, repudiate "obey," and the giving away scene, as unworthy the higher civilization we boast to-day.

March 24, 1870

"Serve and Obey"

. . . So, then, the man is to promise to love, comfort, and honor; three comparatively easy things. But the gentle maiden – the embodiment of all the graces – the angelic creature sent from heaven for the purpose of exercising her miraculous *female influence* on stern man, she who is so ethereal that she must never know aught of the sordid art of money-making promises – to *serve* and *obey*. She is not too spiritual to serve, and the word may be made to comprehend a deal of unpleasant work. If her lord commands her to serve in a minimal capacity, she is to remember "obey" was in her marriage vows. No matter how unreasonable he is, no matter

207

how superior her judgment is to his, his word is law, her promise unconditional. . . .

. . . Again I read, "I pronounce that they are *man* and *wife*." There's a absurdity for you, "a man's a man for a' that;" but the woman is irretrievably lost in the wife wedded; she is no longer a woman – *wife* alone.

Shall we not institute a reform in this matter? Knowing that justice is with us we need never despair of success; "We will find a way or make it."

Hayes
March 2, 1871

Daring Words

"The Cleveland *Herald* thinks the marriage service should be changed to read: 'Who dares take this woman?' and the groom shall answer, 'I dare.'"

There are also some occasions where it might be changed to read, "Then the minister shall say, who dares throw away this woman upon this man?"

September 29, 1870

Leave Tryant-Husbands

"Dear Mrs. Kirk: . . . Your ideas all meet my approval – my intense appreciation – but they do occasionally seem not a little impracticable. You counsel all women who are slighted, ill-treated – put aside for others – to step immediately out of the ranks. It strikes me that is more easily said than done. How is a woman to support herself and children if she voluntarily turns from her husband? . . ."

. . . In regard to the impracticability of my advice to married women who are unfortunate enough to possess tyrants for husbands – wretches who have no regard for the marital obligation – I can only repeat my convictions on the subject, strengthened every day by new developments. I speak from terrible experience, my dear friend, having for the last three years supported myself and a family of children by my own individual exertions. When I finally decided that farther disgrace could not be borne without the burial of the last atom of my self-respect (a quality which, of all others, I disliked to part with), I humbly and tearfully asked a divine blessing – asked that my way might be made plain, arose from my knees with a determination to go it alone, and have never for a moment faltered.

What is the poor-house, the wash-tub, starvation or death, compared to the agony of a woman occupying the position of a slave? second to some female whom the precious husband has entrapped into his wily meshes? It was not practicable with me, why should it be with others? . . .

. . . Form a club, and meet weekly for the discussion of affairs connected with your social and pecuniary interests. Sound the depths, go to the bottom, and see how many women you have in town who can be depended upon; who will make hard warfare against intolerance. There must be a beginning, and this will be a good initiatory movement. Frequent discussings, comparing notes with each other, reading aloud articles from "*The Revolution*" (which I am glad to find is no stranger in [your] town), will give you a breadth and earnestness which will finally do away with this nonsensical squeamishness about the so much talked of unfeminine element. . . .

Eleanor Kirk★
August 6, 1868

[★ See the Appendix for biographical information.]

Facts Without Fancies

Editor of the Revolution:

In the city of Janesville, Wis., living next neighbor to my cousin, with whom I am spending a few weeks, is a couple who, according to human law, have for ten years, sustained the relation of husband and wife. This *legal* husband commenced married life the most despotic of tyrants, and has continued to prove himself the same up to the present time. He *owns* his legal wife, body and soul, and exercises unlimited authority over her, with less mercy than most men show their horse or dog. The first week after their marriage, he brought a whip into the house, and gave his wife to understand that whenever she *failed to please him* it should be used upon her, and true to his original promise, it has, time and again, been used upon the slightest provocation, and often without her knowledge when or wherein she had offended. . . . And yet, notwithstanding all this abuse, this woman feels that she is *obliged* to *continue* living with this brutal husband (although her sufferings are so great that, but for her children, she would long ago have put an end to her earthly existence) and for the following reasons: That neither *society* nor *law* offer *any* haven wherein she can screen herself from his terrible vengeance – nor *any* protection for her individual rights – nor *any* guaranty that to *her* shall be given the custody of the children. . . .

Besides this man's abuse of his wife, he treats his children so unmercifully, they are in constant fear of him – and has been seen to whip his horses until they lay upon the ground from pain and exhaustion, and the neighbors then interfered. But no interference in behalf of the wife, no practical sympathy, no protection for her anywhere, but, on the contrary, a pious neighbor woman tells her it is commanded in the Bible; "Wives obey your husbands." What an outrage upon justice, and what an insult to all womanhood to preach *such nonsense* at *any* time and under *any* circumstances! . . .

Elvira Wheelock Ruggles
July 29, 1869

★★The Real Cause of Child-Murder★★

. . . Women are educated to think that with marriage their individuality ceases or is transferred to their husbands. The wife has thenceforth no right over her own body. This is also the husband's belief, and upon which he acts. No matter what her condition, physical or mental, no matter how ill-prepared she may feel herself for maternity, the demands of his passion must never be refused.

He thinks, or cares nothing, for the possible result of his gratification. If it be that an immortal being, with all its needs, physical, mental or moral, shall come into the world to sin, to suffer, to die, because of his few moments of pleasure, what cares he?

He says he is ready to provide for his children, therefore he feels himself a kind father, worthy of honor and love. That is, he is ready to provide for them food and clothing, but he is not willing to provide for them, by his self-denial, sound bodies, good tempers and a happy ante-natal existence. He gives his wife wealth, leisure and luxury, and is, therefore, a devoted husband, and she is an *undutiful*, unloving wife, if her feelings fail to respond to his.

Devoted husband! Devoted to what? To self-gratification at the expense of the respect of his wife. I know men who call themselves Christians, who would insist that they are *gentlemen*, who never insult any woman – but their wives. They think it impossible that

"What about the babies?"

they can outrage them; they never think that even in wedlock there may be the very vilest prostitution; and if Christian women are *prostitutes* to Christian husbands, what can we expect but the natural sequence – infanticide? . . .

A.

July 8, 1869

A Word to Abused Wives

Let the marriage question alone, did you say, and wait for female suffrage to unsnarl the skein . . . Wait all you that wish; but the writer cannot do it. Ten miserable years of married life, in which every article of the wifely contract was performed to the letter, and, as far as possible, in the required spirit – ten years of abuse, drunkenness, infidelity and poverty – ten years of childbearing and child-nursing – deprived of home comforts – cursed, kicked, and finally deserted – has led me to a place where I may not say "wait." . . . Who ordained that man can violate every marriage obligation – drink, abuse, and then be *obeyed*? Who decided that such men's *wills* should be the *law* for wives? Who said that a man could commit every evil in the calendar, and be winked at by society, while a woman making the smallest misstep from conventional paths shall be everlastingly frowned down, and spit upon? Who declared that a woman must live with a wretch through all sorts of personal ill-treatment and licentiousness? Who determined that marriage shall mean everlasting slavery? Who says that because a woman has borne one child for a man she shall continue to bring others into the world to be knocked about and finally ruined by a miserable, drunken father? You, who are suffering this worse than internal torments, don't believe a word of such stuff; it is the most ridiculous balderdash that ever was repeated. . . .

"Ah!" pleads one, "I know it all; but my husband has money, and with him I can be supported in affluence."

Money! Do I hear aright? Money! Let his cursed money rot with his dirty carcass! Another says:

"Yes; but I love him; and, perhaps, I may, by my patience and perfect unselfishness, be the means of his reformation."

Go away with your nonsense. A man who can be dragged down to such depths with a good wife, can never be raised to manhood by any influence of hers. Free yourself, refuse to live with him. . . .

Eleanor Kirk

June 18, 1868

211

Wed-Lock

. . . There is something monstrous and degrading to both man and woman, for two persons to live together as husband and wife, where there is so much antagonism as to admit of violence on any occasion whatever. . . .

July 23, 1868

What Justifies Marriage?

The institution of marriage is either the greatest curse or the greatest blessing known to society. It brings two people into the closest of all possible relations; it puts them into the same house; it seats them at the same table; it thrusts them into the same sleeping apartment; in short, it forces upon them an intimate and constant companionship from which there is no escape. More than this, it makes any attempt at escape disreputable; the man or woman who seeks to loosen or break the tie he or she finds intolerable, is frowned upon by society. . . .

Man has bound in wedlock many whom God has not joined together. Indeed, it is difficult for a close observer not to come to the conclusion that marriage, as it now exists, is a curse to society and to the human race; it is a source, far more frequently, of misery than of happiness. What God intended for the crowning felicity of mankind has been distorted by the race into its crowning wretchedness.

How can this be remedied? No pair ever entered upon wedlock with the consciousness that they were entering upon a life of torture. Very few marry without the expectation of inward happiness. Why are they so, almost invariably, disappointed? In other words, what justifies a man and woman in marriage? There are some who marry, knowing that other than the highest motives lead them to this step; but those who marry consciously for ambition, from pique or from other equally ignoble reasons, are the exception rather than the rule. Most of those who marry are, or fancy themselves to be, in love with each other. Each imagines the other to possess those qualities which will make a life spent together delightful to both; and this expectation makes the disappointment, when it comes, the harder to bear; the ideal happiness they have hoped for, and failed to find, makes the real wretchedness the more insupportable.

Is it not time that advanced thinkers should give some attention

"What about the babies?"

to the marriage relation, and discover, if possible, upon what basis it may rest securely, peacefully, and happily. . . .

Meanwhile men and women marry in the same old hap-hazard way, learning nothing from each other's experience; and the result is what one might expect, confusion, misery and crime.

August 18, 1870

The Woman Question

The Woman Question – "Can you let me have $20 this morning?" The Man Question – "What did you do with that $1 I gave you last week?" – *Revolution*

August 18, 1870

Housekeeping

. . . [H]ousekeeping is not beautiful; it cheers and raises neither the husband, the wife, nor the child; neither the host, nor the guest; it oppresses woman. A house kept to the end of prudence is laborious without joy; a house kept to the end of display is impossible to all but a few women, and the success is dearly bought.

February 5, 1868

★★The After Meal★★

. . . A reliable city editor informs us that one summer, when Mr. Beecher was left to keep house for himself, he cooked his own breakfast every morning (so far so good) but never washed his dishes, getting out each morning a clean set, for cooking and table purposes, and when he used all the iron, tin and crockery in the establishment, he cooked no more. . . . But we can sympathize with Mr. Beecher in this seeming neglect, for the most depressing and discouraging part of a meal is picking up the fragments, and marshaling pots, pans, knives, forks, spoons, and China in decency and order to their accustomed places. There is some enthusiasm in compounding delicacies, roasting a turkey or boiling vegetables, all to the point of perfection, spreading the table with clean napkins, shining silver, pure white china and vases of flowers, but when the lights are fled, the garlands dead, and all the he's departed, what a scene of desolation dining-room and kitchen reveal. We have often likened it to a deserted field of battle. . . .

October 15, 1868

★★House-Keepers★★

. . . It also occurred to me that the epithet of woman, as the great house-keeper of the world, was about as dignified as it would be to call our merchants *store-keepers*; and I would also suggest that if *house-keepers* should become house-*owners*, the houses would stand a better chance to be well kept. People generally take better care of what belongs to themselves than of what belongs to somebody else.

As store-keepers delight in the grand title of merchant princes, why not call house-keepers household princesses, or Queens of the home? Good reason why; because our houses and their keepers are owned by lords and masters. House-keepers is a very appropriate title for the wife and mother in her present dependent condition. . . .

Mrs. E. O. G. Willard
December 3, 1868

What's "Home" in Poverty?

. . . Oh! what is "home," without a country? What's "home," in ignorance, poverty and debauchery? What's "home," when the chief priest who ministers there is dead to everything but his own passions, appetites and ambition? . . . It is vain we drape the spotless curtain, spread the clean meal and decorate with flowers, wash the little rosy faces and smooth the golden ringlets down; our smiles are smiles of sadness so long as fathers, husbands, sons are moulded in the outer world, while over its highways, honesty, purity, virtue, and love, may not in safety walk.

. . . We have lived thus far under a dynasty of force, which is the male element, hence war, violence, discord, debauchery. . . .

If you shut a woman up within four walls and make the pleasing of man the only object of her life, she will, of course, become narrow, foolish and frivolous; to be otherwise she must have all the variety, discipline, and expanse of thought and training man has. You can make women wise only by changing the conditions of their lives. Give them something better to do and think about, and they will abandon the Grecian bend [a fashionable way for women to carry their bodies bent forward from the hips] and the Italian wiggle; but if you make it the business of their lives to attract men,

214

this can only be done by a succession of new modes and manners. So long as there is a demand for weak-minded women, there will be a plentiful supply. And so long as the mass of men are the unthinking, unreasoning crowd they are today, the demand for fools and finery will continue. . . .

Elizabeth Cady Stanton
December 17, 1868

Tell Us More, Aunt Lucy

Speaking about the bedquilts of many colors and innumerable pieces which take prizes at agricultural fairs, "Aunt Lucy" says, in the *Rural New Yorker*, "I have lived forty-six years and brought up six children, and have never yet found time to buy calico and cut it up into little pieces, half an inch square, for the purpose of sewing them together again, just to see how many I could make of it."

February 11, 1869

Co-operative Housekeeping

Dr. Dio Lewis has introduced it admirably into Boston in one form, in his eight story boarding house. The lower story is a restaurant. The building has a steam elevator and two dum-waiters, sixty large rooms, with hot and cold water in every bedroom, a mile and a quarter of speaking tube connecting every room in the house with the office. The price of suites of rooms ranges from $300 to $2,000 per annum. Parties or families can be served with meals at a few minutes notice, without leaving their rooms, and everything goes on so satisfactorily that it is said the Doctor now only regrets that he had not built twelve stories instead of eight. Here is a good beginning. Now let us have similar establishments at cheaper rates, but as well conducted, to meet the wants of the million.

February 18, 1869

The Eight Hour Law

The New York legislature enacted it just at the close of the protracted session, and the Governor issued a proclamation a few hours after its passage announcing the fact, and calling the attention of the people of the state to its provisions. Eight hours are proclaimed to be the legal measure of a day's work for all classes of

215

mechanics, workingmen, and laborers, "excepting those engaged in farm and domestic labor."

Excepting those, that is, who do the most laborious, most confining and every way most disagreeable work. . . .

Parker Pillsbury
May 5, 1870

★★Scripture: Dishwashing is Man's Work★★

New Interpretation of Scripture. – Phoebe Couzins,★ imitating some late ministerial Scripture renderings, proves clearly enough that dishwashing is man's work more than woman's from 2d Kings xxi, 13: "I will wipe Jerusalem as a *man* wipeth a dish; wiping it, and turning it upside down." Another reading of the passage is, "*he* wipeth and turneth it up on the face thereof." Observe it is *he*, not *she*, in both readings.

May 19, 1870

[★ See the Appendix for biographical information.]

9
"All the rights I want"

Introduction

Whether a person thinks she has all the rights she wants depends upon what she thinks she deserves or can obtain. As *The Revolution* writers were aware, many women were not willing to demand woman suffrage actively.

Throughout the histories of women's movements, men have been able to point out that there are many women who do not want the vote, or the same property rights as men, or the Equal Rights Amendment. Even many women who have worked for women's increased participation in social and political life have believed that women should be allowed in the "public sphere" only after domestic duties have been fulfilled. Others have requested increased recognition and control over the "domestic sphere" rather than expansion into the activities controlled by men. Not only have the women's tactics differed, but also their ideas, aims and objectives.

The Revolution editors and the regular contributors were generally supportive of women who were expanding their ideas of interest and work beyond the stereotypical confines of women's activities, even if those women did not have a primary commitment to the woman's movement. So its columns are filled with information about women starting newspapers, giving public speeches, working in print shops, sculpting public monuments, preaching from pulpits – even if these women were not explicitly supportive of woman's rights. At the same time the writers often argued that these activities were possible in good part because of the work of woman's rights activities. They even called the open opposition from women lecturing against woman's suffrage a promising feature, suggesting that "ladies" who left their homes to speak to mixed-sex groups to ridicule the "strong-minded women" were in danger of being ranked in that category themselves (October 14, 1869).[1]

The Revolution writers also argued that what were called

women's "natural," special virtues and skills were those activities
and characteristics which men allowed women. When the influential
and opposing *Tribune* editor advised that if a woman wanted to
chop wood (that is, take on this type of work which was
stereotypically men's work) then "let her," a contributor pointed
out the paternalism of the remark. Who is to "let her?" The law?
Public opinion? Her husband? Horace Greeley?

Further, the editors pointed out that the enforced division of
labor, with women assigned the unpaid domestic tasks, assumed
that all women would be continually and adequately financially
supported by men, when the evidence was clear that women could
not count on such support.

Working-class women already knew this, of course. Anthony
and Stanton sought allies among them. In 1868 they helped to form
a pioneering, if short-lived, Working Woman's Association to
integrate trade union and woman's rights goals. Anthony, unlike
many middle-class women who disapproved of labor unions and
strikes, wanted women in the factories and workshops to unite to
get better wages and work conditions as well as for independence
from fathers and husbands and to work for the vote (see section 4).
However, the "rights" which these women thought obtainable and
valuable differed depending upon class and work situation.
Anthony found that only a small group of professional workers,
such as journalists, were interested in *The Revolution's* emphasis
upon voting. Stanton reported that working-class women were
much more interested in talks and discussions about marriage and
divorce than in talk about the vote.

There were other objections to increased rights for women. For
example, Greeley repeatedly questioned women's right to the vote
if they weren't willing to accept the "duty" of fighting the wars. In
1867, when Stanton and Anthony were making a plea to a New
York Constitutional Convention chaired by Greeley, for enfranchisement of women, Stanton answered him by saying that yes,
women were willing to fight – just as he had in the Civil War, by
sending substitutes. When he raised the issue again in his *Tribune*, a
Revolution correspondent pointed out that Greeley had not fought,
but he still claimed his right to vote (February 11, 1869).

The strong-minded women's claims for greater autonomy were
designed to clash with men's social policies which assumed gender
divisions to be outside politics and law. However, the claims and
the claimants were also seen as wrong and threatening to many
women living in the web of the policies and in binding relationships

with men. The woman's rights advocates were debating not only issues of the sameness and difference of women and men (such as whether women have special skills and virtues that make them especially designed for domestic work and child care), but also issues of dominance. The woman's rights advocates were challenging the practiced "right" of men to determine the rights of women.

Note

1 The terms "women" and "ladies" were sometimes used interchangeably in the *Revolution* pages, but writers consistently opposed a particular kind of "lady" – the one who, from a position of current economic security, refused to recognize the needs of other women to be independent of men's economic and social control. (This was the kind of "lady" lampooned by feminist theatrical groups of the 1870s, satirizing the opposition of women like Phyllis Schlafly to the Equal Rights Amendment. The actors wore suits, hats and white gloves, or housedresses and aprons, or cheerleading outfits while chanting such slogans as Roses Not Raises; Father Knows Best; Brooms, Not Basketballs; Gold Rings, Not Gold Medals; I'd Rather Be Ironing; Pump Iron: Do His Shirts. They called themselves Ladies Against Women.)

Bibliography

Cott, Nancy F., and Elizabeth H. Peck, eds. 1979. *A Heritage of Her Own: Toward a New Social History of American Women.* New York: Simon & Schuster.

DuBois, Ellen Carol, ed. 1981. *Elizabeth Cady Stanton/Susan B. Anthony: Correspondence, Writings, Speeches.* New York: Schocken.

Helsinger, Elizabeth K., Robin Lauterbach Sheet, and William Veeder. 1983. *The Woman Question: Social Issues, 1837–1883.* New York and London: Garland.

Lutz, Alma. 1940. *Created Equal: A Biography of Elizabeth Cady Stanton 1815–1902.* New York: John Day.

Shapiro, Ann R. 1987. *Unlikely Heroines: Nineteenth-Century American Women Writers and the Woman Question.* New York: Greenwood Press.

"I Have All the Rights I Want"

. . . In view of the sorrow and suffering that envelope the human family like a dark cloud, that woman must be selfish, ignorant and unthinking, who can wrap the mantle of complacency about her and say "I have all the rights I want."

Elizabeth Cady Stanton
March 25, 1869

The Rights Man Gives to Woman

When I see a poor washerwoman breaking her back over the wash-tub, working faithfully a whole day and getting twelve shillings in payment; and a great, strong man with ever so much more back and no brains, get two dollars and a half for holding a lamp while the plummer blackens a lead pipe in a dark closet, and scrapes stars and fancy devices on the pipe that are never to be seen (the same plumber getting from three to four dollars a day), then I want *women* to *vote*, that they may get a better price for their labor.

I have had some interest in finding out the general opinion of *man* kind (or unkind) on the subject, and as a general thing I find he is willing to accord her –

The right to wake when he's asleep,
The right to watch, the right to weep,
The right to rise and light the fire,
The right to keep her needle by her,
The right his ancient clothes to mend,
The right his simplest want t'attend,
The right to pleasantly construe him,
The right to bring his slippers to him,
The right to let him make the laws,
The right to find no fault for cause,
The right to comfort his distress,
The right to wear her same old dress,
The right his every joy to double,
The right to save him every trouble,
The right to clothe and teach the young,
The perfect right to hold her tongue.*

S. X.
April 23, 1868

[* The poem may be a parody of Mrs. E. Little's, "What are the Rights of Women?" published in Ladies Wreath II (1848–9), p. 133,

"All the rights I want"

quoted by Barbara Welter, "The Cult of True Womanhood: 1820–1860," *American Quarterly* 18 (Summer 1966), pp. 151–74.]

The Clergy and Women

These two classes, it is said, are too pure, too spiritual, too exalted to vote. The laws and custom for the clergy are in harmony with this idea, they are treated as a superior class, as a privileged order. The people furnish them houses, food, clothes; lawyers fight their battles for nothing, physicians prescribe for their families without charge, they get railroad tickets, periodicals and newspapers at half prices. The butcher, the baker, the milkman, the blacksmith and the carpenter delight to grant favors to their pastor. He is the special favorite of the law, too. $1500 of his property is not taxed, in fact, all pay more respect to the black coat than any other. But what one of all these privileges is bestowed upon a woman? None, whatever. With her, the practice is all reversed, she does everything for the rest of the world at half price. She is taxed on all she eats and drinks and wears. The poorest widow pays as much as a millionaire for a trip on the cars, for a book or paper. As she owns nothing, has no credit in the marts of trade, and is a beggar in the world of work, she is without influence, and it is nobody's interest to do her favor. Could a ballot bring her down any lower? If, like the Priest, she were, in fact, regarded as a superior being, and because of the "holy office of maternity," enjoyed the long list of privileges he does, one might accept the assertion that woman is too good to vote, but unfortunately, creeds, codes, customs, all point in the opposite direction, that with woman, disfranchisement is degradation.

Elizabeth Cady Stanton
May 8, 1869

Why Not Rev. Mrs. as Well as Rev. Mr.?

It is a sorry old anecdote, that of Dr. Johnson's sneer at female oratory. When asked what he thought of a woman's preaching, he said he had the same opinion of it as of a dog's dancing – of which the marvel was, not that it could be done well, but that it could be done at all. If the prince of lexicographers (and likewise of curmudgeons) were now alive, he might find many profitable opportunities to sit, like other sinners of the same sex, under edifying sermons by preachers of the opposite.

221

The Revolution in Words

A great many women possess by nature, and in a high degree, the functions expressed in the Latin meaning of the word *doctor*, a teacher. Woman's ability as a secular teacher is acknowledged in the day-school; her ability as a religious teacher is equally acknowledged in the Sunday-school. But why should not a schoolmistress who speaks to a thousand pupils in a New York public school have an equally good warrant from public opinion for speaking to any other secular audience? And why should not a gifted woman, who goes with a Bible in her hand to her mission class every Sunday in the Five Points, be permitted by the same public opinion to widen the circle of her sympathetic appeal by uttering it from the church desk?

Of all forms of female oratory – and woman's tongue is eloquent by nature – its highest reach of effectiveness is likely – nay, almost inevitably – to be found, by and by, in religious discourse. If there is one place more appropriate than another for a woman to use her native faculty of public speech, that place is the religious meeting. Three-fourths of all the members of our churches are women, and three-fourths of the ministers of these churches should be women likewise. . . .

Men, by their usurpation of the exclusive prerogative of religious teaching, have given to the world a distorted, one-sided, and half monstrous view of God. It is a masculine theology which is responsible for our prevailing creeds of hate, of wrath, of vengeance, and of fiery penalty. Woman in the pulpit would interpret God in his gentler aspects, as the lover, not the scourger, of the human race. The Christian church now needs a profound reform in its service – not that the priest should be hushed to silence, but that the priestess also should be suffered to speak.

October 13, 1870

"Women Do Not Want to Vote"

. . . It may be urged in proof that women do not wish to vote, that so few have yet come forward to ask for the right. And since it must be acknowledged at the very outset that men have done their utmost to place women, upon this question, in a hopeless dilemma, for they said almost what amounts to this – that, if any woman desires to vote she is unwomanly, and consequently no fair representative of her sex, if she does not desire to vote, well and good, she need not, it results from this that only those women who have very superior firmness of character have had the courage to come out as champions of their sex. And when we see what they have been called upon to endure in consequence, it is no longer a wonder that so few women are ready to battle for the cause; but matter for surprise that any have dared to brave the fearful ordeal.

I believe that never since the world began was any reform movement so villified, so misrepresented, so assailed with most cowardly and contemptible weapons as this has been. It is always possible to ridicule any one, no matter how impracticable he may be in mind, morals, and appearance, and from the time when little, earnest-eyed Lucy Stone [abolitionist, suffragist and orator] was described as a coarse, masculine virago, so that to this day many persons suppose her to be a six-foot stentor-voiced creature, up to last week, when a feeble and absurd caricature in an obscene weekly paper, did flagrant injustice to four of the finest looking women concerned in the movement, there has been a persistent attempt on the part of all the newspapers, by personal ridicule and villification, to choke down the whole thing. And this warfare, too, has not been confined to a few journals, but *all* the influential papers except those devoted to the cause, from the few leading dailies of New York to the small weekly magazines and provincial gazettes have had a fling at the champions of Woman's Rights. . . .

And not content with personal attacks, with describing an assemblage of well-dressed and fine looking women as a "drabbled and dilapidated crowd of spectacled old maids," and asserting that every one carried a "baggy blue cotton umbrella," they have descended to absolute and wilful misrepresentation of them in reporting any meeting of the friends of Woman Suffrage, misstating the numbers and even suppressing the names of those who really took part in the proceedings, and dragging forward as speakers those who had nothing whatever to do with the meeting except as spectators. . . .

And, to quit this public trial that every woman has to undergo, and consider the private view of the question, the numbers of women may be counted by scores who long for suffrage, and would like to plead for it, but they are withheld by the actual *commands* of husbands and fathers. . . .

Considering, then, this public martyrdom which any woman must endure, and the private denunciation she must suffer in joining the Woman Suffrage party, it speaks well for the deep-seated, earnest desire there is among them for political freedom, that so many, and those, too, among the most thoughtful and brilliant women of the land, have come forward to enrol [*sic*] themselves among its members; and each one of these may be taken as representing fifty who would like to join the movement but have not got the strength to defy the old shackles of education and conventionality, and claim for themselves that absolute freedom that is the birthright of every American. . . .

L. D. B.
July 22, 1869

Problems for Ten Thousand Women

Desiring to sit at the feet of the gentle women who "shrink from the notoriety of the public eye" and learn from them, we ask them, in all simplicity, the following questions, trusting that a regard for their own "peace and happiness," which they charge us with having placed in "grave peril," will lead them to give us answers good and true:

Dear ladies, are you "the working women of this country?" and if you are not, how can you understand their trials, their wants or their wrongs, or judge intelligently of the proper remedy?

Have you traveled through the land, visited the homes, and ascertained to a certainty that you "represent the sober convictions of the majority of the women of the country?"

Does the petition of 100,000 women of America, asking for the privilege and immunities of citizenship, indicate only "exceptional discontent?". . . .

Do you watch anxiously for your own names, morning after morning, in the most conspicious columns of the daily press, to see whether the minutest article of the dress you wore the previous evening is properly described; and don't you sometimes wonder that such a faithful record is kept of what you wear, and that nobody seems to remember anything you say?

Can it enter into your delicate minds to conceive that the ladies who find in the same column their names held up to ridicule and contempt; their language and sentiments misrepresented; their aims misunderstood, their reputation wantonly attacked, yet who stand, year after year, in simple traveling dress, before large audiences, steadfastly maintaining the justice, and profoundly believing in the ultimate triumph of their cause, may be as sensitive, as highly bred, as finely organized as you?

If they were not inspired by a noble purpose, reaching far beyond all personal considerations, could they bear so much and bear it so patiently?

"All the rights I want"

If they sought only the admiration of the multitude, would they not take your own easy way to win it? . . .

Mrs. H. C. Spencer
February 23, 1871

Indignant Scorn for *All Men*

Petaluma, Cal.

Dear Friends of the *Revolution*: . . . The sentiments in your valuable paper seem like echoes of my own thoughts years ago on this subject. I can well remember the indignant scorn with which that sentence in the constitution, that *"all men* are created free and equal,"* filled me whenever I heard it read or spoken. . . .

Mrs. A. A. Haskell
September 16, 1869

Man's Chivalry to Woman

The principle of Equal Rights, the key-note of American civilization, is the pivot on which this whole question turns. Here our argument is grounded on a rock. The Declaration of Independence declares that "all men are created equal;" equal, not in capacities, but in rights. The Constitution of Massachusetts, following the Declaration, says: "All men are born free and equal." It must be conceded by all that the word "men" here includes both sexes. . . .

But women do not ask to be enfranchised. True, as a class, they do not, but the question of right and duty is not changed in the least by this fact. Many have already asked, both in this country and in England, but their petitions have been unheeded. Shall we wait, then, till all have asked? There may have been slaves that did not ask for freedom, but was that an argument against emancipation? Because the majority of women do not wish to vote, shall even one woman whose property is taxed be deprived of equal representation? Because one man does not wish to go to the polls, shall his neighbor, therefore, be denied the right to go?

But we are told that the result of the whole ballot would remain the same, and so nothing be gained. This objection, if true, does not in any sense whatever affect the question under consideration. Suppose that two men vote opposite tickets, shall they be disfranchised because their votes neutralize each other? If so, then may one party cancel another of equal number, and so all be disfranchised together. This objection places no value on a vote only as it subserves party interests, and ignores the duty and obligation of all to defend what they believe to be right?

If women vote, they must also do military duty; the ballot and bullet are inseparable. This is but a repetition of the old idea, that one class may rule another by virtue of its power to do so. The idea is neither true in theory nor in practice. If ability to serve in the field is the test by which the right of Suffrage is determined, then let it be applied to man as well as woman. Two-thirds, or more, of men are unfit for military service, on account of age or physical disability; shall they, therefore, be disfranchised? . . . . Men are required only to do that work in public defense for which they are best fitted; let equally rational requisitions be made on women, and they will acquit themselves, as they always have done, in a manner that *should* put to blush many of the aristocratic sex.

But women may relieve themselves of all political responsibility, by intrusting their interests to their husbands, fathers, brothers, or sons. This statement involves a moral impossibility; for it assumes that a right or duty of one may be performed by another, which is simply impossible. It is the old appeal for class power. The same argument has been urged against the operatives in England, and against the negroes in our own country. . . .

It has been said that "the scheme of the ballot for woman would give the country up to Romanism [Roman Catholicism]." If true, this objection is very grave and startling. An examination of facts, however, will show that it is only one of those "blear illusions" by which spectral-sighted conservatism is so often cheated. The Catholic population is about one-eighth of the entire population of the country. The relative strength of Catholicism to Protestantism in the United States, then, is expressed by the ratio of 1 to 8. Now, granting that our vote would be doubled by giving woman the ballot, who would be the gainer? . . .

A certain clergyman, somewhat notorious as the avowed champion of the conservative side of this question, professes to think that by the use of the ballot "woman would unsex herself and become a monster;" that the laws of nature would be reversed; and, more wonderful still, that 30,000 men would be driven from the stores and counting-rooms of Boston and New York and compelled to find homes in the West, thus taking away 30,000 chances of marriage from the females of these two cities. These objections, particularly the last, have, at least, the merit of originality. Of course, it never occurred to the reverend gentleman that wives are as indispensable in the West as here in New England.

"All the rights I want"

It is to be hoped that the ladies of our eastern cities will not take alarm at this novel prediction, and so attempt to anticipate the movement of the other sex by a general stampede to the west on their own part.

But it is unwomanly to vote and hold office. From 1797 to 1807 women were allowed to vote in the State of New Jersey, but history has not recorded a single instance of that wonderful metamorphosis by which woman is supposed to "unsex" herself and become a "monster." . . .

It is alleged that the sentiment of romance would be destroyed. Do not women mingle with the very same men at political meetings that they would meet at the polls? . . .

But women must not come in contact with such disorder, profanity, and vulgarity as is generally witnessed at the polls. Very true, they should not, nor should men. . . .

We have now passed in review the principal objections to giving woman the ballot; and we find that the majority of them, if not all, prove the necessity of the reform. They spring mainly from the conservative instincts of humanity, and are objections to those only who seek to know what is expedient before knowing what is right. Conservatism is always shocked at the idea of reform, and shrinks from it as an unholy thing. Instead of maintaining the right, with all its consequences, it is forever tormenting itself with the problem of expediency. Female Suffrage is right, and therefore expedient. It is one of the essential links in the great chain of progressive civilization. It may meet with opposition, as indeed, every reform does, but all this opposition is but the alarm of the great clock of human progress, which is soon to strike the hour, when all enlightened nations shall recognize not only manhood suffrage, but also Woman Suffrage.

September 30, 1869

Woman As Soldier

The National Women, in Convention assembled, give notice to the country that in claiming the ballot they do not overlook "the logical fact of its being accompanied by the right to be voted for." There is another logical fact which we fear they do overlook. It is that Suffrage has duties as well as privileges. We should like to hear of their accepting the logical fact that they ought not to demand the one and shirk the other. – N. Y. *Tribune.*

"Duties as well as privileges." I presume that shouldering the musket is one of the "duties" that the editor [Horace Greeley] of the New York *Tribune* thinks women would be inclined to "shirk." I should like to know his reasons for not shouldering *his* during the late war. He certainly did not, and yet I have never heard of his resigning his right to the ballot in consequence; he still claims that "privilege" while shirking the aforesaid "duty." . . .

C.

February 11, 1869

Behind Time

A widow . . . writes us the following. She shows that she does not know how much ground we have gone over in twenty years, nor how strongly we have pressed the importance of the very point she never saw until she felt it in her own case:

Dear Friend: . . . "Women's Rights women" do not work at the right end of things; they must educate the young ladies, make it popular for them to study the laws of the state of New York, till they know before they are married what they will be when married – that when married they have lost their identity and their individuality – that they are classed with infants, idiots, and insane people. . . .

We sent this friend one of our speeches made on the laws in 1854. These people who wake up at the eleventh hour are very apt to think that those who went before them "are not working at the right end of things."

March 19, 1868

Slings and Arrows

A fashionable friend writes us:

. . . I hate all great pow-wows for any purpose whatever, and I never have been able to bring myself to mix publicly in the Woman's Movement, perhaps, because I am really more "Woman's Rights" than the agitators of the question. That is, I so hate any recognition of the arbitrary distinctions which men have founded on sex, and so detest the necessity of a woman making a fuss about herself as a woman, and am so certain that a few more years of the rapid progress we are making in all

228

directions will inevitably give woman her right status as a free human being, that I have never felt called to put so much of myself into the movement as perhaps I ought, since I am all right on the theory. And, no doubt I shall make a sorry figure in the day of judgment when Susan B. Anthony & Co., get their crowns of martyrdom. . . .

. . . Tell me what you consider the cause of this progress, on which you are falling back with such charming, self-indulgent reliance. Does progress come like the rising of the sun without human agency? Will it roll on and "inevitably give woman her right status," while she, meanwhile, sits with folded hands? What is progress but the result of persevering, untiring labor! . . .

. . . Your freedom from suffering gives you this calm, delightful trust in the future. It reminds me of a clown in the classic fable who, seeing a man bring down a bird with an arrow, said to him, "you might have saved your arrow, the fall would have killed him!"

May 8, 1869

★★Opposing Strong-Minded Women★★

One of the most promising features of the woman's movement at present, is the open opposition from the women themselves. There are several ladies in different parts of the country, now lecturing against the extensi[on] of Suffrage to women. They probably do not see that taking the rostrum is a fatal step in that direction.

When a woman so far oversteps her prescribed sphere as to express her opinion in a mixed assembly of men and women, it will not be very difficult for her quietly to slip it into the ballot-box in the presence of four inspectors.

We warn Miss Emma Webb, who lectured in Brooklyn, a few evenings since, in ridicule of strong-minded women, that she is in great danger of being ranked in that category herself. . . .

October 14, 1869

★★No More Rights Wanted★★

Portland

Dear Revolution: I have just reached home, but I cannot sleep, until I have answered what follows for your admirable paper. Please give it [the quoted letter] a place, and allow my notes to follow.

229

To the Editor of the R. I. *Bulletin*:

. . . I would not "refuse to relieve a case of destitution, if brought to my notice:" but I do not believe there is a woman in America who can justly complain of oppression, destitution, or suffering, through the laws of the land. . . .

I cannot but think that all this cry for "Woman's Rights" is but the hungry craving of an unsatisfied woman's heart. Her throne and kingdom are her home; her high heaven of heavens is in her husband's heart. And while she retains her proper place, and merits the respect of man, her influence is three-fold stronger than it could be were she masculine as she wishes to become. I agree with the western editor who said, "a true woman, one fitted to be a wife and mother, would no sooner touch a vote than she would a coal of fire or a rattlesnake." . . .

C. P. B.

And so Mrs. C. P. B., the dear creature, is one of the *contented* women of Rhode Island. One of the short-sighted, sleepy women, rather, who, not understanding their true condition, wholly mistake their duty. *Contented*, forsooth! – just so with the *contented* slaves, who had no right to their own earnings, their own bodies, their own souls, not even to their own babies . . .

"I don't believe," she says, "there is *a woman in America who can justly complain of oppression*, destitution, or suffering, through the laws of the land!" What an egregious simpleton! Does she ever read a newspaper? or ever look into the records of our criminal courts? . . .

"I cannot but think that all this cry for Woman's Rights is but the *hungry craving of an unsatisfied woman's heart*." Gracious Heaven, dear sister, do you know what you are saying? This very belief which you so triumphantly or unguardedly avow – I know not which – is just what all these women believe who are clamoring for Woman's Rights, and whom you are taking to task in the newspapers. You are with them therefore, without knowing it. Bethink you, I pray – whence comes "the *hungry craving of an unsatisfied woman's heart?*" Ask yourself and you may reach the truth by intuition, if not by reasoning. . . .

John Neal★
November 4, 1869

[★ Neal had been a supporter of and lecturer on woman's rights since 1832.]

"All the rights I want"
Women Versus Women

A Protest

. . . We feel that our *present* duties fill up the whole measure of our time and abilities; and that they are such as none but ourselves can perform.

Their importance requires us to protest against all efforts to compel us to assume those obligations which cannot be separated from Suffrage; but which cannot be performed by *us*, without the sacrifice of the highest interest of our families, and of society.

It is our fathers, brothers, husbands and sons, who represent us at the ballot-box. Our fathers and brothers love us. Our husbands are our choice, and one with us. Our sons are what *we* make them.

We are content that they represent us in the cornfield, the battle-field, and at the ballot-box, and we them, in the school-room, at the fireside, and at the cradle; believing our representation, even at the ballot-box, to be thus more full and impartial than it could possibly be, were all women allowed to vote.

We do, therefore, respectively protest against legislation to establish "Woman's Suffrage" in our land, or in any part of it.

The above paper, signed by more than one hundred ladies of Lorain country, was presented March 14, 1870, to the legislature assembled at Columbus, Ohio.

That so many signed is not strange, because the non-suffrage side is the popular one at present. Years hence, when it shall be customary for woman to vote, it is questionable whether the lady who drew up this document would have many supporters. . . .

Two things we do certainly find in the Bible with regard to this matter; that women are to bear children, and men to earn bread. The first duty we believe has been confined entirely to the female sex, but the male sex have not kept the other in all cases.

If anybody has belonged for any considerable time to a benevolent institution, he has ascertained that women sometimes are obliged to earn bread and bear children also. . . .

Is it not *barely* possible, seeing that [women's] condition is so constantly changing, that we are not exactly performing all that He intended us to do? that the nineteenth century is not perhaps, after all, the millennium for women? and whether we know definitely *what* duties God has imposed upon us?

In the year 2,000, it is not improbable that women, walking side

231

by side with husbands, fathers and brothers in all great and good things, shall say, if possibly this protest shall go down to posterity, what reason had those good people to say that the golden heights for woman had been reached? . . .

I am glad these ladies made this protest, not only because this is a country where honest views ought to be expressed, but because agitation pushes forward reform. . . .

Sarah Knowles Bolton
April 21, 1870

The True Question

One of the arguments most frequently advocated by those who oppose woman's suffrage is that the majority of women do not themselves desire the franchise. But granting this to be the case, does it prove that a thing is not desirable for a class because that class may not happen to desire it? . . .

Even in our own country the demand for the emancipation of our millions of slaves did not first come from the bondmen. It was the most common argument of the slaveholder that his slaves did not desire their freedom, and, no doubt, this was, in many instances, true; but had not one slave desired liberty, would it have been less desirable?

When the question was asked them privately, "Do you wish to be free?" the reply was almost invariably in the negative. But it occurred to some few of the inquirers that to ask a slave this question when his reply in the affirmative could do him no possible good, and might do him a good deal of harm by exciting suspicion against him, was not the surest way of arriving at the true state of the slave's sentiments.

Did it ever occur to the opponents of woman's suffrage, who so triumphantly proclaim the feminine indifference to the ballot, that very possibly they may not have discovered the exact state of the opinion of the women on this subject. . . .

September 22, 1870

The Anti-Woman's Suffrage Movement

The following petition is now being signed by many ladies in this and other cities:

Should the person receiving this approve of the object in view, his or her aid is respectfully requested to obtain signatures to the annexed petition, which may, after having been signed, be returned to either of the following-named persons:

Mrs. Gen. W. T. Sherman, Mrs. John A. Dahlgren . . . Mrs. Catherine E. Beecher, No. 69 West Thirty-eighth street, New York City.

Please attach to this a paper for signatures.

The petition of the undersigned, to the Congress of the United States, protesting against an extension of the suffrage to women:

We, the undersigned, do hereby appeal to your honorable body, and desire respectfully to enter our protest against an extension of suffrage to women; and in the firm belief that our petition represents the sober, convictions of the majority of the women of the country.

Although we shrink from the notoriety of the public eye, yet we are too deeply and painfully impressed by the grave perils which threaten our peace and happiness in these proposed changes in our civil and political rights longer to remain silent.

Because, Holy Scripture inculcates a different, and for us, higher sphere, apart from the public life.

Because, as women we find a full measure of duties, cares and responsibilities devolving upon us, and we are therefore unwilling to beat other and heavier burdens, and those unsuited to our physical organizations.

Because, we hold that an extension of suffrage would be adverse to the interest of the working women of the country, with whom we heartily sympathize.

Because these changes must introduce a fruitful element of discord in the existing marriage relation, which would tend to the infinite detriment of children, and increase the already alarming prevalence of divorce throughout the land.

Because no general law, affecting the condition of all women, should be framed to meet exceptional discontent.

For these and many more reasons, do we beg of your wisdom that no law extending suffrage to women may be passed, as the passage of such a law would be fraught with danger so grave to the general order of the country.

We are at a loss which most to admire in this singular document, the modesty of the assumption, that the petitioners "represent the sober convictions of the majority of the women of the country," or that "shrinking from the notoriety of the public eye" which induces the ladies who have drawn up this manifesto to thrust themselves into the most prominent position which women could possibly assume.

We cannot admit their first statement. Many women in our country have given little thought to the question of female suffrage, but the majority of those who have arrived at "sober convictions" on the subject, are *not* opposed to the extension of the franchise.

As to the second count, we admit at once their modest shrinking from public notice, but can only say that these ladies have taken a singular method of showing their desire for the seclusioh of private life.

With regard to the third article, as we are unaware what especial duties Holy Scriptures inculcate upon Mrs. Gen. Sherman, Mrs. Dahlgren and the other signers included in the generic term "us," we shall not attempt without further information on the subject to dispute that proposition.

In reply to the fourth plea, for exemption from other and heavier burdens, we would suggest to these ladies that it is not proposed by the most radical of the advocates of the Sixteenth Amendment to force every woman to go to the polls. Perhaps they are not aware that even among men it is not obligatory to cast a ballot. With this crumb of comfort let us pass on to the next reason of the petitioners – the injury the ballot would do to the working woman. Why that instrument of political power which, in the hands of laboring men, raises them into such importance that their interests absorb the attention of every legislative body in the land, and which has made their condition so superior to that of the laboring women, should be fatal to the welfare of their toiling sisters, is a sort of logic which we confess we have not the profundity to grasp. Why is there an eight hour law for working men, and no hint of such a thing for working women? The reply that occurs to us is that the working men are a power which it is worth while for legislators to conciliate, and the working women are not. This answer commends itself to our common sense, although opposed to the logic of the aristocratic ladies who so deeply sympathize with the working women.

As to the most alarming statement, that Woman Suffrage would destroy domestic peace, tend to the detriment of children, and increase the prevalence of divorce, we must beg to know if that much boasted glory of our republic, universal male franshise, is the fruitful source of all domestic woes? This is an entirely new discovery. The subject of matrimonial infelicities has been widely discussed, but never until now has this root of the matter been touched upon. Has feminine intuition hit upon the hidden cause of the ills of our society? If the ballot in the hands of woman would increase all this, does it not follow naturally enough that the ballot in the hands of man must have caused the present social disturbances? Is this logic, good ladies? If withholding the franchise from woman will prevent any increase of family discords, wouldn't taking it from men still further tend to promote the household peace?

The last reason given is, that laws should not be "framed to meet exceptional discontent."

With all deference to the ladies of this petition we would suggest that it is hardly worth while to say what laws should *not* rest upon. It seems a much easier and more comprehensive statement to say that laws should be framed to meet the demands of justice.

It is not for the soothing of discontented men or women that law-makers attempt to frame codes. Justice is invoked for the sake of the best interests of society. And women ask the ballot because it is just that they should in a republican government have a voice in the laws which they equally with men are bound to obey.

If the "many more reasons" which the anti-suffrage ladies tell us lastly they have to offer, but which they kindly refrain from pressing upon us, are no better than the specimens they have given us, we must confess that we are not convinced that it is our duty to sign their petition ourselves or to endeavor to induce others to do so.

July 21, 1870

Advice to the Strong-Minded

In the May number of the *Public Spirit*, a new monthly for the million, Mr. [David] Croly, one of the editors of the *World*, addressed a letter to us on the question of Woman's Rights. . . .

Mr. Croly's article closes with much excellent advice to the women of the metropolis, as to the various public works they should do.

He says they should take charge of the public health, of our streets, tenement houses, jails, prisons, asylums, superintend the schools, the press, the halls of legislation. They should suppress drunkenness, gambling, licentiousness, legislative corruption, and immoral advertisements in public journals, and the wholesale murder of innocents in hospitals and badly ventilated school-rooms;

and after we do all these things systematically and well, then, he thinks, we shall prove our calling and election sure to the right of the ballot. In other words, being women, we are to make bricks without straw, learn to swim without going near the water, regulate public abuses without a voice in the laws, being supernaturally endowed, we are to do without the ballot what man is wholly unable to do with it. These are the very things we want to do; all we ask is the authority of the State. Make us school superintendents, prison and street inspectors, a uniformed police, and pay us for the discharge of these duties! That is the point Mr. Croly forgot! Somehow women's duties are always gratuitous. . . .

Elizabeth Cady Stanton
May 21, 1868

Troublesome Women

A celebrated lawyer once said that the three most troublesome clients he ever had were a young lady who wanted to be married, a married woman who wanted a divorce, and an old maid who didn't know what she wanted. – Trenton (N.J.) *Union Sentinel.*

Yet if that "celebrated" gentleman was like most lawyers he would have held up his hands in conservative horror at the proposition to widen the sphere of these women so as to allow a proper and useful exercise of their misdirected energy. . . .

If this "celebrated" gentleman found himself shut out by a social ostracism stronger than law from every employment to which he found himself congenial, how long would it be before his groping after some direction in which he might spend his God-given powers without offending "delicacy," would make him as "troublesome" to those around him as the women of whom he complains.

June 4, 1868

Let The *Fair* Sex Determine Rights

"The Revolution". – This is the [name] of a weekly journal devoted to Woman Suffrage and the rights of the fair sex in general, and is a very able aid to the cause of Woman's Rights. We like its independence. We want to see the dear creatures have their rights – all the rights nature intended them to have. The terms of subscription are $2.00 a year. [The Delaware (Ohio) *Weekly Herald*]

And let us be the judges of nature's intentions. Somehow, we have lost faith in man's interpretations of higher laws.

July 30, 1868

Who Let Her?

"If a woman wants to chop wood, *why let her.*" – Horace Greeley.

Already comments upon this text have appeared in your paper, on reading which, – this question suggested itself: Who, or what is to let her?

Is it the laws of the land? Is it public opinion? Is it woman's husband as her nearest male relative? or is it Horace Greeley [N. Y. *Tribune* editor]? Perhaps he'd be glad of the chance. I hope he will be gallant enough to turn round and wash the dishes.

There is a great deal implied in the giving of the *gracious* permission. When a woman chops wood, she does it of her own free will, and nobody *lets* or hinders, most especially no one hinders. Women that labor don't generally experience any difficulty of that kind; nobody hinders them from doing all that they possibly can and that of the hardest kind of work too. Women already have such liberties. . . .

Mrs. H. S. Brooks
Chicago
March 31, 1870

★★I Am Not A . . .★★

I am not an advocate, nor even a convert, to the theory of "Woman Suffrage" but am to woman's sufferings. . . .★

F.
April 7, 1870

[★ The preface "I am not a feminist but" to an argument for woman's rights has many historical antecedents, all designed to forestall the often powerful and personally cruel criticism of those opposed to furtherance of woman's rights. In the nineteenth century it was often "I am no ranter for woman's rights, yet. . ." or "I am no supporter of unwomanly women but. . ."]

237

10
Becoming perfect nuisances

Introduction

Working for woman's rights, in both the nineteenth and twentieth centuries, has taken courage. This section contains excerpts detailing some of the courageous activities of the reform workers during these years of *The Revolution* and the advice given to other women to agitate for more control over their lives.

In the women's press of the 1850s, editors and contributors had debated the relative desirability of "talk" and "action." For example, *The Woman's Advocate* editor, Anne McDowell, chided the writers of the more literary woman's newspaper, *The Una*, for seeming to think that writing about heroines in medicine and about woman's rights conventions (which McDowell called "windy resolutions" by "mutual admiration societies") was sufficient for reform. Women needed profitable employment, she stated. In truth, although their focuses and audiences differed somewhat, all the women's press editors believed that women needed opportunities for good education (that is, much more than training in domestic tasks) and for profitable work. And the editors were generally supportive of agitation beyond the writing and publishing of periodicals.

Elizabeth Cady Stanton, who wrote analytic pieces as well as advocate essays for several of the woman's rights papers in the 1850s, declared at a 1852 temperance meeting that it is primarily agitation that convinces the public mind. This includes, she said, giving lectures, distributing tracts, editing and supporting newspapers – and withholding money and efforts from organizations which send the gospel abroad or send men to seminaries or build gorgeous church buildings, while ignoring the suffering in this country's cities. Paulina Wright Davis, a pioneering lecturer on women's anatomy and physiology in the 1840s and editor of the woman's rights newspaper *The Una* in the 1850s, wrote that in order to impress the seriousness of the injustices women suffer "forcibly upon the public mind," woman's rights activists might have to "pass through the fiery furnace" (*The Una*, February 1855). Many of the women working for dress and health reforms themselves wore short skirts and trousers – and were ridiculed by jeers on the streets and in the men's press. (For information on the activists of the 1850s see Russo and Kramarae, 1990.) Women lecturing on women's health, suffrage, temperance, abolition of slavery, and marriage sometimes attracted large, curious crowds out to see a woman speak, and they also attracted much negative criticism in the men's press.

Any openly declared support (signing a petition for woman suffrage, keeping one's name when marrying, attending woman's rights conventions) was courageous, and many had to pass through the fiery furnace of approbation in the media and in their homes. Meanwhile, *The Revolution* editors praised individual and collective actions of independence, self-protection and confrontation.

These actions took many forms. Some women refused to pay taxes or paid under protest. Dr Harriet Hunt of Boston was one of those women. In her efforts to advance woman's rights, she became publicly visible. She applied for admission to Harvard Medical School and was eventually allowed to attend lectures there in 1850, but was forced out by students. (She had already acquired a great deal of medical knowledge and practice; she later received an honorary MD from the Female Medical College of Philadelphia.) She had earlier made connections between women's medical needs and the exploitation of women's labor and exclusion from many educational opportunities. In 1851 she began paying her taxes under protest; her annual letter of protest was published in the woman's press.

In 1858 Lucy Stone refused to pay property taxes and her household goods were sold at auction. (Purchased by a supportive neighbor, they were returned to her.) The author Lydia Maria Child also paid under protest. In Connecticut, sisters Abby and Julia Smith refused to pay; their cows were confiscated. Susan B. Anthony paid the taxes on the sales of *Revolution* copies, but her payment was accompanied by a letter of protest, published in *The Revolution* at the same time.

Another way women took direct action and made perfect nuisances of themselves was in trying to vote. Because of an "error" in a hastily constructed state constitution, women had voted at times in New Jersey until 1807. Lucy Stone led campaigns in that state for women to challenge the state constitution by voting. In 1868, more than a hundred women in Sturgis, Michigan, marched together to the polls to vote for prohibition. *The Revolution* carried an account and reminded women that issues involving schools, poverty and crime were also issues upon which women wanted a voting voice. The women of Vineland, NJ, illegally went to the polls several times. In Rochester, NY, sixteen women (Anthony, four relatives, and eleven neighbors) voted in 1872. Anthony was arrested, charged and tried in a court of law for having "knowingly, wrongfully, and unlawfully voted for a representative to the Congress of the United States." She used the weeks before her trial to campaign for woman's rights throughout the county. The prosecution asked for the trial to be moved to another county, whereupon Anthony and co-worker Matilda Joslyn Gage spoke in all districts of *that* county. Anthony used the trial to speak for what she called "my natural rights, my civil rights, my political rights" which were being violated by "this so-called Republican government." She was fined $100, which she refused to pay.

Anthony and her many supporters were able to publicize her protest in part because she was a nationally known woman's rights campaigner. Many other women who made statements and took actions in contradiction to the social and political law had to then return to houses and situations governed by those laws. Their rebellion often meant increased suffering. (See Carroll, 1989, for discussions of the many direct action protests of feminists through the centuries.)

This section records only a fistful of the many types of women's inciting actions recorded in *The Revolution*. Read the other sections in this volume for additional reports.

Bibliography

Bacon, Margaret Hope. 1986. *Mothers of Feminism: The Story of Quaker Women in America*. San Francisco: Harper & Row.

Carroll, Berenice A. 1989. "'Women Take Action!' Women's Direct Action and Social Change." In Berenice A. Carroll and Jane E. Mohraz, eds. "In a Great Company of Women: Women's Nonviolent Direct Action," special issue of *Women's Studies International Quarterly* 12, No. 1: 3–24.

Hewitt, Nancy A. 1984. *Women's Activism and Social Change: Rochester, New York, 1822–1872*. Ithaca and London: Cornell University Press.

Martin, Theodora Penny. 1987. *The Sound of Our Own Voices: Women's Study Clubs 1860–1910.* Boston: Beacon Press.

Steiner, Linda Claire. 1979. "The Woman's Suffrage Press, 1850–1900: A Cultural Analysis." Doctoral dissertation. University of Illinois, Urbana-Champaign.

Women at the Polls

From an eye witness of that wonderful scene in Michigan, one hundred and fourteen women marching up to the polls to vote, we receive this "spicy" letter. . . .

Sturgis, Mich.

. . . [W]e must tell you what occurred in our town on election day; one hundred and fourteen women went to the polls and put in their ballots for "prohibition," two by two the long line filed along the streets, looking grandly; significant of what is to come we entered the uncleanly place, deposited our votes, the men pressing back to leave room for us to pass around the box and walk out. Our men seemed to take it in good faith and behaved very much to their credit.

S. A. Gray

This settles the common objection that respectable women would not go to the polls. The moment that woman understands that our colleges, schools, streets, tenement houses, jails and prisons are all subjects of legislation, she will feel it is her solemn duty to use her influence to the utmost to improve the surroundings of her sons and daughters in the great world, as well as in the family circle. . . .

May 7, 1868

The People's Party

The two great political parties have met in solemn convention, and declared themselves. With the usual amount of canvassing and maneuvering they have nominated their condidates and built their platforms. The parties are so nearly alike in all they propose that it is not of the slightest consequence to the people which one triumphs. The masses will be no more taxed or oppressed under one dynasty than the other, for they are equally corrupt, selfish and partisan, neither seeking the good of the nation, but their own self aggrandisement. . . .

241

If these political platforms express the average thought of those who think at all, and the masses are ready to follow in their wake to share the fate of all republics that have gone before, then it is vain to propose new leaders, and a new road to peace and safety; but if the murmurs of discontent we hear among women, negroes, working men, and the few great souls that feel the mighty sorrows of the masses, though safe above want and oppression themselves, are as widespread as they seem, then let the educators of public sentiment turn from old parties and old principles, and with one simultaneous move galvanize the laboring classes into a new and higher life, teach them what their true interests are, and what laws are needed to secure to them food, clothes and homes, virtue and education, time to read and rest, and to cultivate that higher nature that is to live for ever. . . .

To this end, as an exhibition of the moral determination of the people to secure the safety and stability of this republic, let us call a national convention of all those outside party trammels [confines], and make a platform worthy the eventful times in which we live, and nominate for the highest offices under government men who are worthy the suffrages of a thoughtful, conscientious people. Until every citizen shall be clothed with all his rights, and feel a personal responsibility for the nation's welfare, our republicanism, our democracy, is a sham, and our boasted experiment of self-government remains untried.

Elizabeth Cady Stanton
July 16, 1868

Voting of Vineland Women

Vineland, N. J.

At a meeting of women held the week before election, a unanimous vote was taken that we would go to the polls on the 3d of Nov. . . .

At 7½ a.m., on November 3d, John and Portia Gage and myself entered Union Hall, where the judges of election had already established themselves for the day. . . .

As time passed, there came more of men and women into the Hall. Quite a number of the latter presented their votes first, at the table where those of men were received. When they were rejected, and this was done with politeness, they were taken to the other side of the platform, and deposited in our box. . . .

Some women spent the day in going after their friends and bringing them to the Hall. Young ladies, after voting, went to the homes of their acquaintances, and took care of their babies, while they came out to vote. Will this fact lessen the alarm of some men for the safety of the babies of enfranchised women on election day? . . .

The result of the ballots cast by the women of Vineland is this: For President – Grant, one hundred and sixty-four; Seymour, four; E. Cady Stanton, two; Fremont, one; and Mrs. Gov. Harvey of Wis., one. . . .

E. A. Kingsbury
November 19, 1868

Vineland Town Meeting

Editors of the Revolution:

Enclosed is the state of the Women's vote in Vineland at our town election, March 9th. Number of votes cast by women of "legal age," one hundred and eighty-two, and some of our best women. The same ticket cast by legal voters, and counted, eighty-nine. The writer of this was present at the polls a considerable portion of the day, but heard no unpleasant remarks made by the *gentlemen* present, curiosity having subsided since the November elections; everything passed off quietly and orderly.

S.
March 18, 1869

Sorosis

This is the name of a new club of literary women, who meet once a month and lunch at Delmonico's to discuss questions of art, science, literature and government.*

Alice Cary,* who is President, in her opening speech, states the object of the club, which is summed up in this brief extract:

We have then, to begin at the beginning, proposed the inculcation of deeper and broader ideas among women, proposed to teach them to think for themselves and get their opinions at first hand, not so much because it is their right as because it is their duty. We have also proposed to open out new avenues of employment to women – to make them less dependent and less burdensome – to lift them out of unwomanly self-distrust and disqualifying diffidence into womanly self-respect and self-knowledge. . . .

243

The editors of the New York press have made known their dissatisfaction that no gentlemen were to be admitted into this charmed circle.

After a calm and dispassionate discussion of this question, it was decided to exclude gentlemen, not because their society was not most desirable and would add brilliancy to the club, but from a fear lest the natural reverence of woman for man might embarrass her in beginning to reason and discuss; lest she should be awed to silence by their superior presence. It was not because they love man less but their own improvement more.

For the comfort of these ostracised ones, we would suggest a hope for the future. After these ladies become familiar with parliamentary tactics, and the grave questions that are to come before them for consideration, it is proposed to admit gentlemen to the galleries, that they may enjoy the same privileges vouchsafed to the fair sex in the past, to look down upon the feast, to listen to the speeches, and to hear "the pale, thoughtful brow," "the silken moustache," "the flowing locks," "the manly gait and form" toasted in prose and verse.

Elizabeth Cady Stanton
May 14, 1868

[* Sorosis was organized as a result of the exclusion of a woman journalist, Jennie June (June Cunningham Croly) from an all-male banquet given by the New York Press Club for Charles Dickens. Within one year there were eighty-three members. Though Sorosis is generally described as the beginning of the US "women's club movement" of the late nineteenth century, there were women's literary clubs as well as numerous (Black and white) women's benevolent societies throughout the century. See the appendix for biographical information on Alice Cary.]

Sorosis and the Woman's Parliament

New York,

To the Editor of The Tribune:

Sir: Sorosis is *not* in the least danger of disruption. None of its members are in favor of committing the society to the "extremely advanced views of Mrs. Elizabeth Cady Stanton and Miss Anna Dickinson," but the reverse. Sorosis desires to hold itself aloof from political claims and discussion. The Woman's Parliament is neither more nor less than a select convention of ladies of talent who meet *by invitation* to discuss questions of social science which properly interest their sex. . . .

. . . It is so anxious to preserve a reputation for discretion and womanly decorum in all things that it will not hesitate to discard any disturbing element with promptness, no matter what it may lose in talent by doing so. It regrets that its record should be misinterpreted. To make womanly women is the highest aim of Sorosis. Very respectfully,

Shirley Dane

When this Paliament is to meet is not yet fully decided, but we hope "the womanly women," throughout the country will be present and take part in its deliberations. We have no doubt after assembling in their conventions a dozen years, to discuss woman's wants and needs, they will be ready for the "extremely advanced views" that Miss Dickinson and Mrs. Stanton hold to-day. . . .★

October 14, 1869

[★ It must have taken courage to join this New York City's woman's club, which was held in suspicion by the men's press and by husbands of some of the women. Sorosis held many receptions to honor women of achievement "to affect the social marks of distinction bestowed by men upon men." In 1873 Sorosis sponsored a meeting to which 400 women responded and formed the Association for the Achievement of Women. In 1890 Sorosis was responsible for the formation of the General Federation of Women's Clubs. Most of the study clubs had educational aims.]

★★Self-Help Clubs★★

Mrs. Celia Burleigh★ well says: "I hold among the best things that the world has in its keeping the friendship of good women, the coming together of such women for something better than mere amusement, or to while away an idle half hour; with a desire for self-improvement, with the earnest wish to make the most and the best of their powers, to be helpful to each other and to humanity, to illustrate the dignity and the power of a cultivated, thoughtful and self-centered womanhood. To promote these ends, I wish every village and neighborhood might have a Woman's Club." We sincerely hope her suggestion will be heeded, and at once.

September 28, 1871

[★ See the Appendix for biographical information on Celia Burleigh.]

A Wife-Whipper Whipped by Women

The Milwaukee *Wisconsin* gives the following account of a scene
which shows that women . . . act in Wisconsin as men are acting
everywhere, showing that they can avenge their wrongs; that they
can fight; and wherefore should they not vote? But to the account:

Last evening one Mr. Downer preferred a charge of assault with
intent to kill against a number of his neighbors. Downer was a
sorry-looking object – his looks giving the truth to the assertion
that he had suffered some hard usage. His clothes were torn and
thoroughly soaked with water, his face was scratched, and he
held in his hand bundles of hair and whiskers which he said had
been pulled out. He was sitting in his house down on the beach,
quietly doing nothing at all to break the peace, when all the
women that lived about there entered, and before he had said a
word, assailed him with clubs, sticks, guns and brickbats, and
beat him shockingly. He knew all the women, and he wanted
them arrested and punished. A well-known citizen entered the
court-room and told the story in a manner which did not add
much to the credit of Downer. The gentleman had been on the
beach for an evening promenade, when his attention was
attracted by loud cries from a knot of shanties some distance
away. Going to them he found Downer indulging in his usual
amusement, whipping his wife, and the woman, suffering from
the blows, was uttering heart-rending cries. The gentleman, well
aware of the danger of interfering between husband and wife
when quarrelling, nevertheless was about to interfere when his
attention was attracted to the actions of a woman, who looked as
though she had the strength of a young Samson in her limbs. She
ran from shanty to shanty calling out the women, who promptly
responded, and it did not seem to be more than ten seconds
before a dozen were assembled, each armed with a mop, a
broom, a fire-shovel, or a pair of tongs. The band marched
directly to the house whence came the cries, and, without the
ceremony of knocking, entered. The gentleman followed, deeply
interested. There was a sound of voices, as if somebody was
ordering somebody else out of the house in very coarse language,
sadly mixed up with oaths. Then there was a general onslaught
upon the wife-whipper. Mops that had been soaked in dirty
water swabbed his face; blows from brooms came thick and fast
upon his head. The astonished wife-whipper dropped the subject
of his blows and looked to his own safety. He struck at one of

the women with his fist, and this brought up the rear-guard of fire-shovels and tongs. On his head came the blows thick and fast. He grappled with one of the women. The rest immediately dropped their weapons and grappled with him. Strong they were, their union perfect, and their cause just. They fairly scratched Downer upon the floor, and scratched him up again. They left the imprints of their nails upon his face, and hands, and neck. They pulled out his hair. Resist he tried to, but he was as a child in the hands of these strong-armed women, and he soon found it out. Cowed, beaten, demolished, he bellowed like a bull, and begged that they would not kill him.

August 6, 1868

Insult Answered

Two Memphis girls were insulted by a young man, who bragged that he had been too familiar with them. The girls found the young man in a depot soon after, and while one held a pistol to his head, the other gave him a good horse-whipping.

June 3, 1869

Unconscious Daring

One dark night not long ago, a burglar entered a private residence on Sixth Avenue. On ascending one flight of stairs he observed a light in a chamber, and while hesitating what to do, a large woman suddenly descended upon him, seized him by the throat, forced him down through the hall, and pushed him into the street before he had time to think. "Heroic repulse of a burglar by a woman" was the way the story appeared in the newspapers next day; but when friends called and congratulated her upon her courage, she exclaimed: "Goodness gracious! I didn't know it was a burglar! If I had, I should have been frightened half to death. I thought it was my husband come home drunk again, and I was determined he shouldn't stay in the house in that condition."

January 5, 1871

Women Casting Out Devils

The Ohio papers tell a good story of the way some brave but quiet women exorcised some evil spirits that had begun to take possession of their husbands and sons. It is said that, in the town of

247

New Paris [Ohio] a number of enterprising ladies, determined to avail themselves of their leap-year privileges, got up a "surprise party," and called upon a couple of gentlemen who had recently established a whiskey shop in that town. Armed with their knitting-work, the party marched to the saloon, helped themselves to seats, made themselves as comfortable as possible, and staid till night. Next morning the same party called again, remained throughout the day, were reinforced by a strong company of recruits toward nightfall, and did not depart till 9 o'clock. The disgusted publicans, swearing that "not a d—d man came in" during the two days, quietly pulled up stakes, packed up their unsold rum, and evacuated the town without waiting for a third visit.

February 26, 1868

Summary Justice

Petersboro, N. Y.
. . . [After an evening's discussion of political parties], we were suddenly roused [from our rest] with the drunken vagaries of some men under our windows. There being no police on duty, we decided after the midnight hour to administer summary justice ourself, in the form of a pail of water, which we found gave them an effectual start. As they staggered off, one said, "by Jove, Jammie, its ranin', let's go home." "Ah," said the other, "my Kate always raises Cain when I come home drunk, I guess I'll stay;" but on returning, another pail of water soon warned him to seek a drier latitude, not subject to such sudden and violent equinoctial gales. We would recommend this mode of warfare to the women of the retired towns, where drunken men are permitted to disturb their pleasant dreams. . . .

Elizabeth Cady Stanton
July 30, 1868

A New Suasion

Moral and legal suasion failing to uproot the liquor traffic in Clyde, Ohio, the women have organized an association called a Knitting Machine, which, without warning, marches into a drinking or billiard saloon, takes possession of the seats and quietly settles down to knitting, their avowed purpose being to "knit all the liquor-sellers out of town." In one saloon, however, the regular customers began smoking in the most furious manner, and the ladies were fairly or unfairly smoked out.

February 25, 1869

Masculinities Flee

The Owego *Times* gives account of the invasion of a gambling saloon in Apalachin, near by, by the wives and sisters of those who were fast coming to haunt and patronize it. So after consultation and due deliberation a solid phallanx of thirty-two marched right into the saloon in good order. The saloon was in full play, crowded with the masculinities of Apalachin. The unexpected sight of mothers, sisters and sweet-hearts bursting right in, was too much for them. They stood not upon the order of their going, but "goed," at once. Hats and caps were left and coat-tails stuck straight out behind. The flight was dastardly, a regular *Bull Run.* Wives saw husbands rapidly vamose, who had left home some hours previously to go up the Creek, others were caught a glimpse of who were supposed to be over at Campville on business. The ladies did not follow up the fugitives or the carnage might have been terrible. . . . It is said that the married ladies on their return, found their husbands very attentive to domestic duties. If there were any children in the house, they had one on each knee, and were kissing and fondling them as if they had never visited a saloon or spent their time and money at a card table.

April 15, 1869

A New Nuisance

An exchange says that women are becoming perfect nuisances, and to substantiate his theory adds that 1,500 women in Center County, Pennsylvania, have petitioned the Court to grant no more liquor licenses.

April 29, 1869

Tobacco

I hate tobacco. I am a clean creature, and it smells bad. Smells bad is a mild word; but I use it, being a woman. I deny your right to smell bad in my presence, or the presence of our clean sisterhood. I deny your right to poison the air of our parlors, or our bed-rooms, with your breath, or your tobacco-saturated clothing, even though you may be our husbands. Terrible creature! I think I hear you say, I am glad you are not my wife. So am I. How would you like it, had you arranged your parlor with dainty fingers, and were rejoicing in the sweet-scented mignonette, and violets, and heliotrope in the pretty vase on your table, forgetting, in your happiness, that Bridget and Biddy had vexed your soul the greater part of the day – and in your nicely-cushioned chair, were resting your spirits even more than your body, to have a man enter with that detestable bar-room odor, and spoil it all? Or worse, light a cigar or pipe in your very presence, and puff away as if it were the heaven to you which it appears to be to him.

Fanny Fern
[Sara Payson Willis Parton]
July 30, 1868

Ardent Spirits

But not to be drank nor in any way absorbed by young bloods who have voluntarily made themselves slaves to vice, are these, as they themselves announce; but young ladies of Tipton, Indiana, who seeing and being disgusted with the low habits of the young men about them have met and resolved thus:

Whereas, we mean business; therefore, be it resolved, that we will not accompany any young man to church, or any place of amusement who uses tobacco in any manner; and resolved, that we discard all young men who play billiards, euchre, or poker; and resolved, that you men who indulge in profane language need not apply; and resolved, that we will not, by "hook, look, or crook," notice any young man who indulges in lager beer or whiskey; and resolved, that we will not harbor young men known to keep late hours at night.

January 13, 1870

E Pluribus Unum

. . . [Shall we change society through restrictive laws] or shall we go deeper down, and having learned that in false marriage, false education, prolonged, monotonous and half-paid labor, we have the causes of these morbid appetites, wisely set ourselves to work, and so change the conditions of the individual, as to secure a healthy, happy, harmonious development, and thus protect society

250

by a recreation of the race. Everything short of this radical work, all attempts at a forcible repression of vice, disease and crime, will prove utterly abortive in the future as the past. Just in proportion as we exalt individual rights above all laws, constitutions, religions and governments we begin the work of moral regeneration. To-day the soldier, the prisoner, the drunkard, the woman, the child are all subordinated, perverted, demoralized, by some false notions of the interests of society, a society that, by its creeds, codes and customs, is daily manufacturing murderers, drunkards, criminals, prostitutes, rogues, thieves and liars, and then for its protection drags to the torture, the rack, the gallows, the prison, the weak and degraded victims of its own crimes and abominations. . . .

Elizabeth Cady Stanton
May 14, 1868

More "Revolution"

. . . Let us all keep our eyes and ears open, making the most of every opportunity to penetrate the rotten fabric, and unearth the multitude of evils which women have borne because they know no better, and teach them a practical solution of their difficulties. You who have suffered, you who are still suffering, look up. Be no longer afraid to speak the words of truth and soberness. Pitch in right and left with the sharp edge of free, earnest utterance. When our soul grows sick with the misery of hope deferred, when our heart aches, as it always has ached, ever since we were old enough to think, for poor fallen, suffering woman, when distressed with some new social aggravation which we are powerless to combat, we ask our Father to show us the way out quickly, a loving voice ever whispers, "*Revolution*," and we are comforted.

"Imagination," is it? Well; have your own way. We know better.

May 21, 1868

Ballot, Bench and Baricade

Boston

Friend [Parker] Pillsbury: . . . [W]oman has *more* than her rights; she has some extra privileges! Truly, she has the privilege of working at starvation prices; of paying for a home, subject to an enforced, and it may be obnoxious and degrading tenantcy; of being hunted down and returned to her master like any other slave. Witness the Boston *Herald* of last week, which says, "an unfaithful wife, belonging to

251

Boston, who had run away from her home with one of the attaches of a circus that exhibited in Taunton, was arrested in that city Friday morning and returned to her family, in *accordance with the request of her husband."* I have anxiously waited, but thus far in vain, hoping to see that gallant pro-slavery league, who once girdled the State House with chains, rise *en masse* to resist such surrender of such fugitive slave to her owner. . . .

My vocation, that of *healer*, brings me in contact with all forms of suffering and wrong; making as I do, the bodily and mental diseases of women and children, more particularly, my specialty; studying into the laws of cause and effect. I see every day more clearly the value, necessity, and sanative qualities of the three B's: Bench, Ballot, Baricade, of home and if need be of battle. My case book is full of interesting sketches, some of which I may hereafter transfer to your columns with your approval. Meantime I will endeavor to get subscribers for *"The Revolution,"* and thus *do I all I can* for the cause. Will do more, just as soon as possible.

Yours for the right,

Aurora C. Phelps*
May 21, 1868

[* Phelps worked to secure homes for women.]

The Right Spirit

It is said that twenty-eight ladies, members in good and regular standing of the Congregational Church in Elmwood, Conn., have seceded, because denied the right of taking part in church proceedings.

September 17, 1868

The Woman's Suffrage Convention

The meetings just held in New York and Brooklyn have been in every way a complete success. The crowded houses, the respectful hearing by the men, the deep and wide-spread interest among the women themselves. . . .

. . . When [unscheduled] a pale, sad woman, mad with oppression, rose up in the midst of that magnificent audience . . . claiming her right to speak, was seized by the Police to be dragged from the platform, the impatience of the audience with her injuries was hushed at once in pity for the woman in the strong arm of the law, and the cry of "Put her out," from many a manly voice was drowned in the nobler one "Let her be heard." . . .

. . . As soon as the officer in uniform laid his hand on the woman she raised herself up to her full proportions, tall and stately, and, with keen satire, said, "I deny your authority, I had no voice in the law that made you my ruler." Her ready wit was greeted with loud applause, and she turned contemptuously from the officer to the audience, who gave her a patient hearing.

Elizabeth Cady Stanton
May 20, 1869

★★New Meaning for "Well Developed"★★

We hope to roll up the largest petition the world has ever seen, before the opening of the next Congress, to prove to American statesmen that the women are ready for the Sixteenth Amendment.

This petition, decorated with flowers and the American flag, will be carried into the National Capitol by a troupe of girls dressed in the National colors, one from each State, District and Territory, of twenty-one years of age. The one chosen for this high honor should be large and well-developed, as the petition will be a very heavy one. Whatever the rules are about the Hall of Representatives they must be set aside for that occasion, as the women propose to present their own petitions and make their own appeals to their rulers.

Elizabeth Cady Stanton
May 20, 1869

The Fourth of July

We would suggest that the Fourth of July this year should be fairly taken possession of by the women of the nation. . . .

Elizabeth Cady Stanton
May 20, 1869

★★No Taxation Without Representation★★

Alfred F. Puffer, Deputy Collector of Internal Revenue

June 4, 1869

Dear Sir: I have your polite note informing me that as publisher of *The Revolution* I am indebted to the United States government in the sum of $14.10 for the tax on monthly sales of that journal.

Enclosed you will find the amount – *fourteen dollars ten cents* – but you will please understand that I pay it under protest. . . .

I am *not* represented in the United States government, and yet that government taxes me; and it taxes me, too, for publishing a paper the chief purpose of which is to point out and rebuke the glaring and oppressive inconsistency between its professions and its practices.

Under the circumstances, the Federal government ought to be ashamed to exact this tax of me. . . .

I am, dear Mr. Puffer, very respectfully yours,

Susan B. Anthony
June 17, 1869

Women Revolutionaries

Fayetteville, N. Y.

. . . It is no new thing for women to protest against taxation. During the struggle of the Colonies, the women of New England held two public anti-tax meetings. These protests against taxation were made as early as 1770, five years before the commencement of the Revolutionary war, and were the real origin of the Boston Tea Party which was held in that harbor three years afterwards. The matrons, at these meetings, entered into a league to use no more tea until the tax upon it was repealed. The anti-tax meeting of the young ladies was held three days afterwards, and these young ladies publicly declared they did not protest against taxation for themselves alone, but as matter of principle, and with a view to benefit their posterity.

The women of to-day are the direct posterity of the women of the Revolution, and as our fore-mothers protested against taxation without representation, so do we, their descendents, protest against being taxed without being represented.

It was the denial of property representation which brought about the Revolutionary war. When our ancestors made that the basis of their demand for all other rights, "they builded better than they knew." James Otis is frequently referred to as one of the shining lights of the Revolution; but he was no more so than was his sister, Mercy Otis Warren, a woman who had great political influence, and who was consulted by Jefferson, the two Adams', and other patriots, on all important steps; and her's was the animating spirit of the Declaration of Independence.

She wrote a history of the American Revolution, from notes she herself kept during the war, and it was long a standard authority. It was only superceded when other histories were written, which drew upon her's for their main facts. Let women search the libraries and read Mrs. Warren's "burning words."

Matilda Joslyn Gage★

August 17, 1871

[★ See the Appendix for biographical information.]

★★Getting Men in a Pickle★★

An illustrious individual remarks that Mrs. Stanton is the salt, Anna Dickinson the pepper, and Miss Anthony the vinegar of the Female Suffrage movement.

The very elements to get the "white male" into a nice pickle.

August 19, 1869

Side Thrusts at Woman Suffrage

Every week of late I have been pained by seeing in print, or by hearing uttered, some sort of attack upon those women who are talkers, as if on that account they could not be workers. At many of the weekly meetings at the Bureau, persons have denounced the holding of Conventions and declared that those who had made speeches in favor of Woman Suffrage might be better employed in works of charity. The daily and weekly press throughout the country has re-echoed some what of this cry, declaring that nothing was gained by all this fuss.

Now it is, I think, high time that some one took up the cudgel in defense of our speechmakers. . . .

The masses of people must be roused and stimulated by direct and public appeal. The cause of Woman Suffrage would progress but at a snail's pace if those who believed in it were to keep their thoughts and arguments locked in their own breasts forever. No cause, since the world began, ever did progress except by earnest speech. . . .

It is easy enough to discover the real reason why the press, hostile to Woman Suffrage, raise this cry which has such a specious semblance of force; that woman had better work than talk, and before they spend their money in holding Conventions they had better try to elevate the degraded of their own sex. All this sounds well and may persuade some superficial reasoners that the women who urge on the reform are out of place, or, worst of all words, "unwomanly," but the friends of this movement ought not to join in these side thrusts. They must remember that the great argument of men against conferring the ballot on women is, that they do not want it, and that only by the public and oft-repeated declaration of many women can they convince the people that they do desire enfranchisement.

Lillie Devereux Blake★
September 30, 1869

[★ See the Appendix for biographical information.]

Local Agitation

There is too much of a disposition on the part of many warm friends of woman's enfranchisement to watch this movement, occasionally indulging in the luxury of a convention in one of the large cities, and applauding the words of its earnest advocates. These conventions are important and those who attend them contribute something to the progress of the cause by giving them their personal presence and support. But this is not enough. There needs earnest, systematic, organized local agitation, to bring the issue directly to the attention of every woman, and every voter, too. And one of the most important services that can be rendered to the cause at the present time, is the organization of its friends in clubs, or associations in every village and town of the land.

It is needless to point out the vast amount of good that such a concentration of our diffused and inoperative strength would accomplish. It would bring together, into active sympathy and co-operation, great numbers of persons who are now but slightly acquainted and practically inactive. It would confirm the hesitating, convince the doubting, encourage the irresolute, and inspire the indifferent and sluggish with enthusiasm. It would collect the scattered sparks and coals into a centre where they would kindle each other, and create a fire, and radiate heat, and diffuse that warmth which is so much needed everywhere. Such a society in a village would bring the issue directly to the notice of everybody within its circuit; it would awaken discussion; it would circulate information; it would draw the lines; it would make converts; it would develop sympathy; it would do a vast deal toward preparing public opinion for the reform which is inevitable, and toward educating the women of our country for new responsibilities and trusts. . . .

July 27, 1871

Take Notice

Miss Susan B. Anthony considers it her mission to keep the world, or at least her part of it, in hot water. Gentlemen, take notice.

October 7, 1869

Sit If You Agree

. . . On the way to the Methodist church where I was to speak, the gentleman who was to introduce me said there were no strong-minded women in McGregor. So I opened my speech by stating the fact and deploring the sad condition of that community; but several voices shouted out, "That is not true, there are plenty of them." So at the close, I took the vote, and the whole audience went solid for Woman's Suffrage.

I have a new way of putting the vote: "Let all those who are in favor keep their seats, and those opposed rise." In this way one gets the most favorable response, because women, like inanimate objects, generally need some external force to put them in motion, and the mass of them would not rise up to save the nation. . . .

Elizabeth Cady Stanton
April 14, 1870

Being and Doing

One of the catch-words or phrases of the time is, that woman ought to be, not do. Goethe's saying, that self-culture is higher than action, is twisted and contorted in a manner the great German doubtless never dreamed of. People talk as if to be good, great, noble and refined, were simply the result of assertion, and not of endeavor. What does culture imply but intense mental activity? Culture which is directed to no purpose and fulfils no end, is very dreary. Women have heard enough of it, and have too frequently been misled by the high sounding claptrap of its advocates.

A city clergyman, as reported by a daily paper, recently said:

"The great thing for woman is not to vote but to *be*; not to dabble in politics, but to acquire personal and moral power; not

257

to strut and storm on platforms and fill the papers with echoes of their rantings, but to fill themselves with ennobling culture and make the world better by their beneficence. The emancipation of woman is not to come from her getting something but from her being somebody, and acting upon society as an intellectual and moral force like the sunlight and gravitation. It is strength and not splutter that tells, whether for individual or public welfare.

If the great thing is to be, men had better stop dabbling in politics at once, for, from a human stand-point, culture is as necessary to them as to the other sex. . . .

. . . The real activities of women, that lie above and beyond all sound and fury, are making extraordinary progress; and those men who call out to the busy workers, and tell them to hold their hands, might as well speak to the dead.

March 2, 1871

Appendix
Women of *The Revolution*

Following are brief biographical sketches of some of the women (and two men) affiliated with *The Revolution*. Unfortunately a number of women have almost disappeared from twentieth-century memory, and most history books tell us almost nothing about the ways women worked together so prodigiously to increase woman's rights. As a consequence, we have not been able to include all of the women who we know had some affiliation with *The Revolution*. The women we have included here are those we know worked with Stanton and Anthony to see that the paper was published and those who were officially cited in *The Revolution* as contributors. We have tried to point out where possible the role of these women as active communicators – lecturers, writers, publishers, organizers. References cited at the end of each sketch should be consulted for additional, relevant information. More information on archival sources can be found in Andrea Hinding, ed., *Women's History Sources: A Guide to Archives and Manuscripts*, New York: Bowker, 1979.

Mary Clemmer Ames (1831–84)

A *Revolution* contributor, Mary Clemmer Ames was also a prominent journalist at the same time. She first wrote as a correspondent for *The Springfield Republican*, made a name for herself as a New York journalist and Washington correspondent following the Civil War, and became the highest paid newspaper-woman of her day at a salary of $5,000. She wrote book reviews, columns and advertising copy from 1869 to 1872 for the Brooklyn, New York, *Daily Union,* and her column, "A Woman's Letter from Washington," appearing in the New York weekly, *The Independent*, was well-known. She was a champion of women's suffrage and a supporter of the newly emanicipated Black population. (See Marion

The Revolution in Words

Marzolf, *Up From the Footnote: A History of Women Journalists*, New York: Hastings House, 1977; Phebe A. Hanaford, *Daughters of America: Or Women of the Century*, Augusta, Maine: True, 1883; Archives: Schlesinger Library; New York Public Library; Rutherford B. Hayes Library, Fremont, Ohio.)

Mathilde Franziska Giesler Anneke (1817–84)

Anneke was a revolutionary and woman's rights activist in Germany before fleeing to the US in 1849 and settling in Wisconsin. Before leaving Germany, she wrote two books of prayers for women, put together collections of poetry, wrote a play later produced in Germany and the US, and published two revolutionary newspapers, one entitled *Frauenzeitung*. When revolution broke out in Germany in 1848, she cut her hair short and rode into battle. In 1852, she began a radical women's journal in Wisconsin, the *Deutscher Frauenzeitung*, hiring women compositors. She moved the paper to New York and Jersey City, where it was published until 1854 or 1855. She joined the American woman's rights movement in the 1850s and became a prominent lecturer on woman's rights and abolition. During the Civil War she lived in Switzerland, writing for Swiss newspapers. When she returned, she supported herself by lecturing, writing and selling insurance. She helped found the Wisconsin Woman Suffrage Association in 1869 and was a contributor to *The Revolution*. (See Alden Whitman, ed., *American Reformers*, New York: H. W. Wilson, 1985; *Notable American Women* 1971; Marzolf, *Up From the Footnote*; Archives: State Historical Society of Wisconsin.)

Mary Stafford Anthony (1827–1907)

Susan B. Anthony's younger sister Mary was a supporter of woman's rights and of *The Revolution*, though her contributions have been overshadowed by those of her famous sister. Mary Anthony was a school teacher and eventually a principal in Rochester, New York, where she lived and managed the family household. A lifelong supporter of women, she attended woman's rights conventions that spanned the years from the second woman's rights convention in Rochester in 1848 to the International Council of Women in Berlin in 1904. In the summer of 1869, she spent her

260

Elizabeth Cady Stanton and Susan B. Anthony (Smithsonian Institution Photo no. 74–847)

summer working in *The Revolution* office so that her sister Susan could attend suffrage conventions and enlist support and subscriptions for the newspaper. She even lent Susan all her small savings to help keep the paper going. Every year Mary protested the taxes she paid on the family home in Rochester, writing a long explanation that occasionally appeared in a local newspaper. (See Katharine Anthony, *Susan B. Anthony: Her Personal History and Her Era*, Garden City, NY: Doubleday, 1954; Rheta Childe Dorr, *Susan B. Anthony: The Woman Who Changed the Mind of a Nation*, New York: Frederick A. Stokes, 1928; Alma Lutz, *Susan B. Anthony: Rebel, Crusader, Humanitarian,*

Boston: Beacon Press, 1959; Archives: University of California Berkeley, The Bancroft Library; Los Angeles County Museum of Natural History; California Historical Society; The Huntington Library; University of Rochester Library, Rochester, NY.)

Susan Brownell Anthony (1820–1906)

It was Susan B. Anthony who first discussed with George Francis Train the possibility of establishing *The Revolution*, and it was she who eventually paid off the $10,000 debt incurred before it was passed into the hands of Laura Curtis Bullard. Her official title was proprietor. She drummed up subscriptions, advertising and financial contributions. Her own money went into keeping the newspaper afloat. In the last two months before she left it, she contributed $1,300 earned from lecturing. She had gained newspaper experience working on her brother's newspaper in Leavenworth, Kansas, and she was a meticulous and seemingly tireless organizer and businessperson. None the less, she was not able to get the newspaper, one of the most radical feminist newspapers ever printed, on solid financial ground. Susan B. Anthony saw her work on *The Revolution* as some of the most important that she did in a lifelong career in the movement for woman's rights; she long regretted its demise. (See Anthony, *Susan B. Anthony*; Kathleen Barry, *Susan B. Anthony: A Biography of a Singular Feminist*, New York: New York University Press, 1988; Dorr, *Susan B. Anthony*; Ida Husted Harper, *The Life and Work of Susan B. Anthony*, Indianapolis: Hollenbeck Press, 1898; Lutz, *Susan B. Anthony*; Archives: Library of Congress; Schlesinger Library; Vassar College; University of Rochester, Rochester, NY; Huntington Library.)

Lydia Becker (1827–91)

The British activist Lydia Becker joined *The Revolution* as a foreign correspondent early in 1870. Becker, an often overlooked figure of the nineteenth-century British suffrage movement, was an effective organizer and campaigner in the constitutional movement for women's suffrage. Self-taught in such diverse areas as science and constitutional law, she published her first book, *Botany for Beginners*, and became president in 1867 of the Manchester Ladies Literary Society before becoming an active suffragist. In 1870 she began publishing the *Woman's Suffrage Journal*, which continued

262

under her editorship until her death in 1891. (See Dale Spender, *Women of ideas and What Men Have Done to Them*, London: Ark, 1982.)

Lillie Devereux Blake (1833–1913)

A contributor to *The Revolution*, Lille Devereux Blake was also a popular writer and an orator. She had been writing stories appearing in popular and literary magazines since 1857, and by one count she had published about 500 stories and articles by 1882, as well as several books, including a novel, *Fettered for Life*, about women's work. She was also a Washington correspondent for the New York *Evening Post* and *The World*. Her writing was her primary source of income through much of her life. She began her work in the woman's suffrage movement in the late 1860s, becoming a regular speaker at the annual conventions of the National Woman Suffrage Association. On November 5, 1872, the same day that Anthony cast her famous ballot, she attempted to vote in her own precinct but was turned away. She began an agitation for the education of women which eventually led to the establishment of Bernard College. She served as president of the New York State Woman Suffrage Association from 1879 to 1890 and of the New York City Woman Suffrage League from 1886 to 1900. (See Mary Cunningham Logan, *The Part Taken by Women in American History*, Wilmington, Del.: Perry-Nalle, 1912; *Notable American Women*; Frances E. Willard and Mary A. Livermore, eds, *A Woman of the Century: 1,470 Biographical Sketches Accompanied by Portraits of Leading American Women*, Buffalo: Charles Wells Mouton, 1893 [1967]; Archives: California Historical Society; Smith College, Sophia Smith Collection; Missouri Historical Society; Cornell University; University of Rochester Library, Rochester, NY.)

Elizabeth Boynton [Harbert] (1845–1925)

"Lizzie" Boynton, a contributor to *The Revolution*, was a journalist, author and lecturer. She earned a PhD degree from Ohio Wesleyan University and was an active member of a number of women's organizations through the years, serving as president of the Illinois Equal Suffrage Association for twelve years, associate president of the World's Unity League and vice president of the Southern

California Woman's Press Association. She published several books, including *Out of Her Sphere*, and edited "The Woman's Kingdom," which appeared in a leading Chicago daily, *Inter-Ocean*, and edited a woman's suffrage newspaper in Illinois in 1885, *The New Era*. (See Willard and Livermore, *A Woman of the Century*; *Who Was Who in American, 1897–1942*, 1968; Steven M. Buechler, "Elizabeth Boynton Harbet and the Woman Suffrage Movement, 1870–1896," *Signs* 13, No. 1: 78–97; Archives: Huntington Library; Schlesinger Library.)

Laura Curtis Bullard

A contributor to and supporter of *The Revolution* when it was in the hands of Anthony and Stanton, Bullard assumed editorial control of the paper after the May 26, 1870 issue. As the heir to the Mrs Winslow's Soothing Syrup patent medicine fortune and the wife and daughter of wealthy and prominent men, she apparently was in a financial position to sustain the paper through its next year and a half before it was sold to publisher J. N. Hallock. Bullard was a supportive and active member of the National Woman Suffrage Association from its beginning, serving as its first corresponding secretary. She was a popular writer of her day, publishing at least two books, *Now-A-Days!* in 1854 and *Christine, or Woman's Trials and Triumphs* in 1856. An extensive European traveler, she sent *The Revolution* letters from abroad while she served as correspondent. *The Revolution* became more of a literary and social journal under her editorship, though it continued to advocate many of the same causes. In her final editorial, "Valedictory" (*The Revolution*, October 12, 1871), she explained that she was leaving behind *The Revolution* because her European travels made it impossible for her to do justice to it. *The Revolution* had claimed civil as well as social equality for women, she stated. "These claims I have endeavored to press with firmness, but with moderation also, and as I have been accused by some of too much gentleness, and by others of too much vehemence, I conclude, that, having suited neither party of extremists, I must have succeeded pretty well in my attempt." (See Lutz, *Susan B. Anthony*.)

Celia Burleigh

A contributor to *The Revolution* when it was under Stanton and Anthony's leadership, Celia Burleigh's name appears regularly in its pages under Bullard's editorship. Burleigh had been a teacher, a personal secretary to Emma Willard, and one of the first women in the Universalist ministry. She was a member of the National Woman Suffrage Association and Sororis, and she started the Brooklyn Women's Club. She was also a member of the Working Women's Association, started by Anthony in the offices of *The Revolution*. (See DuBois, *Feminism and Suffrage*; Karen J. Blair, *The Clubwoman as Feminist: True Womanhood Redefined, 1868–1914*, New York: Homes & Meier, 1980.)

Alice Cary (reproduced from Mary Clemmer Ames, *A Memorial of Alice and Phoebe Cary, with Some of Their Later Poems*, New York: Hurd & Houghton, 1873)

Alice Cary (1820–71)

A strong supporter of *The Revolution* from its beginnings, Alice Cary contributed poetry, an unfinished novel and emotional support to Stanton and Anthony. Cary, along with her sister Phoebe, was a prominent and popular writer at the time. Leading literary periodicals as well as the popular press published her work, which eventually included five volumes of verse, three collections of fiction and three novels. The novel she was writing at the time of her death, *Born Thrall*, was being serialized in *The Revolution*. Alice Cary was a founding member of the women's club Sorosis in 1868 and became its president. (See *Notable American Women*; Ida Husted Harper, *Life and Work of Susan B. Anthony*, Vol. 1, New York: Arno and *The New York Times*, 1969; Mary Clemmer Ames, *A Memorial of Alice and Phoebe Cary, with Some of Their Later Poems*, New York: Hurd & Houghton, 1873; Archives: Huntington Library; Iowa State Historical Department, Boston Public Library; Schlesinger Library.)

Phoebe Cary (reproduced from Mary Clemmer Ames, *A Memorial of Alice and Phoebe Cary, with Some of Their Later Poems*, New York: Hurd & Houghton, 1873)

Phoebe Cary (1824–71)

Phoebe Cary also lived most of her life by her pen, writing hymns, ballads, nature poems and other verse. Phoebe's contributions to *The Revolution* were not only literary; she worked in the office, often helping Stanton put the newspaper out. Her role became even greater when Bullard took the paper over, when she and Augusta Larned provided most of the editorial assistance to Bullard. The Cary home, within walking distance of the *Revolution* offices, was a meeting place for artists, writers and reformers, including Stanton and Anthony. Anthony frequently called at the sisters' home, and Stanton wrote in the November 18, 1869 issue of *The Revolution*: "Hungering that day for gifted women, I called on Alice and Phebe Cary, and Mary Clemmer Ames, and together we gave the proud 'white male' such a serving up as did our souls good. . . . the *Tribune* says, 'The idea of a *home* without a man in it!' In visiting the Carys one always feels that there is a home, and a very charming one, too, without a man in it . . ." (See *Notable American Women*; Lutz, *Susan B. Anthony*; Ames, *A Memorial of Alice and Phoebe Cary*; Willard and Livermore, *A Woman of the Century*; Archives: Boston Public Library; Schlesinger Library.)

Phoebe Couzins (1839?–1913)

While Phoebe Couzins was a contributor to *The Revolution*, she was also attending law school at Washington University in St Louis, graduating in 1871 as one of the first women in Missouri to get a law degree. She apparently remained active in the woman's rights movement at the same time, attending the 1869 American Equal Rights Association and joining Stanton and Anthony in founding the National Woman Suffrage Association. She was a regular speaker at NWSA meetings and became a popular lecturer on woman's rights, temperance and other reforms. She served briefly as a US marshal in 1887 when her father, who held that position, died. She was reportedly the first woman to serve in such a position. In 1893 she became secretary for the Board of Lady Managers of the Women's Building of the World's Columbian Exposition in Chicago. (See *Notable American Women*; Hanaford, *Daughters of America*; Jeanne Madeline Weimann, *Fair Women*, Chicago: Academy Chicago, 1981; Archives: University of California Berkeley, Bancroft Library; Filson Club, Louisville, KY; Missouri Historical Society.)

Paulina Kellogg Wright Davis (1813–76)

Paulina Wright Davis had been an activist, organizer and newspaper editor long before her association with *The Revolution*. She began her work on woman's rights as early as the mid-1830s, when she worked on a petition drive for a New York married woman's property Act, and 1850, when she organized a woman's rights convention. She used the wealth of her two husbands in the cause of woman's rights, financing conventions and her own monthly

Paulina Kellogg Wright Davis (reproduced from the collections of the Library of Congress)

periodical, *The Una* (1853–5), one of the earliest papers devoted to woman's rights. (Excerpts are included in *Radical Women's Press of the 1850s*, a companion to this volume.) When *The Revolution* was begun, she made a generous financial contribution, contributing again when Anthony was trying to keep the paper afloat. She contributed strong arguments supporting the paper's stand on the Fifteenth and Sixteenth Amendments. When Parker Pillsbury left *The Revolution* for a better-paying position, Davis became associate editor. There was a brief plan that never materialized for her participation with other women to form a stock company to finance *The Revolution*. Davis was one of the few New England supporters of the National Woman Suffrage Association. Her dream was to have a "Woman's Congress" (advocated in *The Revolution*) that would meet in Washington at the same time as (men's) Congress was in session. (See *Notable American Women*; *American Reformers*; Paulina Wright Davis, *A History of the National Woman's Rights Movement for Twenty Years, from 1850 to 1870*, New York: Journeymen Printers' Cooperative Association, 1871; Lutz,

Women of The Revolution

Susan B. Anthony; Hanaford, *Daughters of America*; Archives: Boston Public Library; Schlesinger Library; Rhode Island Historical Society Library.)

Jenny P. d'Héricourt (1809–75)

French citizen Jenny d'Héricourt lived only about ten years in the US, but those ten years happened to encompass the time *The Revolution* was being published. The English translation of her work that critiqued the theories of women and men's relations by major nineteenth-century male writers, *A Woman's Philosophy of Woman, or Woman Affranchised: An Answer to Michelet, Proudhon, Girardin, Leqouvé, Comte, and Other Modern Innovators*, appeared in 1864. She lived in Chicago while in the US, and came to know Kate Newell Doggett and Mary Livermore (founder and publisher of *The Agitator*) and Anthony and Stanton. She apparently played a significant role in establishing connections between US and continental women, bringing news of woman's rights debates in France to the US and assisting American women when they visited the Continent. She lectured, wrote novels and practiced medicine. (See Karen Offen, "A Nineteenth-Century French Feminist Redis-covered: Jenny P. d'Héricourt, 1809–1875, *Signs* 13, No. 1 [Autumn 1987]: 144–58).

Anna Elizabeth Dickinson (1842–1932)

Anna Dickinson often visited the offices of *The Revolution*, giving cheer and support to her many friends there, in particular to her close friend Susan B. Anthony. She also made generous financial gifts to the newspaper. Dickinson was clearly one of the most popular platform speakers of her time, speaking for woman's rights as well as temperance and abolition of slavery. The large fees that she was able to command – earning her more than $20,000 some years – made it possible for her to support herself and her family. Her popularity as a lecturer was at its peak through the decade of 1863 to 1873. She wrote two books on reform, *What Answers?* in 1868 and *A Paying Investment* in 1876. She went on to write plays and to become a dramatic performer. (See *American Reformers*; James Parton et al., *Eminent Women of the Age*, Hartford, Conn.: S. M. Betts, 1869; Lutz, *Susan B. Anthony*; Anthony, *Susan B. Anthony*; Archives: Trinity College, Watkinson Library,

Anna Elizabeth Dickinson (reproduced from the collections of the Library of Congress)

Hartford, Conn.; Library of Congress; Women's Christian Temperance Union National Headquarters, Frances Willard Memorial Library, Evanston, Ill.; Iowa State Historical Department; Schlesinger Library; Columbia University.)

Kate Newell Doggett (1828–84)

Kate Doggett is perhaps best remembered as the founder in 1874 of the first literary association for women in Chicago, the long-lived Fortnightly Club. She was an artist, educator, lecturer, translator and botanist as well. In 1869, while a contributor to *The Revolution*, she was elected to the Academy of Science and given charge of its herbarium. In the same year she was elected a vice-president of the National Woman Suffrage Association and served as a delegate to the Woman's Industrial Congress in Berlin. She was reported to have worn her hair short and had radical opinions (quoted in Jeanne

Women of The Revolution

Weimann, *The Fair Women*, Chicago: Academy Chicago, 1981, p. 13). (See *Appleton's Cyclopaedia of American Biography*, 1888; Hanaford, *Daughters' of America*; Muriel Beadle and the Centennial History Committee, *The Fortnightly of Chicago, The City and Its Women: 1873–1973*, Chicago: Henry Regnery Company, 1973; Archives: Newberry Library; Rutherford B. Hayes Library, Fremont, Ohio.)

Emily Faithfull (1835–95)

Under Bullard's editorship, Emily Faithfull became a regular contributor to *The Revolution*, providing columns of correspondence on the condition of women and on the suffrage movement in England. According to a column in the October 20, 1870 issue of *The Revolution*, in 1860 Faithfull, believing that women needed more opportunities for paying jobs, gathered together a group of women compositors and established the Victoria Press. The press gained a reputation for its high quality work, and she earned the favor of Queen Victoria. She went on to publish *The Victoria Magazine* in 1863, "the production of women's brain as well as women's fingers," a monthly publication for woman's rights. The magazine was still being published at the time she was contributing to *The Revolution*. (See Sir J. A. Hammerton, ed., *Concise Universal Biography*, London: Educational Book Co., 1934.)

Emily Ellsworth Ford (1826–93)

Emily Ford contributed a series of literary columns to *The Revolution* that could best be described as a form of feminist literary criticism. She was a poet and essayist whose works also appeared in *Harper's* and *The Atlantic*, and two collections of her poetry were published in 1872 and 1879. She was active in bringing about reforms in a county poorhouse, among other causes. In her literary columns in *The Revolution* she analyzed such topics as "The Typical Women of American Authors" and "The Type [of] Husbands of American Stories." While not generally critical of literary portrayals of men and women, she does call James Fenmore Cooper's women characters "wooden" and praises novels in which equality in marriage is demonstrated. (See *The National Cyclopedia of American Biography*; Archives: The New York Public Library.)

271

Matilda Joslyn Gage (reproduced from the collections of the Library of Congress)

Matilda Joslyn Gage (1826–98)

A historian and theorist, Matilda Joslyn Gage made contributions to the woman's movement of the nineteenth century that have been generally overlooked. She began her public work for woman's rights in 1852, followed by a lifetime of organizing, lecturing, researching and writing. Her main interest was in the recovery of women's history of achievements and the causes of women's subordination to men (which occurred in the main through religious teaching, she believed). She helped found the National Woman Suffrage Association in 1869 and wrote for *The Revolution*, to which her major contribution was a series of articles on women's historic role as inventors, published as a book in 1870. She went on to write *Woman, Church and the State* (1893) and to collaborate with Anthony and Elizabeth Cady Stanton on the *History of Woman Suffrage* (1881–6). She edited the monthly paper *National Citizen and*

Ballot Box, the organ of the NWSA, from 1878 to 1881. She was one of the most scholarly of the radical women of this period. (See *American Reformers* 1985; *Notable American Women*; Spender, *Women of Ideas*; Archives: Stowe-Day Library, Hartford, Conn.; Chicago Historical Society; Schlesinger Library; Smith College, Sophia Smith Collection.)

Marie Goegg

Formally listed as a contributor to *The Revolution*, Marie Goegg was instrumental at the same time in establishing the Woman's International Association at her home of Geneva, Switzerland. The association began in July of 1868 with Goegg as president. She also established a bimonthly newspaper the *Woman's Journal (Journal des femmes)*, which survived only a few months. The association ended at the outbreak of the Franco-German war, but was revived two years later as Solidarity, with Goegg assuming its presidency again in 1875 and founding and editing its official newspaper, the *Solidarity Bulletin*. Both the newspaper and organization were discontinued in 1880. Goegg was not only active in organizing women internationally, but she was also instrumental in working for political reforms for women in Switzerland. (See Elizabeth Cady Stanton, Susan B. Anthony and Matilda Joslyn Gage, eds, *History of Woman Suffrage*, Vol. 3, New York: Arno and *The New York Times,* 1969, pp. 910–11; Susanna Woodtli, *Du Féminisme à l'Éqalité Politique: Un Siècle de Luttes en Suisse, 1868–1971*, Lausanne: Payot, 1977; and France Pieroni Bortolotti, *La Donna, La Pace, l'Europa: l'Associazione International Delle Done Dalle Origini All Prima Guerra Mondiale*, Milan: Franco Angeli Libri, 1985.)

Isabella Beecher Hooker (1822–1907)

Isabella Beecher Hooker did not join the woman's movement until the 1860s, but she soon became an important part of its radical arm. A member of the influential and respectable Beecher family (she was a half-sister to Henry Ward Beecher and Harriet Beecher Stowe), she sought to bring respectability to the movement but increasingly became willing to support even its more controversial aspects (such as the ideas of Victoria Woodhull). Though she was one of the founders in 1868 of the New England Woman Suffrage Association, she remained loyal to the National Woman Suffrage Association in 1869 when the movement split, taking, in fact, a

Isabella Beecher Hooker (reproduced from the collections of the Library of Congress)

leadership position in 1871. Hooker persuaded Harriet Beecher Stowe that the two of them should become associate editors of *The Revolution* when Anthony was desperately trying to keep the paper going. Stanton and Anthony could not be persuaded to change the name to something more moderate, however, and during the discussions of their involvement *The Revolution* took an unpopular stand on a well-publicized scandal (the "Richard-McFarland Affair"). As a consequence, Stowe and Hooker withdrew from these publishing plans, a decision Hooker apparently regretted. Hooker had also been part of a plan with Paulina Wright Davis and Laura Curtis Bullard to establish a stock company to finance *The Revolution*, another proposal that did not materialize. (See *American Reformers*; *Notable American Women*; Dorr, *Susan B. Anthony*; Lutz, *Susan B. Anthony*; Archives: Stowe-Day Library, Hartford, Conn.; Library of Congress; The Filson Club, Louisville, KY; Schlesinger Library; Smith College, Sophia Smith Collection; Vermont Historical Society.)

Eleanor Kirk [Easterbrook Ames] (1830–?)

Despite her success as a writer and her efforts on behalf of working women, Eleanor Kirk has all but disappeared from twentieth-century memory. She was a regular contributor to *The Revolution*, providing fiction and articles. Her story, "Up Broadway," about the economic and moral hardships of a working woman, was a popular serialization in the paper (published in book form in 1870). She appears to have made her living as a writer, becoming a regular contributor to *Packard's Monthly* and publishing books such as her *Information for Authors* (1891), a book of advice for aspiring authors on how to get published. She operated an "Authors' Bureau," charging a fee to read manuscripts and give authors publication advice. Kirk was particularly concerned for the welfare of working women. She was a forceful member of the Working Women's Association, advocating practical reforms and assistance to help women's working conditions and contributing a series of articles in *The Revolution* describing those conditions. (See DeBois, *Feminism and Suffrage*.)

Augusta Larned (1835–1924)

August Larned was instrumental in the publication of *The Revolution* during Laura Bullard's tenure with the newspaper. While Bullard was traveling in Europe, Bullard gave Larned the credit for publishing the newspaper. Larned also contributed long pieces such as her "Galileo's Daughter, Sister Maria Celeste" in the November 3, 1980 issue. Larned became a professional writer in 1867, writing stories, correspondence and editorials for many magazines and newspapers. She also published six volumes of stories for young people after 1872. (See *The National Cyclopedia of American Biography*.)

Olive Logan (1839–1909)

Olive Logan claimed at the 1869 American Equal Rights Association convention that a year before she had never read a page of *The Revolution* and did not care to. Yet by November of 1869 she was officially listed as one of the newspaper's contributors. Having given up in 1868 a career in acting begun in childhood, Logan took to the stage as a lecturer. During the next year she apparently became convinced of the need to support woman's rights, perhaps because of the difficulties she encountered as a lecturer. She lectured for another decade, as well as translating French plays for American production. She published several books, including *Chateau Frissac* (1862), *They Met by Chance: A Society Novel* (1873), and three collections of commentary on social problems and the theater. She also published a number of stories in pamphlets and wrote newspaper and magazine articles supporting suffrage. (See *Notable American Women*; *The National Cyclopedia of American Biography*; Archives: University of Texas at Austin, Humanities Research Center; State Historical Society of Wisconsin.)

Clemence Sophia Harned Lozier (1813–88)

A close friend and supporter of Susan B. Anthony, Clemence Lozier was often used in example by Anthony as one of many single women keeping a home and making their own way financially. Lozier (who did the unwomanly act of obtaining a divorce from her husband) trained for the medical profession and began an obstetrical practice in 1860. She gave lectures to women in their home on anatomy, physiology and hygiene and wrote popular health books for women (*Child-birth Made Easy* in 1870 and *Dress*, date unknown). With a lucrative practice (reported to be $25,000 a year), she founded and served as dean of the New York Medical College and Hospital for Women in 1863, a homeopathic institution. She also made substantial financial contributions to *The Revolution*, supported the Working Women's Association and served as president of the New York City Woman Suffrage Association and the National Woman Suffrage Association. (See *American Reformers*; *Notable American Women*; DuBois, *Feminism and Suffrage*.)

Clemence Sophia Harned Lozier (reproduced from the collections of the Library of Congress)

Elizabeth Smith Miller (1822–1911)

Elizabeth Smith Miller is best known for her advocacy of the reform dress which became known as the "bloomer" (after Amelia Bloomer publicized it in her newspaper, *The Lily*); however, she was active in all areas of woman's rights, her activism beginning as early as 1850. She was a member of the National Woman Suffrage Association, and according to Alma Lutz (*Susan B. Anthony*, p. 166), "gave money, encouragement, and invaluable aid [to *The Revolution*] with her translations of interesting letters which *The Revolution* received from France and Germany." As Stanton's cousin and close friend, she was a source of feminist inspiration and encouragement. (See also *American Reformers*; *Notable American Women*; *Radical Women Challenge Maledom*; Archives: Schlesinger Library; New York Public Library; Madison County Historical Society, New York; State Historical Society of Wisconsin.)

Lily Peckham

Lily (Lilia or Lila) Peckham of Milwaukee, Wisconsin, has almost been lost to modern feminists. After a very active part in the movement around the time of *The Revolution*, she died suddenly and at a young age. In addition to being a *Revolution* contributor, she was an agent or distributor in Milwaukee. In 1869 she and Dr Laura Ross issued the call for the 1869 Milwaukee suffrage convention, where Peckham was elected secretary. She attended and spoke at other Wisconsin conventions and conventions in Ohio, Illinois and Rhode Island. Olympia Brown called her "a bright young lawyer" (Olympia Willis, ed., "Olympia Brown," unpublished manuscript, Racine, Wisconsin, 1960, p. 44). She died before fulfilling her plan to become a minister by attending the Cambridge Divinity School that fall. (See *The Revolution*, March 11, July 1, October 21 and November 4, 1869 and January 27 and February 3, 1870; and *History of Woman Suffrage*, Vol. 3, pp. 640–3.)

Elizabeth B. Phelps

Elizabeth B. Phelps' dream of having a center for women was realized for a short time. *The Revolution* occupied the first floor of the large and reportedly elegant house on East Twenty-Third Street in New York City – the "Woman's Bureau" – that Phelps purchased for just such purposes. She planned to rent the rooms to women's organizations and enterprises, with space available for receptions, readings and concerts. For some reason, other women's organizations did not take up the offer – it has been suggested that *The Revolution* kept them away – and Phelps' plan was discontinued. She also gave generously to Anthony in support of *The Revolution*. She was well-known in New York as a philanthropist. She served as vice president of the National Woman Suffrage Association when it was founded. (See Harper, *Life and Work of Susan B. Anthony, Vol. 1*; Lutz, *Susan B. Anthony*.)

Parker Pillsbury (1809–98)

A man who supported woman's rights could become the target of ridicule as much as women. Parker Pillsbury was called "Miss Pillsbury" or "Mrs. Pillsbury" by other newspaper editors in scorn of his loyal position as co-editor (with Elizabeth Cady Stanton) of

Parker Pillsbury (reproduced by permission of the New Hampshire Historical Society)

The Revolution. Pillsbury, a minister, had already had a long career in the service of anti-slavery before coming to *The Revolution.* He was an experienced editor, having been editor of the *Herald of Freedom* in the 1840s and the *National Anti-Slavery Standard* in the 1860s. He was one of the few male abolitionists to support woman's suffrage, even resigning his position at the *Standard* over the principle. As an editor for *The Revolution,* he worked for little pay and wrote strong editorials in support of woman's rights. He was active in organizations for woman's rights and brought his writing and lecturing skills to the cause. Pillsbury left the paper for a time in 1869 for a better paying position but returned temporarily at Anthony's request in 1870. After leaving *The Revolution,* he returned to lecturing and preaching. (See *American Reformers*; Lutz, *Susan B. Anthony*; Archives: Boston Public Library; Harvard University Library.)

Elizabeth Cady Stanton (1815–1902)

Elizabeth Cady Stanton was a lifelong champion of woman's rights as a writer, lecturer and organizer. Her association with *The Revolution* was not her only experience with woman's rights periodicals. As early as 1849 she had been writing for Amelia Bloomer's publication *The Lily,* then Paulina Wright Davis' *The Una* in the 1850s. In addition to writing for numerous other (men's) magazines and newspapers, she wrote for Clara B. Colby's *The Woman's Tribune* in the 1890s. During the years of *The Revolution,* Stanton was a prolific contributor of editorials as well as letters of correspondence while on her many lecture tours. She continued to write addresses and letters, to chair conventions and to attend hearings. She was an important theorist for the movement and an important link between the many women and their various methods of communication during the time period. (See *American Reformers*; *Notable American Women*; Elisabeth Griffith, *In Her Own Right: The Life of Elizabeth Cady Stanton,* New York: Oxford University Press, 1984; Alma Lutz, *Created Equal: A Biography of Elizabeth Cady Stanton, 1815–1902,* New York: John Day, 1940; Archives: Library of Congress; Boston Public Library; Schlesinger Library; Rutgers University; Douglass College Library.)

Helen Ekin Starrett (1840–1920)

Anthony and Stanton's work in Kansas during the campaign for woman suffrage was aided by the work of such women as Helen Ekin Starrett, who were already active for the cause. Credited with being a contributor to *The Revolution,* Starrett went on to become an educator and author, founding a classical school for girls in Chicago, the Kenwood Institute, and then the Starrett School for Girls. She wrote a number of books, such as *Future of Educated Women* (1880), *Letters to a Daughter* (1882) and *After College, What For Girls?*, contributed to magazines and journals, and wrote poetry. (See *Twentieth Century Biographical Dictionary of Notable Americans*; *Who Was Who in America*; DuBois, *Feminism and Suffrage*; Elizabeth Cady Stanton, Susan B. Anthony, and Matilda Joslyn Gage, eds, *History of Woman Suffrage,* Vol. II, New York: Fowler & Wells, 1882, pp. 250–5.)

Women of The Revolution
Elizabeth Tilton (1834–97)

Unfortunately Elizabeth Tilton's contributions to the woman's rights movement have been overshadowed by her husband, Theodore, who was editor of *The Independent* and active in the leadership of the National Woman Suffrage Association after its split with the American Woman Suffrage Association. She is best remembered, also unfortunately, for the scandal that was made public in the early 1870s, her affair with minister Henry Ward Beecher, a leader in the American Woman Suffrage Association. She was apparently a loyal supporter of *The Revolution*, a contributor, and the one who selected its poetry. Her other contributions to the woman's movement await further discovery. (See Inez Haynes Irwin, *Angels and Amazons*, Garden City, NY: Doubleday, 1933.)

George Francis Train (1829–1904)

Perhaps George Francis Train's greatest contribution to *The Revolution* was the notoriety he brought to it. Train was a well-known Democrat and financier who had made large sums of money on a shipping firm in Australia and on American railroads. He was willing to take public stands on unpopular causes, including the cause for woman's rights. Out of his association with Anthony in Kansas campaigning for woman's suffrage grew his offer for financial backing of *The Revolution*. Train subsequently made little financial or editorial contribution to the paper, but the paper would even over a hundred years later be thought of in the light of his (limited) association. Abolitionists used him as an excuse to further dissociate themselves from the women of *The Revolution* and the cause of woman's rights. Though Train was racist, as abolitionists claimed him to be, he apparently tempered his racism while in the company of Anthony and Stanton. (See *Dictionary of American Biography* 1936; Willis Thornton, *The Nine Lives of Citizen Train*, New York: Greenberg, 1948; George Francis Train, *The Great Epigram Campaign of Kansas*, Leavenworth, Kansas: Prescott & Hume, 1867.)

Charlotte Beebe Wilbour (1833–1914)

Charlotte Wilbour had an active role in both Sorosis, the New York women's club, and the National Woman Suffrage Association

George Francis Train (reproduced from the collections of the Library of Congress)

at the same time that she served as a contributor to *The Revolution*. Wilbour was one of the founders of Sorosis, as well as president of the organization from 1870 to 1875. She served as executive secretary of NWSA during the period of conflict and attempted reunion with the American Woman Suffrage Association. Wilbour was a lecturer and writer and was among the first to issue a call for a Woman's Congress. She appeared before the New York legislature on a number of occasions to testify on behalf of reform measures for women. (See Hanaford, *Daughters of America*; *The National Encylopedia of American Biography*; Archives: Library of Congress.)

Index

enforced 73–90 *passim*, 158, 191; not obstacle to voting 199; not substitute for other work 193–4; ownership of children 198; *see also* voting

Mott, Lucretia 16, 69, 148

motto 19–20, 41–3; *Revolution* 153

names: diminutive for women 180; "married" 168–71; of women's schools 177; to criticize women 188

National Anti-Slavery Standard 279

National Citizen and Ballot Box 7, 272–3

National Colored Labor Union 93

National Labor Union 93

National Part of New America 20

National Union of Cigar Makers 93

National Woman Suffrage Association 8, 49, 66, 70, 71, 72, 263, 264, 265, 267, 268, 270, 272, 273, 277, 278, 281

National Woman Suffrage Association Report: history 66, 67–70

nature: men's interpretation 236–7

Neal, John 230

needlework 91–114 *passim*; 111; poor work for women 92, 102

needleworkers: equal pay for equal work 100

Negrophobia 173; *see also* colorphobia

NeSmith, Georgia 13

networks of women 1–13 *passim*, 7

neuter dress 145–6; *see also* dress reform; bloomers; costume

New England Woman Suffrage Association 273

New Era 264

New Jersey voting laws 239

New Northwest 8, 197

New York City Woman Suffrage League 263

New York Medical College and Hospital for Women 276

New York State Woman Suffrage Association 263

Newman, Louise Michele 13

newsgirls: *Revolution* 24–5, 133–4

newspapers: men ignore women's topics 185, *see also* men's press; women's press

nincompoop: man who does not know 120

noodledom 165

Norton, Sarah F. 102

novel reading 156, 157

novelists: representation of women 157

"obey" in vows 183, 191, 206–8, 210

old maid: a slight on man's vanity 201; as described by media 223; redefinition 166, 200–2

old woman 156

Oliphant, Mrs. Margaret 143

Opodeloc 206

orations 139, 222, 263; *see also* speaking

Organ, Mrs. M. Stephenson M. D. 147

Parton, James 269

Parton, Sara Payson Willis 167

patent medicine advertising 16, 196

paternalism: of Horace Greeley 218

paternity 206

Peck, Elizabeth H. 219

Peckham, Lilly 39, 188, 278

Peterson, Agnes B. 105

petticoats: as worn by women and men 123–4

Phelps, Aurora C. 252

Phelps, Elizabeth B. 34, 69, 278

Phillips, Wendell 50, 51, 189; sexist 50–1, 58

physical education: relationship to

291

weaker sex: men 138–9
wealth: men's display of house, wife's dress 113–14
Webb, Emma 229
Weimann, Jeanne Madeline 267, 271
Welter, Barbara 13, 118, 221
Wendt, Mathilde F. 69–70
Wertheimer, Barbara Mayer 93, 94
Wheelock, Elvira 26
white: mischievous word 171
"white male" 166, 255; abolitionists 72; criticized 29, 116, 119, 267; interpretation of Bible 204; writing about man's sphere 118–19
white men: suffrage 47–72 *passim*; *see also* racism
white women: immigrant 74; property of men 56; racism 3–4, 12, 47–8, 62
Whitman, Alden 260
widow 170–1, 178; *see also* property laws
widowhood 170
Widstrand, Frans H. 146
wife: as slave 207–9; enforced sex 205; little protection from poverty 130
wifebeater: beaten himself 246
wifebeating 83, 116, 134, 205; *see also* battered women; violence
Wilbour, Charlotte Beebe 8, 39, 69, 188, 281–3
Willard, Frances E. 263
Winslow's Soothing Syrup 196, 264
Wisconsin Woman Suffrage Association 260
Woman: as toy of man 203; defined 176; how related to "lady" 219; meaning of 182; redefinition 3, 11, 74, 127–8; *see also* womanhood
Woman, Church and the State 272
womanhood 170, 175, 197; annual

holocaust 158; men's use of term 129; redefinition 48
womanish 179
womanliness 179
Woman's Bureau 69, 278
Woman's Congress 268, 283
Woman's Industrial Congress in Berlin 270
Woman's International Association 273
Woman's Journal (Journal des femmes) 44–5, 71, 273
woman's movement *passim*
woman's rights activist 238–58
woman's rights international xxvi
woman's suffrage: arguments and opposition 217–37 *passim*
Woman's Suffrage Association of America 59–60
Woman's Suffrage Journal 7, 262
Woman's Tea Company 25
woman's tongue 27
Woman's Tribune 280
women: all compared to slave 56; as police 134; as slaves 72; ignored except when existence conflicts with men's 56; required to imitate men's interests 126; *see also* slavery analogy
women of color 75
women revolutionaries 238–58
women worthies xxix, 4
Women's Building of the World's Columbian Exposition 267
Women's Bureau, New York 33
Women's Christian Temperance Union National Headquarters 270
Women's Cooperative Printing Union 105
women's duties: as gratuitous 235–6
Women's Medical College in Cleveland 109

For Product Safety Concerns and Information please contact our EU
representative GPSR@taylorandfrancis.com
Taylor & Francis Verlag GmbH, Kaufingerstraße 24, 80331 München, Germany